# ANCIENT ANATOLIA

# WISCONSIN STUDIES IN CLASSICS

*General Editors*
Barbara Hughes Fowler and Warren G. Moon

---

# Ancient Anatolia

## Aspects of Change and Cultural Development

Essays in Honor of Machteld J. Mellink

Edited by Jeanny Vorys Canby, Edith Porada,
    Brunilde Sismondo Ridgway, and Tamara Stech

THE UNIVERSITY OF WISCONSIN PRESS

Published with the assistance of the J. Paul Getty Trust

Published 1986

The University of Wisconsin Press
114 North Murray Street
Madison, Wisconsin 53715

The University of Wisconsin Press, Ltd.
1 Gower Street
London WC1E 6HA, England

First printing

Printed in the United States of America

For LC CIP information see the colophon

ISBN 0-299-10620-9

# CONTENTS

# ABBREVIATIONS

| | |
|---|---|
| *AA* | *Archäologischer Anzeiger* |
| *AASOR* | *Annual of the American Schools of Oriental Research* |
| *AfO* | *Archiv für Orientforschung* |
| *AHR* | *American Historical Review* |
| *AJA* | *American Journal of Archaeology* |
| *AJPA* | *American Journal of Physical Anthropology* |
| *AnatSt* | *Anatolian Studies* |
| *AnnLiv* | *Annals of Archaeology and Anthropology, Liverpool* |
| *AnnPisa* | *Annali della R. Scuola Normale Superiore di Pisa, Sezione di Lettere* |
| *ANYAS* | *Annals of the New York Academy of Sciences* |
| *AZ* | *Archäologische Zeitung* |
| BAH | Bibliothèque Archéologique et Historique |
| BAR | British Archaeological Reports |
| *BASPR* | *Bulletin of the American School of Prehistoric Research* |
| BibMes | Bibliotheca Mesopotamica |
| *BibO* | *Bibliotheca Orientalis* |
| *BMQ* | *British Museum Quarterly* |
| *BSA* | *British School at Athens, Annual* |
| *CAH*³ | *Cambridge Ancient History*, 3rd ed. |
| *CRAI* | *Comptes Rendus de l'Académie des Inscriptions et Belles Lettres* |
| *CTH* | *Catalogue des textes hittites* (Paris 1971) |
| *DialAr* | *Dialoghi di Archeologia* |
| *HH* | E. Laroche, *Les Hiéroglyphes hittites* (Paris 1960) |
| *IrAnt* | *Iranica Antiqua* |
| IstForsch | Istanbuler Forschungen |
| *IstMitt* | *Mitteilungen des deutschen archäologischen Instituts, Abteilung Istanbul* |
| *JAOS* | *Journal of the American Oriental Society* |
| *JCS* | *Journal of Cuneiform Studies* |
| *JdI-EH* | *Jahrbuch des k. deutschen archäologischen Instituts, Ergänzungsheft* |
| *JFA* | *Journal of Field Archaeology* |
| *JKF* | *Jahrbuch für kleinasiatische Forschung* |
| *JNES* | *Journal of Near Eastern Studies* |
| *JRAS* | *Journal of the Royal Asiatic Society* |
| *JSAH* | *Journal of the American Society of Architectural Historians* |
| *KUB* | *Keilschrifturkunden aus Boghazköi* |
| *KZ* | *Kuhnes Zeitschrift = Zeitschrift für vergleichende Sprachforschung* |

| | |
|---|---|
| *Manuale* | P. Meriggi, *Manuale di Eteo-geroglifico* I, I.1, II.2–3 (Rome 1966, 1967, 1975) |
| *MDOG* | *Mitteilungen der deutschen Orient-Gesellschaft* |
| Meriggi, *Glossar* 1 | P. Meriggi, *Mitteilungen der vorderasiatisch-aegyptischen Gesellschaft* 39.1 (Leipzig 1934) 91–174 |
| Meriggi, *Glossar* 2 | P. Meriggi, *Hieroglyphisch-hethitisches Glossar* (Wiesbaden 1962) |
| *MVAG* | *Mitteilungen der vorderasiatisch-aegyptischen Gesellschaft* |
| OIC | Oriental Institute Communications |
| OIP | Oriental Institute Publications |
| OlForsch | Olympische Forschungen |
| *OLZ* | *Orientalische Literaturzeitung* |
| *OrAnt* | *Oriens Antiquus* |
| PK | Propyläen Kunstgeschichte |
| *PPS* | *Proceedings of the American Philosophical Society* |
| *ProcPS* | *Proceedings of the Prehistoric Society* |
| *PSBA* | *Proceedings of the Society of Biblical Archaeology* |
| *RA* | *Revue Archéologique* |
| *RAssyr* | *Revue d'Assyriologie et d'archéologie orientale* |
| *RGZM* | *Römisch-germanische Zentralmuseum, Mainz, Jahrbuch* |
| *RHA* | *Revue Hittite et Asianique* |
| *RLA* | *Reallexikon der Assyriologie und vorderasiatischen Archäologie* |
| *SAOC* | *Studies in Ancient Oriental Civilization* |
| *SBÖstAkadWiss* | *Sitzungsberichte der Österreichischen Akademie der Wissenschaften* |
| SIMA | Studies in Mediterranean Archaeology |
| *StClOr* | *Studi Classici e Orientali* |
| TAVO | Tübinger Atlas der Vorderorients (Wiesbaden 1972–   ) |
| *TPSoc* | *Transactions of the Philological Society* |
| TTKY | Turk Tarih Kurumu Yayinlarindan |
| *TürkArkDerg* | *Türk Arkeoluji Dergisi* |
| *TürkTarDerg* | *Türk Tarih Arkeologya ve Etnografya Dergisi* |
| *TürkTarSB* | *Türk Tarih Sunulan Bildirler* |
| *WVDOG* | Wissenschaftliche Veröffentlichungen der deutschen Orient-Gesellschaft |
| *ZAssyr* | *Zeitschrift für Assyriologie* |

Machteld Johanna Mellink, Leslie Clark Professor of Humanities at Bryn Mawr College,
President of the Archaeological Institute of America, 1981–1984

# INTRODUCTION

Anatolia, by virtue of its geographic accessibility to its neighbors, was in the early days of its exploration regarded by European travelers and scholars as a bridge between East and West, the conduit through which passed the "light from the Orient." In 1965, at the American Philosophical Society for Promoting Useful Knowledge, Machteld J. Mellink reviewed this historical tradition and clearly demonstrated the strength of Anatolia's independent cultures and political entities. "Anatolia appears neither as an assemblage of oriental and classical colonies nor as a transit station but as a land with a character of its own. It is seen to have developed cultural characteristics which are native, tenacious, and of potential impact on both the east and the west."[1] The intensification of archaeological research in all parts of Anatolia can be measured in Machteld Mellink's annual analytical summary, "Archaeology in Asia Minor," published in the *American Journal of Archaeology*. In 1966 about fifty foreign and Turkish excavations were taking place; in 1983 there were "about one hundred excavations, reconstructions, surveys and research projects . . . some small, but several with large staffs including engineers and technicians; many of the new excavations . . . with diversified teams of specialists in environmental studies."[2]

Sheer numbers are not the measure of progress, but rather indicators of expanded research goals. We are now beginning to appreciate subtle regional differences and preferences and to refine the broad perspective. The immense amount of evidence which has been produced in the past twenty years, coupled with the ever-increasing array of scientific techniques to examine it, has allowed deeper insight into man's activities in Anatolia and the formulation of more sophisticated questions about them, as the papers which make up this volume show. The scholars whose contributions are presented here have been in the forefront of their respective areas of research, and their collected wisdom is the product of long years in the field and at the desk.

Robert and Linda Braidwood, pioneers in piecing together diverse strains of evidence to explain early human settlement and food production, now seek the immediate background to the village-farming way of life in Southwest Asia. Although they can give no certain answers to the question of how effective village-farming communities developed out of the incipient level, the very fact that the question can be posed represents progress. In the Levant, the phase of incipiency has to a certain extent been identified, particularly in terms of stone artifacts, but it has not yet been recognized in Anatolia. The very early site of Çayönü (ca. 7250–6750 B.C.), with its extraordinary monumental architecture, excavated by the Braidwoods for the University of Chicago with Professor Halet Çambel of Istanbul University, is already over the "threshold of incipiency." Isolating the background of sites such as Çayönü, if such exists locally, is now a priority in prehistoric research in Anatolia, and the Braidwoods suggest where it may be sought.

J. L. Angel and S. C. Bisel of the Smithsonian Institution bring us closer to the lives of Early Bronze Age Anatolians by examining how and how successfully they dealt with the natural and human perils of their environment and by acquainting us with what a population needs in order to be well nourished, energetic, intelligent, and socially well adjusted. This extraordinary reconstruction, the result of rigorous anthropological methods and imaginative reading of "clues," on the evidence of relatively scanty skeletal remains, is aided by Angel's wide experience in forensic anthropology. At Karataş, the site Machteld Mellink and the Bryn Mawr

Expedition have excavated, there are indications that newcomers were absorbed into the community without apparent disruptions in local culture.

Tahsin Özgüç has directed excavations for nearly forty years at the great central Anatolian city of Kaneš with its suburbs of Assyrian merchants. Here he presents for the first time concrete evidence of contact between that city and her southern neighbors in the third millennium B.C. —evidence which gives increased credence to the later legends about military and commercial ventures at the time of the Mesopotamian monarch Sargon of Akkad and his grandson Naramsin (ca. 2400–2300 B.C.), an idea suggested long ago by Machteld Mellink.[3] The possibility that some historical reality lies behind such legends may explain their particular popularity in second-millennium Anatolia.

Nimet Özgüç, excavator of Acemhöyük and an expert on Anatolian glyptic, uses seals and sealings to illustrate internal as well as external patterns of commercial contact in the second millennium B.C. A sealing stylistically at home in North Syria or Assyria appeared on documents at both Kültepe and Acemhöyük, a clear demonstration of the relationship between Anatolia and the south.

Much has been learned in recent years about the early history of the Hittites because of the identification of several phases in the development of their script and language. The revised linguistic chronology has allowed philologists to reassign important historical events to earlier periods. Newly discovered texts have also broadened our knowledge of the Hittites' relations with their neighbors. Concrete archaeological evidence for these connections is scarce, but careful study of several seals by specialists in glyptic provides here some new insights into the nature of Anatolian iconography and cultural exchange with its neighbors. Nimet Özgüç discusses a seal which confirms the long-suspected link between local artistic styles of the Old Assyrian Colony period in the early second millennium, when the Hittites were not yet in power, and those of the Imperial period. In the same vein J. V. Canby focuses on a puzzling figurine made of rock crystal during the Imperial Hittite period to explore the use of the image of the child in art to express political and theological propaganda, as well as certain religious concepts, from the late third millennium through the Neo-Hittite period.

In the mid-second millennium, Assyrians and Hittites, according to the texts, fought and traded with each other and exchanged diplomatic correspondence, but their interaction is expressed in few known monuments. Drawing on her vast knowledge of the entire corpus of ancient art, Edith Porada of Columbia University, dean of glyptic experts, calls attention to a rare cylinder seal

of the Middle Assyrian period from Nineveh, which incorporates what look like Hittite cultic elements. The adoption of ritual iconography argues for a close contact which is unusual in the context of a more general exchange, but which may be documented in areas not yet explored.

Edibe Uzunoğlu, of the Ancient Near Eastern section of the Istanbul Archaeological Museum, also illuminates the artistic dialogue between north and south in publishing for the first time a cylinder seal which she classifies as Imperial Hittite but which, as she points out, shows the confluence of Syrian and Hittite ideas. The intrusion of Hittite iconography into the southern realm is little documented and, as in the case of the Middle Assyrian cylinder discussed by Porada, must result from some special type of exchange. An example of this unusual relationship in the first millennium is seen in a cylinder seal found at Carchemish, which is carved in an Assyrianizing style and bears an unusual Hittite Hieroglyphic inscription. Ali M. and Belkıs Dinçol of Istanbul University append some speculations on the significance of this unique inscription.

R. D. Barnett, long the keeper of Western Asiatic Antiquities in the British Museum, well illustrates the complex relationships among eastern Anatolia (Urartu), Syria, and the Aegean in the Iron Age as he reviews the arguments about the provenience of the giant "Urartian" bronze cauldrons with figural attachments. His suggestion that these vessels were used in funeral feasts may help explain their widespread distribution.

The importance of Anatolian evidence for the general history of the ancient Near East is demonstrated by J. D. Hawkins of the University of London, who examines a newly discovered inscription in Hieroglyphic Luwian from Aksaray, which—together with inscriptions from Carchemish and Sultanhan—can be linked with Old Babylonian (early second millennium) and late Neo-Assyrian (seventh century B.C.) statements of "ideal prices." The new inscription not only allows the decipherment of difficult passages in the other Anatolian texts, but also demonstrates the perpetuation of an old Mesopotamian political ploy—the public statement that "the economy was in good shape when I was in power."

The long continuation of ancient traditions is seen in another light in Kurt Bittel's meticulous reexamination of the strange ensemble of carvings on Kızıldağ. The excavator of Boğazköy and former President of the German Archaeological Institute suggests the possibility that this rock sculpture of King Hartapus (ninth–eighth centuries) was an object of veneration in later, Classical times, further proof of the continuity and strength of Anatolian culture.

The rediscovery by Hans G. Güterbock, of the Oriental Institute of the University of Chicago, of a long-missing but well-known Hittite tablet—a ritual for a prince—along with a collection of bulls' heads and a ram's head spout in a small American midwestern college shows that not all treasures lie under the ground. The letter accompanying the finds at the time of their bequest to Grinnell College reveals how an educated member of the clergy living in late nineteenth-century Turkey viewed the Anatolian past—as part of the world of the Bible and Homer. This historiographic footnote illustrates the enormous strides made in our understanding of Anatolia during the last century.

No longer seen merely as a bridge between Asia and Europe, Anatolia can now be perceived as an indepen-dent entity receptive to foreign ideas, such as cuneiform writing, the cylinder seal, some literary traditions, and some elements of iconography. But the core of its culture, life, and art remained indigenous, and the thread of continuity can be traced from the third through the first millennium, as the papers in this volume so clearly demonstrate, in a fitting tribute to Machteld Mellink's vision.

NOTES
1 M. J. Mellink, "Anatolia: Old and New Perspectives," *PPS* 110.2 (1966) 115.
2 M. J. Mellink, "Archaeology in Asia Minor," *AJA* 88 (1984) 441.
3 "An Akkadian Illustration of a Campaign in Cilicia?" *Anadolu* 7 (1963) 101–15.

# BIBLIOGRAPHY OF MACHTELD J. MELLINK
(Compiled with the help of Nancy Westneat Leinwand)

**1943**
*Hyakinthos* (Utrecht).

**1946**
"De Leeuw van Babylon," *Handelingen van het Nederlandsche Philologencongres* (April) 81–82.

**1950**
"Karatepe. More Light on the Dark Ages," *BibO* 7, 141–50.
Review of A. J. B. Wace, *Mycenae*, in *AJA* 54, 433–34.

**1951**
Review of P. Bourboulis, *Apollo Delphinios*, in *AJA* 55, 432.

**1952**
Review of C. W. Blegen, J. L. Caskey, M. Rawson, and J. Sperling, *Troy* 1.1. *General Introduction, The First and Second Settlements*, in *AJA* 56, 149–51.
Review of J. L. Angel, *Troy. The Human Remains*, in *AJA* 56, 151–52.
Review of W. Otto and R. Herbig, *Handbuch der Archäologie im Rahmen des Handbuchs der Altertumswissenschaft*, in *AJA* 56, 217–19.

**1953**
Review of O. R. Gurney, *The Hittites*, in *AJA* 57, 288.
Review of E. Kunze, *Olympische Forschungen* 2. *Archaische Schildbänder*, in *AJA* 57, 228–30.
Review of *Troy* 1, *Troy* 2, and *Troy. The Human Remains*, in *BibO* 10, 52–61.

**1954**
"Bronze Age Settlements along the Coast of S.W. Asia Minor from Halicarnassus to Antalya," *Yearbook of the American Philosophical Society*, 326–27.
Review of C. H. E. Haspels, *Exploration archéologique de la Phrygie* 3. *La Cité de Midas. Céramique et trou-*

*vailles diverses*, in *AJA* 58, 167–69.
Review of C. L. Woolley, *Carchemish. Report on the Excavations at Jerablus on Behalf of the British Museum* 3. *The Excavations in the Inner Town*, and R. D. Barnett, *The Hittite Inscriptions*, in *AJA* 58, 247–50.
Review of R. Dussaud, *Prélydiens, Hittites et Achéens*, in *AJA* 58, 250–51.
Review of J. Garstang, *Prehistoric Mersin. Yumuk Tepe in Southern Turkey*, in *BibO* 11, 13–15.
Review of P. Dikaios, *Khirokitia. Final Report on the Excavation of a Neolithic Settlement in Cyprus*, in *BibO* 11, 59–61.

**1955**
"Archaeology in Asia Minor," *AJA* 59, 231–40.
Review of *Harvard Studies in Classical Philology* 61 (1953), in *AJA* 59, 183–84.
Review of H. Z. Koşay, *Alaca Höyük*, in *AJA* 59, 184.
Review of *Staatliche Museen zu Berlin. Vorderasiatische Abteilung, Wegleitung* 1/52, in *AJA* 59, 184.
Review of *Istanbul Arkeoloji Müzeleri Yilliği. Annual of the Archaeological Museums of Istanbul* 6, in *AJA* 59, 185.
Review of B. Hrozný, *Ancient History of Western Asia, India and Crete* (trans. J. Procházka), in *AJA* 59, 185.
Review of J. Vercoutter, *Essai sur les relations entre Égyptiens et Préhellènes*, in *AJA* 59, 185–86.
Review of S. I. Rudenko, *Der zweite Kurgan von Pasaryk* (trans. I. M. Gorner), in *AJA* 59, 243–44.
Review of B. B. Piotrovsky, P. N. Schultz, V. A. Golovkina, and S. P. Tolstov, *Ourartou; Néapolis des Scythes; Kharezm*, in *AJA* 59, 244–45.
Review of F. Matz, *Torsion. Eine formenkundliche Untersuchung zur ägäischen Vorgeschichte*, in *AJA* 59, 337.
Review of H. Biesantz, *Kretische-mykenische Siegel-*

bilder: Stilgeschichte und chronologische Untersuchungen, in *AJA* 59, 337–38.

Review of G. C. Miles ed., *Archaeologica Orientalia in Memoriam Ernst Herzfeld*, in *BibO* 12, 122–23.

Review of M. Gough, *The Plain and Rough Places*, in *BibO* 12, 182.

## 1956

*A Hittite Cemetery at Gordion* (Philadelphia).

"Neolithic and Chalcolithic Pottery," in H. Goldman, *Excavations at Gözlü Kule, Tarsus* 2. *From the Neolithic through the Bronze Age* (Princeton) 65–91.

"The Royal Tombs at Alaca Höyük and the Aegean World," in S. S. Weinberg ed., *The Aegean and the Near East. Studies Presented to Hetty Goldman* (Locust Valley) 39–58.

"Archaeology in Asia Minor," *AJA* 60, 369–84.

Review of A. Gabriel, *La Cité de Midas. Topographie. Le site et les fouilles*, in *AJA* 60, 191–92.

Review of M. Riemschneider, *Die Welt der Hethiter*, in *AJA* 60, 457–58.

## 1957

"Turkey: A Decade of Discovery," *Archaeology* 10, 238–39.

Review of F. Matz, *Kreta, Mykene, Troja. Die Minoische und die Homerische Welt*, in *AJA* 61, 195–96.

Review of E. Akurgal, *Phrygische Kunst*, in *AJA* 61, 392–94.

Review of C. L. Woolley, *Alalakh. An Account of the Excavations at Tell Atchana in the Hatay*, in *AJA* 61, 395–400.

Review of C. W. Blegen, J. L. Caskey, and M. Rawson, *Troy. The Sixth Settlement*, in *BibO* 14, 235–39.

## 1958

"Archaeology in Asia Minor," *AJA* 62, 91–104.

Review of F. Matz, *Geschichte der griechischen Kunst* 1. *Die geometrische und früharchaische Form*, in *AJA* 62, 334–35.

Review of D. Opitz and A. Moortgat, *Tell Halaf* 3. *Die Bildwerke*, in *AJA* 62, 438–40.

Review of C. Descamps de Mertzenfeld, *Inventaire commenté des ivoires phéniciens et apparentés découverts dans le Proche-Orient*, in *Gnomon* 30, 29–33.

## 1959

"Archaeology in Asia Minor," *AJA* 63, 73–85.

"The City of Midas," *Scientific American* 201 (July) 100–109.

Review of K. Bittel, W. Herre, H. Otten, M. Rohrs, and J. Schaeuble, *Die hethitischen Grabfunde von Osmankayası*, in *AJA* 63, 291–92.

Review of F. Cassola, *La Ionia nel mondo miceneo*, in *AJA* 63, 294–95.

Review of R. Naumann, *Architektur Kleinasiens von ihren Anfängen bis zum Ende des hethitischen Zeit*, in *Gnomon* 31, 69–73.

## 1960

"Ancient Gordion," in *Encyclopedia Yearbook, Grolier Society*, 242–44.

"Archaeology in Asia Minor," *AJA* 64, 57–69.

"An Archaic Fresco Found at Gordion in Asia Minor," *Yearbook of the American Philosophical Society*, 563–65.

Review of X. de Planhol, *De la plaine pamphylienne aux lacs pisidiens. Nomadisme et vie paysanne*, in *AJA* 64, 378–79.

Review of R. Ghirschman, *Bichapour* 2. *Les mosaïques sassanides*, in *BibO* 17, 197–98.

Review of C. W. Blegen, C. G. Boulter, J. L. Caskey, and M. Rawson, *Troy* 4. *Settlements VIIa, VIIb and VIII*, in *BibO* 17, 249–53.

## 1961

"Archaeology in Asia Minor," *AJA* 65, 37–52.

Review of R. J. Braidwood and B. Howe, *Prehistoric Investigations in Iraqi Kurdistan*, in *AJA* 65, 195–96.

Review of A. Goetze, *Kleinasien*, in *BibO* 18, 74–75.

## 1962

"Archaeological Evidence for Akkadian Contacts with Asia Minor," in *Proceedings of the 25th Congress of Orientalists* (Moscow) 297–98.

About 30 entries in *The Interpreter's Dictionary of the Bible* 1–4 (New York and Nashville).

"Archaeology in Asia Minor," *AJA* 66, 71–85.

"The Prehistory of Syro-Cilicia," review of L. and R. J. Braidwood, *Excavations in the Plain of Antioch* 1, in *BibO* 19, 219–26.

Review of C. G. Starr, *The Origins of Greek Civilization 1100–650 B.C.*, in *AJA* 66, 212–14.

Review of V. R. d'A. Desborough and N. G. L. Hammond, "The End of Mycenaean Civilization and the Dark Age," *CAH*[3] 2, ch. 36, in *JAOS* 82, 573.

Review of J. M. Cook, "Greek Settlement in the Eastern Aegean and Asia Minor," *CAH*[3] 2, ch. 38, in *JAOS* 82, 573–74.

## 1963

"An Akkadian Illustration of a Campaign in Cilicia?" *Anadolu* 7, 101–15.

"Archaeology in Asia Minor," *AJA* 67, 173–90.

Review of J. Deshayes, *Les outils de bronze de l'Indus au Danube (IVe au IIe millénaire)*, in *AJA* 67, 306–7.

Review of G. Mylonas, *Aghios Kosmas. An Early Bronze Age Settlement and Cemetery in Attica*, in *BibO* 20, 192–93.

## 1964

Ed. and contributor, *Dark Ages and Nomads c. 1000 B.C.: Studies in Iranian and Anatolian Archaeology*

(Publications de l'Institut historique et archéologique néerlandais de Stamboul 18).

"A Hittite Figurine from Nuzi," in K. Bittel et al. eds., *Vorderasiatische Archäologie. Studien und Aufsätze: Festschrift Anton Moortgat* (Berlin), 155–64.

"The Concept of Syro-Cilicia and New Developments in Anatolian Archaeology," in *Compte Rendu de l'onzième Rencontre Assyriologique* (Leiden) 34–38.

"Excavations at Karataş-Semayük in Lycia, 1963," *AJA* 68, 269–78.

"Excavations at Karataş-Semayük 1964," *TürkArkDerg* 13.2, 49–57.

"Lycian Wooden Huts and Sign 24 on the Phaistos Disk," *Kadmos* 3, 1–7.

"Report on the First Campaign of Excavations at Karataş-Semayük," *TürkArkDerg* 13.1, 97–98.

"A Votive Bird from Anatolia," *Expedition* 6, 28–32. (Translated in *Die Umschau in Wirtschaft und Technik* 64, no. 17, 536.)

Review of S. Lloyd and J. Mellaart, *Beycesultan I. Chalcolithic and Early Bronze Age Levels,* in *AJA* 68, 303–5.

Review of O. E. Ravn, *A Catalogue of Oriental Cylinder Seals and Impressions in the Danish National Museum,* in *BibO* 21, 61.

Review of A. R. Bellinger, *Troy. The Coins,* in *BibO* 21, 64–65.

Review of J. Mellaart, "Anatolia before c. 4000 B.C. and c. 2300–1750 B.C.," *CAH*³ 1, ch. 7, sect. 11–14, and ch. 24, sect. 1–4, in *JAOS* 84, 473–74.

Review of J. L. Caskey, "Greece, Crete and the Aegean Islands in the Early Bronze Age," *CAH*³ 1, ch. 26(a), in *JAOS* 84, 473–74.

**1965**

"Anatolian Chronology," in R. W. Ehrich ed., *Chronologies in Old World Archaeology* (Chicago) 101–31.

"Archaeology in Asia Minor," *AJA* 69, 133–49.

"Excavations at Karataş-Semayük in Lycia, 1964," *AJA* 69, 241–51.

"Excavations at Karataş-Semayük 1965," *TürkArkDerg* 14.1–2, 223–29.

"Mita, Mushki and Phrygians," *Anadolu Araştirmalari Helmuth Bossert in Hatirasina Armağan. JKF* 2.1–2, 317–25.

Review of D. B. Thompson, *Troy. The Terracotta Figurines of the Hellenistic Period,* in *BibO* 22, 180–82.

Review of F. H. Stubbings, "The Expansion of Mycenaean Civilization," *CAH*³ 2, ch. 22(a), in *JAOS* 85, 418.

**1966**

"The Art of Anatolia until c. 1200 B.C.," in *Art Treasures of Turkey* (Smithsonian Institution, exhibition catalogue, Washington, D.C.) 3–20.

"Anatolia: Old and New Perspectives," *PPS* 110 (April) 111–29.

"Archaeology in Asia Minor," *AJA* 70, 139–59, 279–82.

"Excavations at Karataş-Semayük in Lycia, 1965," *AJA* 70, 245–57.

"Excavations at Karataş-Semayük 1966," *TürkArkDerg* 15.2, 73–80.

"The Hasanlu Bowl in Anatolian Perspective," *IrAnt* 6, 72–87.

Review of *Persica: Annuaire de la Société Néerlando-Iranienne* 1 (1963–1964), in *BibO* 23, 80–81.

Review of F. H. Stubbings, "The Recession of Mycenaean Civilization," *CAH*³ 2, ch. 27, in *JAOS* 85, 229.

Review of W. Orthmann, *Frühe Keramik von Boğazköy,* in *OLZ* 61.1–2, 40–41.

**1967**

"Foreword," in *A Land Called Crete* (Smith College Museum of Art, exhibition catalogue, Northampton), 1–10.

"Sea Peoples," in *Encyclopedia Britannica* suppl., 130–31.

"Archaeology in Asia Minor," *AJA* 71, 155–74.

"Beycesultan: A Bronze Age Site in Southwestern Turkey," *BibO* 24, 3–9.

"Excavations at Karataş-Semayük in Lycia, 1966," *AJA* 71, 251–67.

"Excavations at Karataş-Semayük 1967," *TürkArkDerg* 16.1, 107–12.

Review of W. S. Smith, *Interconnections in the Ancient Near East,* in *AJA* 71, 92–94.

Review of E. Akurgal, *Die Kunst Anatoliens von Homer bis Alexander,* in *BibO* 24, 192–94.

Review of T. Özgüç, *Altintepe. Architectural Monuments and Wall Paintings,* in *BibO* 24, 347–49.

Review of *Persica* 2 (1965–1966), in *BibO* 24, 367.

Review of E. Porada et al., *Ancient Iran. The Art of Pre-Islamic Times,* in *BibO* 24, 367–68.

**1968**

"Archaeology in Asia Minor," *AJA* 72, 125–47.

"Excavations at Karataş-Semayük in Lycia, 1967," *AJA* 72, 243–59.

"Excavations at Karataş-Semayük 1968," *TürkArkDerg* 17.2, 145–50.

Review of C. J. and J. Deshayes, *Index de l'outillage. Outils en métal de l'Age du Bronze, des Balkans à l'Indus,* in *AJA* 72, 79–81.

Review of H. W. Catling, "Cyprus in the Neolithic and Bronze Age Periods," *CAH*³ 1, chs. 9(c), 26(b); 2, chs. 4(c), 22(b), in *JAOS* 88, 539–40.

Review of J. L. Caskey, "Greece and the Aegean Islands

in the Middle Bronze Age," *CAH*³ 2, ch. 4(a), in *JAOS* 88, 540–41.

Review of O. R. Gurney, "Anatolia c. 1600–1380 B.C.," *CAH*³ 2, ch. 15(a), in *JAOS* 88, 541–42.

**1969**

"Archaeology in Asia Minor," *AJA* 73, 203–27.

"The Early Bronze Age in Southwest Anatolia: A Start in Lycia," *Archaeology* 22, 290–99.

"Excavations at Karataş-Semayük in Lycia, 1968," *AJA* 73, 319–31.

"Excavations at Karataş-Semayük 1969," *TürkArkDerg* 18.2, 137–39.

"Excavations of a Lycian Painted Tomb near Elmalı, Kızılbel," *TürkArkDerg* 18.2, 141–44.

"A Four-Spouted Krater from Karataş," *Anadolu* 13, 69–76.

"The Pratt Ivories in the Metropolitan Museum of Art— Kerma—Chronology and the Transition from E.B. to M.B.," *AJA* 73, 285–87.

Review of W. Orthmann, *Das Graberfeld bei Ilıca*, in *AJA* 73, 80–81.

Review of *Anatolica* 1 (1966–1967), in *BibO* 26, 92–93.

**1970**

"Archaeology in Asia Minor," *AJA* 74, 157–78.

"Excavations at Karataş-Semayük and Elmalı, Lycia, 1969," *AJA* 74, 245–53.

"Excavations at Karataş-Semayük and Elmalı, 1970," *TürkArkDerg* 19.1, 157–68.

"Observations on the Sculptures of Alaca Höyük," *Anadolu* 14, 15–27.

Review of L. Vanden Berghe, *Het archaeologisch Onderzoek naar de Bronscultuur van Luristan. Opgravingen in Pusht-i Kuh 1. Kalwali en War Kabud (1965 en 1966)*, in *AJA* 74, 103–4.

Review of *Anatolica* 2 (1968–1969), in *BibO* 27, 44.

**1971**

"Archaeology in Asia Minor," *AJA* 75, 161–81.

"Excavations at Karataş-Semayük and Elmalı in Lycia, 1970," *AJA* 75, 245–55.

Review of W. Schirmer, *Die Bebauung am unteren Büyükkale-Nordwesthang in Boğazköy*, in *OrAnt* 10, 83–85.

**1972**

"Archaeology in Asia Minor," *AJA* 76, 165–88.

"Excavations at Karataş-Semayük and Elmalı, Lycia, 1971," *AJA* 76, 257–69.

Review of *CAH*³ 1.1, in *Archaeology* 25, 314–26.

Review of *Anatolica* 3 (1969–1970), in *BibO* 29, 199–200.

Review of *Persica* 4, in *BibO* 29, 243.

**1973**

"Archaeology in Asia Minor," *AJA* 77, 169–93.

"Excavations at Karataş-Semayük and Elmalı, 1972," *AJA* 77, 293–303.

"Karataş-Semayük and Elmalı, 1971," *TürkArkDerg* 20.2, 155–66.

"XXe Rencontre Assyriologique in Leyden, July 3–7, 1972," with D. Hansen and E. Porada, *Archaeology* 26, 139–44.

Review of *CAH*³ 1.2, in *JNES* 32, 487–88.

**1974**

*Frühe Stufen der Kunst*, with J. Filip and others (Berlin).

"Hittite Friezes and Gate Sculptures," in *Anatolian Studies Presented to Hans Gustav Güterbock on the Occasion of His Sixty-Fifth Birthday* (Istanbul) 201–14.

"Notes on Anatolian Wall Painting," in *Mélanges Mansel: Mansel'a Armağan* (Ankara) 537–47.

"Archaeology in Asia Minor," *AJA* 78, 105–30.

"Excavations at Karataş-Semayük and Elmalı, Lycia, 1973," *AJA* 78, 351–59.

"Excavations at Karataş-Semayük and Elmalı, 1972," *TürkArkDerg* 21.1, 125–32.

Review of J. D. Muhly, *Copper and Tin. The Distribution of the Mineral Resources and the Nature of the Metals Trade in the Bronze Age*, in *Science* 185/4145, 52–53.

Review of *Anatolica* 4 (1971–1972), in *BibO* 31, 283.

**1975**

"Hurriter. Kunst," in *RLA* 4 (Berlin) 514–19.

"Neolithic Female Idol," in I. E. Rubin, *The Guennol Collection* 1 (Metropolitan Museum of Art, New York) 53–57.

"Wall Paintings from the Persian Period at Gordion," in *Fifth International Congress of Iranian Art and Archaeology* 2 (Teheran) 357–59.

"Archaeology in Asia Minor," *AJA* 79, 201–22.

"Excavations at Karataş-Semayük and Elmalı, 1974," *AJA* 79, 349–55.

"Excavations at Karataş-Semayük and Elmalı, 1973," *TürkArkDerg* 22.1, 71–78.

Review of R. Fleischer, *Artemis von Ephesos und verwandte Kultstatuen aus Anatolien und Syrien*, in *AJA* 79, 108–8.

Review of R. M. Boehmer, *Die Kleinfunde von Boğazköy aus den Grabungskampagnen 1931–1939 und 1952–1969*, in *BibO* 32, 228–30.

**1976**

"Archaeology in Asia Minor," *AJA* 80, 261–89.

"Excavations in the Elmalı Area, 1975," *AJA* 80, 377–84.

"Excavations at Karataş-Semayük and Elmalı, 1974," *TürkArkDerg* 23.1, 87–92.

"Local, Phrygian and Greek Traits in Northern Lycia," *RA* (Mélanges Pierre Demargne), 21–34.
Review of G. M. A. Hanfmann, *From Croesus to Constantine. The Cities of Western Asia Minor and Their Arts in Greek and Roman Times*, in *AJA* 80, 439–40.

## 1977
"Archaeology in Asia Minor," *AJA* 81, 289–321.
"Excavations at Karataş-Semayük and Elmalı, 1975," *TürkArkDerg* 24.1, 137–43.
Review of A. Parrot, *Mari, capitale fabuleuse*, in *AJA* 81, 115.

## 1978
"Mural Painting in Lycian Tombs," in *Proceedings of the Xth International Congress of Classical Archaeology* (Ankara) 805–9.
"Archaeology in Asia Minor," *AJA* 82, 315–38.
Review of K. Bittel, *Die Hethiter. Die Kunst Anatoliens vom Ende des 3. bis zum Anfang des 1. Jarhrtausends vor Christus*, in *AHR* 83, 135–36.

## 1979
"Midas in Tyana," in *Florilegium Anatolicum. Mélanges offerts à Emmanuel Laroche* (Paris) 249–57.
"The Symbolic Doorway of the Tumulus at Karaburun, Elmalı," *VIII. Türk Tarih Sunulan Bildirler* 1 (Ankara) 383–87.
"Archaeology in Asia Minor," *AJA* 83, 331–44.
Review of J. Borchhardt, *Myra*, in *AJA* 83, 123–25.
Review of C. Burney, *The Ancient Near East*, in *JSAH* 38, 176.

## 1980
"Archaic Wall Paintings from Gordion," in K. DeVries ed., *From Athens to Gordion* (University Museum, Philadelphia) 91–98.
"Hetty Goldman," in B. Sicherman, C. Hurd Green, et al. eds., *Notable American Women* (Cambridge, Mass.) 280–82.
"A Sample Problem from the Painted Tomb at Kızılbel," in H. Metzger ed., *Actes du Colloque sur la Lycie Antique* (Paris) 15–20.
"Archaeology in Asia Minor," *AJA* 84, 501–18.
"Excavations at Karataş-Semayük and Elmalı, 1976," *TürkArkDerg* 25.1, 175–86.

"Fouilles d'Elmalı en Lycie du Nord (Turquie). Découvertes préhistoriques et tombes à fresques," *CRAI* 476–96.
"Rhys Carpenter, Necrology," *AJA* 84, 260.
Review of *CAH*³ 2.2 and plates to vols. 1 and 2, in *JNES* 39, 71–73.

## 1981
Contribution to R. S. Young, *Gordion Excavations 1. Three Great Early Tumuli* (Philadelphia).
"Temples and High Places in Phrygia," in *Colloquium on Temples and High Places in Biblical Times* (Jerusalem) 96–104.
"Turchia, Archeologia," in *Enciclopedia Italiana di Scienze, Lettere ed Arti* (G. Treccani), IV Appendice 1961–1978 (Rome) 704–7.
"Archaeology in Asia Minor," *AJA* 85, 463–79.
Review of M. N. van Loon ed., *Korucutepe 2*, in *BibO* 38, 115–18.

## 1982
"Archaeology in Asia Minor," *AJA* 557–76.
"John Langdon Caskey, Necrology," *AJA* 86, 317, and *American Philosophical Society Yearbook 1982*, 454–59.

## 1983
"Comments on a Cult Relief of Kybele from Gordion," in R. M. Boehmer and H. Hauptmann eds., *Beiträge zur Altertumskunde Kleinasiens. Festschrift für Kurt Bittel* (Mainz am Rhein) 349–60.
"Archaeology in Asia Minor," *AJA* 87, 427–42.
"The Hittites and the Aegean World 2. Archaeological Comments on Ahhiyawa-Achaians in Western Anatolia," *AJA* 87, 138–41.

## 1984
"The Native Kingdoms of Anatolia," with O. Masson, in J. Boardman ed., *CAH*³ 3, Plates (Cambridge) 164–76.
"Archaeology in Asia Minor," *AJA* 88, 441–59.
Review of O. Aurenche, *La maison orientale. L'Architecture du Proche Orient ancien des origines au milieu du quatrième millénaire*, in *AJA* 88, 407–8.
Review of R. M. Boehmer, *Die Kleinfunde aus der Unterstadt von Boğazköy. Grabungskampagnen 1970–1978*, in *AJA* 88, 408–9.

# ANCIENT ANATOLIA

# Prelude to the Appearance of Village-Farming Communities in Southwestern Asia    1

LINDA S. BRAIDWOOD and ROBERT J. BRAIDWOOD

Machteld Mellink has herself not yet undertaken research reaching as far back as the appearance of effective village-farming communities in Anatolia. She has, however, always given attention to the prehistory of the region in her excellent yearly news articles in the *American Journal of Archaeology*. We hope these modest jottings will serve to complement her interest in the prehistoric background to the great era of later cultural developments and changes in Anatolia with which she has been so fruitfully concerned.

In this essay in Machteld Mellink's honor, we propose to examine, very briefly, the available evidence for the immediate background to the appearance of effective food production and the village-farming community way of life as it evolved in the Southwest Asiatic instance. We have long tended to think of the range of time and developments within this background as an era of incipience—that is, as an inchoate buildup to effective food production.[1] Earlier, we tended to consider only the materials of the Natufian and Karim Shahirian types of assemblages as of the incipient era. Now, it seems wise to us to include the preceding materials of Kebaran and Zarzian types as also essentially incipient.

We are particularly interested here in whether there are materials now available in Anatolia which can usefully be considered as incipient. The outlook is not at all hopeful, as yet, when one compares the materials available from the Levantine region and, in a more restricted sense, from the Zagros flanks.

We wish to make it clear (as usual) why we shall not use the term "Neolithic." The old word has come to include a confusing bundle of meanings: chronological, descriptive (i.e., a phase with ground stone, with pottery, or merely "aceramic" or "proto-" etc.), and interpretative (as, for example, in the phrase "Neolithic way of life"). To compound the confusion, there is Childe's well-known conception of a "Neolithic Revolution," with its definite implications of a food-producing economy.[2] Incidentally, we find a kind of wry amusement in Perkins and Daly's title "A Hunters' Village in Neolithic Turkey,"[3] which implies that "Neolithic" had to be explained in order to be understood by readers.

Thus, our interest here is not in "Neolithic" beginnings, nor for that matter would we really choose to speak of our interest as "Mesolithic" or "Epipaleolithic," although many of our respected colleagues do so. Again, the question we face is what evidence is now available, natural and cultural, that may lead to an understanding of the appearance of effective food production in southwestern Asia. We shall not, however, concern ourselves greatly with "models" of exactly how and why the development happened. We doubt that there is yet enough sound evidence anywhere in the region for elaborate "model building."

As the chronological evidence now stands, what we take to be the overall level of incipience probably spanned about ten thousand years. There tends to be general agreement that the level's time span was from sometime after 20,000 to just after 10,000 years ago—in effect, from terminal Pleistocene into early Holocene times.

Knowledge of the paleoenvironmental sequences within the above time range is increasing. During the 1959–1960 field season of the Oriental Institute's Prehistoric Project near Kermanshah, Iran, our geological colleague Herbert E. Wright, Jr., undertook pioneering palynological studies at Lake Zeribar; he was soon joined by Willem van Zeist.[4] The published results of a symposium held at the Biologisch-Archaeologisch Instituut at Groningen in 1980 show how much has already been learned about *Palaeoclimates, Palaeoenvironments and Human Communities in the Eastern Mediterranean in Later Prehistory.*[5] Naturally, there are conflicting interpretations and qualifications of some details. For example, in pollen studies, Bottema commends Leroi-Gourhan for now stressing that samples from terrestrial contexts are very poor in pollen compared with samples from lacustrine or peat deposits.[6] Of course, few (if any?) pollen samples from directly excavated contexts in southwestern Asia actually come from lacustrine or peat deposits. In addition, climatic reconstruction based on the proportionate numbers of animal bones from excavated sites must take into account Reed's idea of the "cultural filter"[7] and also the fact that the remains of smaller (and environmentally more sensitive) species have received less attention than those of larger mammals.

The general paleoenvironmental picture seems to suggest that Pleniglacial and Late Glacial conditions were already relatively clement in the southern Levant (where the Huleh basin provides the best pollen evidence)[8] and generally tended to improve as time went on. However, grading northward through northwestern Syria, east to the Zagros flanks, and up into Anatolia, conditions were less clement than in the south and ameliorated more gradually.

The pollen diagrams for the southern Levant show that although open forest was replaced by forest steppe during the Pleniglacial (24,000–14,000 B.P.),* a Late Glacial expansion of oak accompanied more rain and warmer weather (14,000–10,000 B.P.). After 10,000 B.P., temperatures seem to have increased still further but there was less rainfall, resulting in a decline in tree pollen and a consequent buildup of herbaceous pollen. After 7,400 B.P., there was again an increase in tree pollen but with fluctuations.

In the Ghab valley in northwestern Syria, there were two phases of high herbaceous pollen in the 25,000–11,000 B.P. time range, indicating a dry climate. Thereafter, forests expanded rapidly to a peak by 8,000 B.P., then decreased somewhat, with temperature as well as rainfall probably also decreasing.[9]

Along the Zagros, from 35,000 to 14,000 B.P., the snow line was much lower than it is today, and low temperature and dryness were responsible for an artemisia steppe condition and the almost complete lack of trees. During the Late Glacial (14,000–10,000 B.P.), the number of trees increased slightly but the level of herbaceous pollen remained high. Thereafter followed an oak-pistachio forest steppe, with Zagros oak forest replacing the forest steppe by ca. 6,000 B.P.[10]

In southeastern Turkey, conditions seem to have been essentially the same, although changes came about more slowly than in the Zagros, with the oak forest beginning only ca. 6,500 B.P. and reaching present conditions at about 3,400 B.P. In southwestern and south central Turkey, tree pollen began to replace herbaceous pollen—doubtless because of a rise in humidity—just before 9,000 B.P. The predominance of oak and juniper implies a drier climate than the present one, however. The present tree cover would be pine, were the area not so overcut and overgrazed. At Beyşehir in south central Anatolia, the shift from cedar to pine came ca. 6,000 B.P., suggesting an increase in humidity which brought it near current levels.[11]

Thus, the general environmental picture for southwestern Asia during the Pleniglacial, Late Glacial, and earliest Holocene seems to have been one of relatively marked climatic amelioration with some fluctuations. It is doubtless worth bearing in mind, however, that these generalities refer to the broader subregions named and that there may well have been more localized variations due to altitudinal, coastal, and other more restricted situations.

Although orderly surface surveys for sites have not yet been undertaken over most of the area of concern here (as well as in the more arid desert portions of the whole region), there is good reason to believe that hunter-collectors were at home from the shores of the Caspian to the Sinai and west to the Aegean. Without question, however, the available artifactual evidence from the time range of the incipient era is best represented in the Levant (i.e., essentially the regions from the middle Euphrates and west of it, especially along the Mediterranean). There is less information from the trans-Euphrates–Zagros flanks region, where far less excavation had taken place even before work became impossible in Iran (and to some extent in Iraq).[12] In Anatolia, almost nothing useful is yet known of the incipient range.

The most recent venture at a general culture-historical summary of the incipient range for all southwestern Asia is that of Henry.[13] Bar-Yosef's excellent papers treat only the materials from the Levant[14]; J. Cauvin's study of 1978 is now somewhat dated.[15] Each of these authors retains the term "Epipaleolithic" for the incipient range. Henry takes his "Epipaleolithic" to have "encompassed the terminal Pleistocene and early Holocene, a time of marked and rapid climatic-environmental oscillation" within an area "that displayed considerable environmental and cultural diversity," and states that "it is not surprising that considerable variation in adaptive strategies existed among the region's inhabitants."[16]

In the Levant, the range of our concern begins with

---

*We propose to list all our chronological assessments, based on radiocarbon age determinations in standard uncalibrated Libby half-life terms, as "before present" (B.P.)—that is, before 1950 A.D. There is simply too much confusion about what is meant when "B.C.," "B.C.E.," "b.c.," etc., are used.

the appearance of the Kebaran complex ca. 19,000 B.P. It consists of a number of regionally or temporally different assemblages, typified by microlithic blade tools. The sites, in the open as well as in caves, tend to be small and are most frequent in the present Mediterranean park–forest zone of the central and northern Levant. At one site, Ein Gev I, the remains of semisubterranean pit houses some 6 m in diameter were found, along with mortars and pestles (probably implying plant-food processing).[17] Farther south, following assemblages not so characteristically Kebaran, Henry sees the later geometric Kebaran as having spread into the Negev and Sinai, and notes that presently the Helwan retouch appeared, suggestive of a northeast African linkage.[18]

Henry proposes a date around 12,500 B.P. for the beginning of the much more full-bodied Natufian assemblage,[19] and follows Wright[20] in linking its appearance to the general temperature rise in the Levant at that time. Earlier, wild cereals (barley and emmer wheat) appear to have grown—no doubt poorly—in restricted areas of sandy soil at low elevations in the Dead Sea valley and along the Mediterranean coast. Henry sees the Natufian inventory as an expression of a new adaptive strategy attending the temperature increase. The Natufian was, he believes, based on increasingly intensive collection of the wild cereals and nuts which were then spreading up into zones with better soils, as well as on the successful hunting of various artiodactyls.

Well over a quarter-century ago, Perrot first demonstrated, through his work at the Natufian site of Ain Mallaha, that the peoples of the incipient range lived in open settlements as well as in caves.[21] The Natufian assemblage, as it is now generally known, includes the remains of stone-founded circular houses. Intramural burials with grave goods are common; a goodly variety of ground stone and bone artifacts have been recovered, and there is a rich variety of chipped stone tools, including microlithic flints as well as larger tools.

Elements of both the earlier Kebaran types of assemblage and those of the Natufian have been found well to the northeast of the coastal portions of the Levant.[22] Such finds have been made in Kowm, a present-day oasislike region north of Palmyra, in Syria. Beyond, on the middle Euphrates, modest exposures were made on the riverside mounds of Mureybit and Abu Hureyra as part of the Euphrates salvage effort in Syria. There is disagreement as to whether their basal yields should be called Natufian without considerable qualification. Both sites have traces of round house structures and "it seems probable"[23] that wild einkorn wheat was being deliberately cultivated.

So far, however, no reliable claims for domesticated plants or animals—save for the dog—have been advanced for the Natufian, which is generally taken to have

ended about 10,500 years ago. Quite soon afterward, ca. 9,750 B.P., evidence of domesticated emmer wheat, lentils, and peas appears at Tell Aswad, near Damascus, in what seems to be an early village type of assemblage.[24] There were also a few kernels of hulled barley and emmer wheat in the "PPNA" levels of Jericho[25] at essentially the same time. Thus, we assume, the threshold of incipience had been definitely crossed in the Levant, and village-farming communities had come into being.

Turning now to the Zagros flanks region, we suggested above that the available evidence for the range of incipience is in no way as substantial here as it is in the Levant. In addition, there are still too few age determinations (some sites having none) to suggest an overall chronological span. We need also note that Henry's general summary,[26] excellent for the Levant, is understandably not so full for the trans-Euphrates regions, where it relies in part on Mellaart's decidedly secondary source.[27] Howe's and Dittemore's final reports on Karim Shahir and M'lefaat have now appeared.[28] Briefer summaries of some of the other Oriental Institute Prehistoric Project test excavations and sites encountered along the Zagros[29] and Wahida's useful account of his reexcavation of Zarzi[30] also need to be noted.

As in the case of the Kebaran in the Levant, we are inclined to consider the so-called Zarzian materials along the Zagros as an early aspect of the incipient level. These materials were first exposed in the cave of Zarzi, near Sulaimaniyah, by Garrod.[31]

The Zarzian, as it is so far known, consists almost entirely of neatly made chipped flint tools, many microlithic, with a few rare obsidian artifacts. Rare grooved abrading stones (two examples only), beads and pendants of various materials, simple bone tools, and perhaps a boulder mortar or quern complete the assemblage as we now know it. Garrod's excavations at Zarzi disclosed the characteristic chipped stone tools as comprising burins, notched pieces, backed blades and bladelets, and a variety of scrapers (including end and thumb nail). Only in the uppermost part of the layer did she encounter geometric microliths—mainly scalene triangles, rare lunates, and shouldered points. Wahida's careful reexamination of Zarzi in 1971 unfortunately could not definitely affirm the two-part division, or deny it. It thus remains a question, even at Zarzi, whether the presence of geometric microliths in a Zarzian-like assemblage makes that industry late Zarzian.

A substantial deposit of Zarzian materials (with a variety of geometric microliths) was excavated by Howe at Palegawra in northern Iraq.[32] He also found what he considers Zarzian traces in various soundings that he made in shelters farther north—Barak, Hajiyah, and Babkhal—unfortunately all much disturbed. These were without geometric microliths, as were collections made on two surface sites. These extremely interesting open-air sites, Turkaka and Kowri Khan, not far from Jarmo, have tentatively been assigned to the Zarzian by Howe. In addition to the absence of geometric microliths, the characteristics of the excellent chipped stone industries represented on the surface of these sites seem closer to those of the Zarzian than to the following Karim Shahirian. The question remains, however, whether one or both of these sites should be considered an aspect of the Zarzian or whether they are earlier than the Zarzian or later.

Three Zagros shelters/caves have Zarzian materials immediately overlying Bardostian levels. The entire range of geometric microliths was found in Pa Sangar,[33] and apparently a variety of triangular microliths at Shanidar in the Zarzian level B 2,[34] but only scalene triangles were found by Howe in the Warwasi Zarzian.[35]

Since at present our detailed knowledge of the Zarzian comes only from the site of Zarzi itself, we shall not know how closely related the various Zarzian occurrences actually are until the other sites have been studied and reported. Should each of the above occurrences be called Zarzian, and over what range of time does the Zarzian occur? At present, the time range accounted for by the radiocarbon determinations would extend from ca. 14,000 B.P. (based on numerous Palegawra samples)[36] until around 12,000 B.P. In actuality, it may well have begun much earlier and continued considerably later.

Nothing substantial can be said of the flora exploited in this time range, but we know more about the fauna. Turnbull and Reed announced the finding of the lower jaw of a domestic dog at Palegawra, but the identification has been questioned.[37] Reed reviewed the matter and asserted that the probability of domestication is strengthened by "the finding of a complete skeleton of a young Canis (not a jackal) buried beneath a human skeleton at Mallaha,"[38] the Natufian site in northern Israel. The most common bones at Palegawra were of wild equids, cervids, and sheep/goats. There seem to have been only a very few bone fragments at Zarzi.

Following the Zarzian, we are confronted with a few sites whose materials seem to belong without question to the incipient level. The names of Karim Shahir and Zawi Chemi (Shanidar) in the Iraqi Zagros and M'lefaat to the west in piedmont country immediately come to mind. These sites seem to have little in common with the preceding Zarzian other than the rare grooved abraders and a possible boulder mortar. There is no longer any doubt about the presence of ground stone—it occurs in great variety and quantity.

The discovery and excavation of the open-air site of Karim Shahir were closely followed by the fortunate excavation of Shanidar Cave, where materials thought to be fairly similar to Karim Shahir were found stratified directly above the Zarzian. This particular aspect of the Shanidar materials was confirmed by the subsequent excavation of the open-air site of Zawi Chemi, a short distance from the cave. The site of M'lefaat, although only briefly tested, is also alluded to as being generally related to Karim Shahir and Zawi Chemi and of the same general time range. There are only two radiocarbon age determinations—that of the Zawi Chemi B 1 level in Shanidar cave, 10,600 ± 300 B.P. and that of the open site of Zawi Chemi, 10,870 ± 300 B.P.[39] Unfortunately, the depth of Karim Shahir was too shallow to provide reliable samples for radiocarbon determination; the M'lefaat matrix was also contaminated in the areas tested, but the site of M'lefaat should provide reliable samples if and when it is excavated in the future.

With the recent final publication of the Zawi Chemi finds,[40] Karim Shahir,[41] and M'lefaat,[42] there is now a possibility of seeing how closely related the three sites may be. As regards Shanidar cave proper, in 1963 Ralph Solecki noted that "Shanidar B 1 is contemporary with the basal layer of the Zawi Chemi village site, which has a carbon-14 date of about 8900 B.C. . . . The artifact contents of cave and village layers are quite similar."[43] Rose Solecki later added that "although many of the same tool types are found at both sites, there are slight differences between the two assemblages."[44] Most recently, in the final publication on Zawi Chemi, she says little more than "A Zawi Chemi occupation is found in Shanidar Cave."[45] Unfortunately, until the Shanidar B 1 level is published, there is no way of judging how comparable its materials are with those of Zawi Chemi. We believe that it will be extremely useful generally, and especially for this important range of time, to be able to make such a comparison.

Karim Shahir and Zawi Chemi both produced sizable excavated samples of the materials of this incipient range—the various exposures of Karim Shahir totaled ca. 600 m², but since the depth of deposit was always shallow, the total amount of cultural matrix cleared was ca. 300 m³. Zawi Chemi tests and cuts exposed only ca. 100 m²; however, there was greater depth to the deposits—2 m at the most—and the total amount cleared was thus ca. 200 m³. Since the soundage made by Broman on M'lefaat in the piedmont zone near Erbil lasted only four and a half days, the two exposures amounted to 36 m², with a total of about 25 m³ excavated;[46] as a result, the sample of materials is relatively small compared to samples from Karim Shahir and Zawi Chemi.

As with the Zarzian, the great bulk of material from each site is represented by the chipped flint category. But the pecked/ground and flaked/polished stone items are impressive in their variety: boulder mortars, querns, mullers, grooved rubbing stones, hammerstones and a variety of hand stones, celts (mainly chipped and polished), and ornamental items such as polished stone beads and pendants and (at Karim Shahir) bracelets. Also newly appearing, but rare, are lightly fired small clay figurines and various shaped bits of clay (Karim Shahir and M'lefaat). There are a variety of bone tools, such as awls, two knife hafts (Zawi Chemi and Shanidar B 1), some beads, and some decorated bone fragments. We can now also speak of architectural traces and hints: circular to oval emplacements of stones (Zawi Chemi and M'lefaat), an alignment of stones (Shanidar B 1), and a puzzling extensive and intensive scatter of cracked rocks and stream pebbles, all brought up from the valley floor (Karim Shahir). Shanidar B 1 also served as the burial ground for twenty-eight individuals.

In the following descriptive summary of the chipped stone industry, we deal in generalities, since Rose Solecki and Howe give valuable detailed comparisons. Obsidian, to all intents, seems to be virtually absent from this range of time (although present, it is definitely rare in the Zarzian), being limited to one piece at Zawi Chemi, five items at Karim Shahir (in situ or brought in by workers from Jarmo?), and nine pieces at M'lefaat (where there was the chance of later intrusion).

All three flint industries have a strong microlithic component, only a small proportion of carefully shaped, neatly retouched tools, with the great bulk showing only retouch by use and serving as multipurpose tools. The shapely, well-made tools are, for the most part, microlithic backed bladelets (most abundant in Zawi Chemi), microlithic lunates (only at Zawi Chemi, and relatively abundant there), drills (Karim Shahir), and perforators (M'lefaat). Aside from the great number of artifacts simply showing various signs of use retouch—multipurpose tools—the largest proportion of artifacts with distinctive traits at Karim Shahir and M'lefaat consists of notched and also nibbled blades and bladelets (mainly bladelets at M'lefaat). At Zawi Chemi the next most numerous category of tools (after retouched-by-use blades and flakes) comprises denticulated blades and flakes and scalar flakes in the standard-sized tool category, and backed bladelets, followed by lunates in the microlithic-sized category. End and side scrapers, shaped mainly by use—whether on blades, bladelets, or flakes—are found in numbers at each site. Drills or perforators are also fairly common. Although some burins are found at each site, they are poor specimens and rare. A few pieces with sheen were found at Karim Shahir and Zawi Chemi—none at M'lefaat.

There are definite differences among the industries at each site, and some have already been mentioned above. Other unusual features include an enormous amount of cores, core fragments, and parts found at Karim Shahir (23 percent, versus 13 percent for M'lefaat and 9 percent for Zawi Chemi). Zawi Chemi had an additional industry—although small in numbers—of large-sized flaked pebble tools. The M'lefaat flint industry was overwhelmingly microlithic. In addition to the differences, from site to site, in the individual tool types as percentages of the industry, there is a marked difference in the overall percentage of microlithic-sized artifacts in the industry and a great difference as well in the extent to which an individual site favored blade tools or flake tools.[47]

The real question is how much stress to lay on the differences among these sites—can some of the differences be attributed to a time differential or to coping with differing living conditions and surroundings? There is no doubt whatever that the overall assemblages have much in common, including the sharing of new elements. Still, we would not feel justified in assigning one name—whether Karim Shahirian or Zawi Chemian—to the assemblages at either of the other two sites.

Finally, moving southeastward into the Iranian Zagros, the site of Asiab should definitely be mentioned as part of this incipient horizon. A substantial sample was excavated (ca. 130 m² in the various test pits and main exposure, and ca. 122 m³ in total matrix removed; the depth was ca. 1.50 m in the excavated portion of a large oval pit dug into virgin soil). Howe's detailed description shows that the Asiab materials, although perhaps somewhat later (one charcoal-based radiocarbon determination gives 9755 ± 85 B.P.), have much in common with the above sites.[48] Layer E of Ganj Dareh may possibly also be part of this horizon, but too little of it is yet published—and perhaps too little yet excavated (36 m² cleared but amazingly "few" grinding stones and no milling stones were found;[49] the early site of Qazemi, east of Ganj Dareh, found on survey by Mortensen and Smith, also had no grinding stones or pestles and suggested to them similarities with Layer E of Ganj Dareh).[50] We have not included the Bus Mordeh phase of Ali Kosh in our incipient stage, since we heartily agree with Howe's assessment that Bus Mordeh is "well subsequent to the horizons of Karim Shahir and similar sites and closer to the time and cultural phase of Jarmo."[51]

Curiously enough, at present we know of no sites in the general Zagros area that would definitely fill the gap between the incipient level of Zawi Chemi or Karim Shahir and the fully developed food-producing level of Jarmo. Only recently, our attention was drawn to a piedmont site in northern Iraq, Telul el-Rihan III, excavated in 1979 within the salvage area of the Hamrin.[52] A modest exposure, ca. 118 m², made in the substantial settlement of ca. 4,000 m², revealed no pottery but did reveal architecture consisting of oval or round huts, 3 to 4 m in diameter, partially dug into the virgin soil. There were well-made clay floors; assorted post holes and debris seem to indicate simple wattle-and-daub structures. The chipped stone industry consisted of blades, scrapers, burins and few sickle blades in flint, and a considerable amount of obsidian microcores and microlithic-sized tools (presumably microblades used as is). The excavator assumes that the site is pre-Jarmo, and it may well be. We eagerly await the publication.

Data on the flora of the incipient phase are meager. As with the lack of trustworthy radiocarbon samples in the relatively shallow depth of the Karim Shahir deposit, we did not feel that any plant materials could be reliably dated to the phases of occupation at Karim Shahir. At Zawi Chemi, Leroi-Gourhan reports a definite increase in Gramineae pollen of the Cerealia type in Shanidar 1 and Zawi Chemi, but cautions that "Il est impossible, par la palynologie de différencier les graminées, sauvages, ancêtres de nos céréales, de ces dernières, cultivées."[53] The evidence for domestic animals also presents a somewhat complicated situation. Reed provides a thoughtful assessment of the evidence for and against the presence of domestic sheep at Zawi Chemi and of goats at Asiab; he does not actually reject either claim.[54] In Asiab, Karim Shahir, and Zawi Chemi, the major hunted animals were deer, sheep, and goat; apparently less frequently hunted were pig, cattle, and gazelle.

In sum, there is as yet no clear proof of effective food production during the time range of the Karim Shahir–Zawi Chemi–Asiab–M'lefaat occupations.

Coming at last to Anatolia, we consider first the piedmont of the eastern Taurus. Essentially, we still know nothing of cultural developments in this region for the time of incipience. The Joint Prehistoric Project of the Universities of Chicago and Istanbul undertook a surface survey within the general region in 1963, but unfortunately we could not then examine the lower slopes of the piedmont in the Urfa-Viranşehir-Mardin-Cizre region,[55] although Howe was able to visit one site just east of Urfa, Göbekli (site V52/1). He also made restricted tests on two sites near the town of Bozova, Biriş (site U51/1) and Soğut (site U51/2).

The most that can be said about all three sites is that they had blade tool industries, made on excellent flint, producing many burins but few microliths. They seem to have had no relationship with the Çayönü industry or the flint component of any later assemblage of the general region.

Finally, in the autumn of 1980, we were able to spend a full day near Mardin, where, with the director of the local museum, Abdulhalik Ekmen, we visited a promising site called Hirbet Selim, at least two hectares in area and 4.5 m in depth. A portion of this low mound had been cut through by a minor road. The material we collected consisted mainly of flint blades and flake tools, some obsidian, and some fragments of heavy ground stone tools. Darkened hearth areas appeared in the road-cut face, but there were no traces of structures.

There may be some significance in the fact that our 1963 survey along the higher piedmont and flanks of the eastern Taurus did not encounter traces of an assemblage related or equivalent to the Natufian or Karim Shahirian–Zawi Chemian type. We return to this point in our conclusion.

The next later step along the southern piedmont of the Taurus is—at present—to be seen at Çayönü, and Çayönü is already over the threshold.[56] The main prehistoric phase at Çayönü itself is dated by a cluster of seven radiocarbon age determinations on reliable samples from good contexts: these span a half-millennium, ca. 9,250–8,750 B.P. Both einkorn and emmer wheat and certain pulses (strangely, not barley) appear as domesticates from the beginning. Save for the dog, however, domesticated sheep, and probably goats, seem to appear only in the upper levels. The full Çayönü inventory is not our immediate concern here, but we shall, later, refer to the quite remarkable architectural evidence the site yields. There are now, also, hints of possible Çayönü-like materials from at least three sites—Boy Tepe, Cafer, and Gritille—all in the region of the upper Euphrates salvage effort.[57]

A case for the presence of materials belonging to the level of incipience in the rest of Anatolia has not really advanced much since general summaries were made by Esin and Benedict and by Bostancı.[58] The proposal that there are Natufian-like elements in Layers B and C of Beldibi cave and in Layer II of Belbaşı cave (both on the southern coast near Antalya) is well known. The caves certainly yielded a generous variety of microblades and lunates, but Bostancı observes that Natufian lunates "are very different from the specimens found at Beldibi and Belbaşı."[59] The evidence produced which bears on the reconstruction of the general subsistence pattern and the environmental situation while the caves were occupied is minimal. The summaries by Esin and Benedict and by Bostancı note other occurrences of microlithic industries, both on the plateau and on the Black Sea coast, but really useful information does not appear to be available.

What happened next in Anatolia proper is downright confusing. In the mid-1960s Todd undertook a number of summer surface surveys in central Anatolia, encountering—among other things—sites without pottery surface scatter but with microlithic chipped stone, often of obsidian. From one site, Aşıklı, near Aksaray, he reports five radiocarbon determinations (8,950–8,600 B.P.), made on samples acquired during surface collection.[60] For about the same time span—on the basis of a single determination of 8,700 B.P.—Mellaart's basal exposure of the "aceramic" levels at Hacilar yielded a few traces of rectilinear house plans in an essentially open area of ca. 150 m². The total count of chipped stone tools is given as eleven pieces, and there were a few stone bowl fragments and polished celts.[61] Helbaek, however, reported the identification of domesticated emmer wheat, hulled barley, and lentils, although only the dog is given as a domestic animal.[62] Thus, it appears as if the threshold of incipience had already been crossed. Nevertheless, in the same general region, the site of Suberde—the "Hunters' Village in Neolithic Turkey"—has a group of seven radiocarbon determinations with the somewhat long span of 8,520–7,584 B.P.[63]

Suberde forcefully reminds us that food production and an effective village-farming community way of life did not appear suddenly, at one magic moment, over all southwestern Asia, sweeping away all the older hunting-collecting patterns of subsistence. We feel bound to wonder how many other instances of the same thing may already be in hand, but with too little evidence for correct assessment, or are yet to be found as field research continues.

Before we attempt to draw some general conclusions, an aside regarding two regions adjoining southwestern Asia and one to the east of it seems justified.

For Egypt, it is worth observing that the very early assays (ca. 17,000 B.P.) for grain from the Wadi Kubbaniya are now definitely subject to question. In a letter dated 27 May 1983 from the excavator, Fred Wendorf, to R.J.B., new determinations on barley seeds were given as 2,670 B.P. and 4,800 B.P. A more recent note asserts that a "determination on the Tucson accelerator showed Wadi Kubbaniya grain to be less than 1000 years old."[64] Clearly we must await new information on Wadi Kubbaniya's relevance to early cereal domestication. The possibility did seem fascinating in relation to Wright's suggestion of a Pleniglacial floral refuge in North Africa.[65]

Note should also be taken of the long sequence (ca. 25,000–5,000 B.P.), covering the pertinent range of time and extending later, at the Franchthi cave in southern Greece.[66] There does not, as yet, appear to have been any particular ties with Southwest Asia, although the hint of an early overseas trade suggested by the movement of Melian obsidian is fascinating. Domestic sheep and goat appear rather suddenly at 8,000 B.P. at the Franchthi cave.[67]

Recent excavations at Mehrgahr in Pakistani Baluchistan now clearly indicate a level of primary village-farming community life on "the eastern margin of the Middle East" by at least the seventh millennium B.C.[68] It will indeed be fascinating to see whether evidence of a level of incipience will be found along this eastern margin.

We have now briefly reviewed the available evidence for the incipient level in southwestern Asia. The ever-fascinating question is: how did the level of effective village-farming communities develop out of the incipient level?

As we have observed in earlier publications, the matter of how and why food production appeared has—over the last thirty years or more—become a fashionable focus for archaeological "model building." Indeed, it has seemed to us that some of the most firmly asserted "models" have come from those model builders having the least familiarity with the southwestern Asiatic region and the evidence available from it.

The model we take to be most restrained and reasonable at the moment is that of Henry.[69] In brief, he proposes that a new and more intensive adaptive strategy developed as the temperature increased and as the wild cereals spread into the better soils of higher elevations. This hypothesis bears primarily on the Natufian of the Levant, but Henry admits that it might also work for the Zagros flanks. He sees the possibility for consequent important societal changes, including an approach to matrilineal-matrilocal patterns and even chiefdomships, as a result.

Obviously, in order to understand the role that the lower flanks and piedmonts of the Zagros and Taurus may have had in the development of effective food production, we need much more field work, far broader exposures, and the use of such procedures as flotation for the recovery of plant materials. There has been a tendency to assume that the threshold was first crossed in the Levant, where many more sites have been excavated, and more area has been exposed. Even more significantly, the supposition has existed for some time that the place of origin of cultivated emmer (the more important of the two yearly wheats) was the upper Jordan catchment area. In assessing the botanical evidence, however, Zohary notes that "with the discovery of Turkish and Iranian wild wheats identical with Palestinian dicoccoides and durum . . . the north and east parts of the fertile crescent have become candidates as well" for the place of origin of cultivated emmer.[70]

Although the settlement of Çayönü appears to be only five hundred years later than that of Tell Aswad

(Damascene)—at present, the earliest known site with fully domesticated cereals—the difference between the two assemblages (as now available) is marked. Çayönü has buildings whose purpose—whether secular or sacred—can hardly have been simply domestic.[71] At least three building plans approach monumentality: may we see here some indications of Henry's "chiefdomship"? At the same time, why did we not locate evidence of incipient assemblages in our 1963 survey along the high Taurus piedmont? Since there were then restrictions on travel close to the frontier, we may perhaps have been too far up on the piedmont to find the antecedents of Çayönü's forerunners—hence our fascination with the Mardin region and the lower reaches of the Turkish courses of the Euphrates and Tigris.

In his conclusion to the large "Origins of Agriculture" symposium of 1973, Reed lists some twenty "Capsulated Conclusions" on factors possibly involved in how an agricultural way of life came into being. He then very sagely adds a twenty-first conclusion: "Many unsolved problems remain."[72]

## NOTES

In preparing this contribution we have had the benefit of many discussions on the topic with Professor Halet Çambel of Istanbul University.

1 L. Braidwood and R. J. Braidwood, "On the Treatment of the Prehistoric Near Eastern Materials in Steward's 'Cultural Causality and Law,'" *American Anthropologist* 51 (1949) 665–69; R. J. Braidwood and L. S. Braidwood, "The Earliest Village Communities of Southwestern Asia," *Journal of World History* 1 (1953) 278–310.

2 V. G. Childe, *New Light on the Most Ancient East* (London 1934).

3 D. Perkins, Jr., and P. Daly, *Scientific American* 219 (1968) 96–106.

4 W. van Zeist and H. E. Wright, Jr., "Preliminary Pollen Studies at Lake Zeribar, Zagros Mountains, Southwestern Iran," *Science* 140 (1963) 65–67; H. E. Wright, Jr., "Climatic Change in the Zagros Mountains—Revisited," in L. S. Braidwood et al. eds., *Prehistoric Archeology Along the Zagros Flanks* (OIP 105, Chicago 1983) 505–10.

5 J. L. Bintliff and W. van Zeist eds., *Palaeoclimates, Palaeoenvironments and Human Communities in the Eastern Mediterranean Region in Later Prehistory* (BAR Int. Series 133, Oxford 1982).

6 S. Bottema, "Final Invited Comments," in Bintliff and van Zeist (supra n. 5) 533.

7 C. A. Reed, "The Achievement and Early Consequences of Food-Production: A Consideration of the Archeological and Natural-Historical Evidence," in R. J. Braidwood and C. A. Reed eds., *Cold Spring Harbor Symposium on Quantitative Biology* 22 (1957) 19–31, esp. 23 n. 12.

8 W. van Zeist and S. Bottema, "Vegetational History of the Eastern Mediterranean and the Near East during the Last 20,000 Years," in Bintliff and van Zeist (supra n. 5) 277–321, esp. 283.

9 Van Zeist and Bottema (supra n. 8) 282.

10 Van Zeist and Bottema (supra n. 8) 278.

11 Van Zeist and Bottema (supra n. 8) 279.

12 The total exposure made so far of sites on the Zagros flanks of the later aspects of the incipient era (i.e., Karim Shahir, Zawi Chemi Shanidar, M'lefaat and Asiab; see the discussion below) is just under 900 m², and the bulk of the matrix cleared is around 700 m³. Although we have not attempted to determine the exact figures, the amount of exposure and bulk cleared at sites with various Natufian components must be triple those amounts.

13 D. O. Henry, "Adaptive Evolution Within the Epipaleolithic of the Near East," *Advances in World Archaeology* 2 (1983) 99–160.

14 O. Bar-Yosef, "Prehistory of the Levant," *Annual Review of Anthropology* 9 (1980) 101–33; and "The Epipaleolithic Complexes in the Southern Levant," in J. Cauvin and P. Sanlaville eds., *Préhistoire du Levant* (Paris 1981) 389–408.

15 J. Cauvin, *Les premiers villages de Syrie-Palestine du IX au VII millénaire avant J.C.* (Lyon 1978).

16 Henry (supra n. 13) 99.

17 M. Stekelis and O. Bar-Yosef, "Un habitat du Paléolithique Supérieur à Ein Gev (Israël). Note préliminaire," *L'Anthropologie* 69 (1965) 176–83.

18 Henry (supra n. 13) 122.

19 Henry (supra n. 13) 150.

20 H. E. Wright, Jr., "Environmental Change and the Origins of Agriculture in the Old and New Worlds," in C. A. Reed ed., *Origins of Agriculture* (The Hague 1977) 281–318.

21 J. Perrot, "Le mésolithique de Palestine et les recents découvertes à Eynan (Ain Mallaha)," *Antiquity and Survival* 2.2/3 (1957) 91–110.

22 M.-C. Cauvin, "L'épipaléolithique du Levant," in Cauvin and Sanlaville eds. (supra n. 14) 439–41.

23 A. M. T. Moore, "Agricultural Origins in the Near East: A Model for the 1980s," *World Archaeology* 14 (1982) 224–36, esp. 228.

24 H. de Contenson et al., "Tel Aswad (Damascene)," *Paléorient* 5 (1979) 153–76.

25 M. Hopf, "Plant Remains and Early Farming in Jericho," in P. J. Ucko and G. W. Dimbleby eds., *The Domestication and Exploitation of Plants and Animals* (London 1969) 355–59.

26 Henry (supra n. 13).

27 J. Mellaart, *The Neolithic of the Near East* (London 1975).

28 B. Howe, "Karim Shahir," in L. S. Braidwood et al. eds. (supra n. 4) 23–154; M. Dittemore, "The Soundings at M'lefaat," in Braidwood et al. eds. (supra n. 4) 671–95.

29 R. J. Braidwood, B. Howe, et al., *Prehistoric Investigations in Iraqi Kurdistan* (Chicago 1960) 25–62.

30 G. Wahida, "The Re-excavation of Zarzi, 1971," *ProcPS* 47 (1981) 19–40.

31 D. A. E. Garrod, "The Palaeolithic of Southern Kurdistan: Excavations in the Caves of Zarzi and Hazar Merd," *BASPR* 6 (1930) 339–46.

32 Braidwood, Howe, et al. (supra n. 29) 28–29, 57–59.

33 F. Hole and K. V. Flannery, "The Prehistory of Southwestern Iran: A Preliminary Report," *ProcPS* 33 (1967) 147–206.

34 R. S. Solecki, "Prehistory in the Shanidar Valley, Northern Iraq," *Science* 139 (1963) 179–93; and "Shanidar Cave, a Late Pleistocene Site in Northern Iraq," in *Report of the VIth International Congress on Quaternary Research, Warsaw 1961* 4 (Lodz 1964) 413–23. In the latter publication (p. 414), Solecki states that "[t]here was evidently some mixture between Layers B 1 [with Zawi Chemian affinities] and B 2."

35 B. Howe, personal communication.

36 Henry (supra n. 13) 104, table 3.1

37 P. F. Turnbull and C. A. Reed, "The Fauna from the Terminal Pleistocene of Palegawra Cave, a Zarzian Occupation Site in Northeastern Iraq," *Fieldiana Anthropology* 63.3 (1974) 81–146.

38  C. A. Reed, "Archeozoological Studies in the Near East," in L. S. Braidwood et al. eds. (supra n. 4) 511–36, esp. 521.

39  Henry (supra n. 13) 104, table 3.1.

40  R. L. Solecki, "An Early Village Site at Zawi Chemi Shanidar" (BibMes13, Malibu 1980).

41  Howe (supra n. 28).

42  Dittemore (supra n. 28).

43  R. S. Solecki 1963 (supra n. 34) 179–93, esp. 180.

44  R. L. Solecki, "Zawi Chemi Shanidar, a Post-Pleistocene Village Site in Northern Iraq," in *VIth . . . Congress on Quaternary Research* (supra n. 34) 405–12, esp. 410.

45  R. L. Solecki (supra n. 40) 63.

46  Dittemore (supra n. 28).

47  In the Karim Shahir industry, of the total number of tools—both microlithic- and normal-sized—the microliths made up 49 percent; at Zawi Chemi, 25 percent; and at M'lefaat, ca. 90 percent. The proportion of blade tools in the Karim Shahir industry (based on the total number of all blade and flake tools, of both microlithic and standard size) is ca. 63 percent; at Zawi Chemi, only 39 percent; and at M'lefaat, ca. 82 percent.

48  Howe (supra n. 28) 115–17.

49  P. E. L. Smith, "Ganj Dareh Tepe," *Iran* 6 (1968) 158–60; *Iran* 13 (1975) 178–80; and "An Interim Report on Ganj Dareh Tepe, Iran," *AJA* 82 (1978) 538–40.

50  P. E. L. Smith and P. Mortensen, "Three New 'Early Neolithic' Sites in Western Iran," *Current Anthropology* 21 (1980) 511–12.

51  Howe (supra n. 28) 122.

52  The site was first identified by our colleague at the Oriental Institute, McGuire Gibson, who recommended it for excavation to Sebastiano Tusa. Dr. Tusa has supplied us with the information on the site published here.

53  A. Leroi-Gourhan, "Analyse pollinique de Zawi Chemi," in R. L. Solecki (supra n. 40), appendix 3, 77–79, esp. 78.

54  Reed (supra n. 38) 521.

55  H. Çambel and R. J. Braidwood eds., *Prehistoric Research in Southeastern Anatolia* 1 (Istanbul and Chicago 1980) 37.

56  H. Çambel and R. J. Braidwood, "Çayönü Tepesi: Schritte zu neuen Lebensweisen," in R. M. Boehmer and H. Hauptmann eds., *Beiträge zur Altertumskunde Kleinasiens. Festschrift für Kurt Bittel* (Mainz am Rhein 1983) 155–66; W. Schirmer, "Drei Bauten des Cayonu Tepesi," in Boehmer and Hauptmann eds., 463–76.

57  R. Whallon, "Boy Tepe," in R. Whallon, *An Archaeological Survey in the Keban Reservoir Area in East-Central Turkey* (Museum of Anthropology, University of Michigan, Memoir

11, Ann Arbor 1979) 246–49; J. Cauvin and O. Aurenche, "Le Néolithique de Cafer Hüyük," in *Cahiers de l'Euphrate* (Paris 1982) 123–38; M. M. Voigt and R. S. Ellis, "Excavations at Gritille, Turkey: 1981," *Paléorient* 7.2 (1981) 87–100. One further site in the Keban region, Nevalla Çori, has yielded materials which may be only slightly later: H. Hauptmann, "Die Ausgrabungen in der akeramisch-neolithischen Siedlung von Nevalla Çori," in press.

58  U. Esin and P. Benedict, "Recent Developments in the Prehistory of Anatolia," *Current Anthropology* 4 (1963) 339–46; E. Bostancı, "The Mesolithic of Beldibi and Belbaşı and the Relations with the Other Findings in Anatolia," *Ankara Üniversitesi, Dil ve Tarih-Coğrafya Fakültesi Dergisi* 3 (1968) 41–137.

59  E. Bostancı, "The Belbasi Industry," *Belleten* 26 (1962) 252–78, esp. 255 n. 8.

60  I. Todd, *The Prehistory of Central Anatolia 1. The Neolithic Period* (SIMA 60, Göteborg 1980) 149.

61  J. Mellaart, *Excavations at Hacilar* (Occasional Publication of the British Institute in Ankara 9, Edinburgh 1970) 3–7.

62  H. Helbaek in Mellaart (supra n. 61) 198–99; B. Westley in Mellaart (supra n. 61) 246–47.

63  J. Bordaz, "Current Research in the Neolithic of South Central Turkey: Suberde, Erbaba and Their Chronological Implications," *AJA* 77 (1973) 285–87.

64  F. Wendorf, *New Scientist* 99.1367 (21 July 1983) 182.

65  H. E. Wright, Jr., "The Environmental Setting for Plant Domestication in the Near East," *Science* 194 (1976) 385–89.

66  T. W. Jacobsen, "Excavations in the Franchthi Cave 1969–1971," *Hesperia* 42 (1973) 45–88, 253–83; cf. also, most recently, "Franchthi Cave and the Beginning of Settled Village Life in Greece," *Hesperia* 50 (1981) 303–19.

67  S. Payne, "Faunal Evidence for Environmental/Climatic Change at Franchthi Cave (Southern Greece)," in Bintliff and van Zeist eds. (supra n. 5) 133–34.

68  R. H. Meadow, "Animal Domestication in the Middle East: A View from the Eastern Margin," in J. Clutton-Brock and C. Grigson eds., *Animals in Archaeology 3. Early Herders and Their Flocks* (BAR Int. Series 202, Oxford 1984) 309–37.

69  Henry (supra n. 13) 149–54.

70  D. Zohary, "Origin of South-west Asiatic Cereals: Wheats, Barley, Oats and Rye," in P. H. Davis et al. eds., *Plant Life of South-west Asia* (Edinburgh 1971) 235–63, esp. 241.

71  Schirmer (supra n. 56).

72  C. A. Reed, "Origins of Agriculture: Discussion and Some Conclusions," in C. A. Reed ed. (supra n. 20) 941–44.

# Health and Stress in an Early Bronze Age Population

## 2

J. L. ANGEL and S. C. BISEL

As the successful challenge of death, health is more than mere survival—it is living usefully despite the various diseases and stresses which challenge all of us. Here we provide measures of health and of stresses in two populations from Karataş and Kalınkaya, well-excavated Early Bronze Age sites in different areas of Anatolia.

Machteld Mellink and the Bryn Mawr College Expedition between 1963 and 1977 carefully recovered the skeletal remains of 584 people from a cemetery dating from about 2700 to 2300 B.C. at Karataş-Semayük in the fertile and mountain-protected Elmalı plain in ancient Lycia, northwest of Antalya in southwestern Turkey. In 1971, 1973, and 1974, Raci Temizer, former director of the Museum of Anatolian Civilizations, Ankara, and his staff excavated the remains of 72 people in 34 graves dating from 3100 to 2300 B.C. (Chalcolithic as well as Early Bronze) at the site of Kalınkaya, northwest of Alaca Höyük and Boğazköy.

We acknowledge with gratitude the help of Machteld J. Mellink and all the people at Elmalı—archaeologists, Turkish commissioners, and staff—who made our work possible. My wife Peggy and I (J. L. A.) recall with particular pleasure the nicknames bestowed on us—"Mother and Father Bones." And the three of us remember most happily the key member of the Bryn Mawr Expedition staff, jeep driver Abdullah Aytulun (and his wife and daughters and son), and Machteld Mellink's rest-day explorations on which he drove us to other sites or to mountain summer pastures, the seashore, or the lake near Elmalı to fish.

The Early Bronze Age sample from Karataş has an infant:child:adult ratio of 6− :5:10 (N = 897), corrected from 1:4:10 (534) by inclusion of empty pithoi of different sizes and careful guesses at rates of infant death and disposal.[1] Of the skeletons, 395 are fragmentary, but were recovered by extremely careful excavation designed to preserve all bony remains. The 82 good and complete skeletons constitute a larger proportion than would be expected in any eastern Mediterranean Bronze Age site. This relatively good preservation is a result of physical and to some extent chemical protection by burial inside large, Ali Baba–type pottery jars or pithoi. The surrounding soil, in use for over 200 generations for growing cereal crops, vines, and grass for cattle, is a slightly clayey loam kept fertile by crop rotation and manuring; it is much less acid than the red earth–derived soils in the valleys of Greece, but still not as good for bone preservation as the sandy soil of the Sea Clan burials of Middle Bronze Lerna.[2]

The Kalınkaya people, on the other hand, were often in unprotected earth burials; sometimes these burials were secondary. Chalcolithic burial M-31 G/12 p² was in a cist (sandık), and there were 13 pithos burials, mostly of Early Bronze date. There are 5 infants, 13 children, and 54 adults, a ratio of 1:3− :10 (best corrected to 4− :3:10 by multiplying the 5 infants by four and doubling the 3 children aged 1 to 4; N then = 90). Skeletons are fragmentary: 6 adult skeletons are fairly complete; information on stature is available from 19 people and information on skull type from 18.

Three aspects of health should be considered: general, nutritional, and psychological. The stress of living may restrict health through disease or injury (sometimes in combination with genetic fault), through various degrees and types of malnutrition, or through social pressures, religion, or even warfare. Genetic factors will promote different degrees of stress-resistance in each person, depending on the previous and current effects of natural selection, which operates in human societies through differential fertility and not only survival (see table 2-5 below). Different individuals age at strikingly different rates, and the aging of each bodily system also varies, depending on genes as well as environment. For example, the modern villagers in the Elmalı plain appear older than Americans of the same chronological age, particularly the men, with their weathered skin. This condition probably derives in part from the cold winters, the use of giant juniper logs in stoves for heat, the hot summer sun, and the 4,000-foot altitude of the plain. Disease may be more frequent too, but the variation in aging is also genetic in origin.

The best measure of overall health, therefore, is adult longevity, determined from changes in the pubic symphysis, skeletal exostoses and bone loss, and suture closure.[3] The survival rate of children and infants is also important, and, obviously, evidence of disease and injury is essential information.

We determine nutritional health by bone trace elements and morphology, remembering that teeth record enamel organ action and mouth chemistry and that bone grows against gravity and against the force of muscle pull in every action of a child's, adolescent's, or subadult's life. Also important is archaeological evidence of foods eaten: bones of domestic and wild meat animals and fish, plant remains, and evidence of food preparation.

Psychological health, reflecting the useful and creative cooperation of individuals, shows in the number and kind of injuries from fighting and to some extent in the level of variability (sigma ratio) as a measure of population mixture. The positive cultural aspects, such as artistic creativity, numbers of inventions, strength of family bonds, will not show up biologically except to the extent that they inhibit disease (medical care) and promote child growth (loving care and education).

In general, all three aspects of health interact positively. All are affected by illness and injury. Stress starts with climate and with the hard work needed to get food; it continues with the stress of childbirth and childrearing and the need to protect the community; and it ends with disease and such effects of population pressure as malnutrition, epidemics, migrations, and warfare.

### ENVIRONMENTS

Both Karataş and Kalınkaya are in mountain valleys with good mixed forest growth on the hillsides, at a slight altitude (3,300 feet, or over 1,000 m above sea level), with excellent water supply and streams; both are far enough inland to have cold, snowy winters (5° C) and hot summers. But the Elmalı plain in Lycia is 5 degrees farther south than Kalınkaya, so it is overall slightly warmer. It is also quite wide, flat, and easily cultivable, with plentiful game in the mountains (boar, deer, goat, bear, fox, etc.), fish in the streams, and stands of conifers, such as giant juniper, to burn for winter heating of gabled houses of mudbrick on stone foundations, with doors (on pivot-stones) to contain heat. Huge pithoi were used for grain storage.[4] The northern edge of the central plateau where Kalınkaya is located has steeper and narrower valleys and more rocky terrain.[5] Farming may be more difficult in the north, but the settlements were in a good position for trade to the east and west, or with Assyria or the Black Sea area, and were more defensible than Karataş. Although Karataş was less accessible from the plateau, and in a sense Lycia was more isolated than the future Hittite centers in the bend of the Halys River, trade and migration certainly occurred through mountain passes and stepping-stone plateaux, as well as directly up the Finike valley from the Mediterranean, Cyprus, and the Levant. Land travel was still on foot; wheeled wagons were not used in the third millennium.

Both sites shared the Early Bronze Age culture of Anatolia and represent slightly different versions of the local farming population before and during the entrance from the east of the wagon-using Indo-European speakers (Hittites and Lycians respectively).

### DIET AND CLOTHING

By the third millennium B.C. in Anatolia, barley, emmer, and wheat were standard crops.[6] The plow (oxdrawn?) was in use in some places; evidence for the döğen (threshing sledge) is not clear. There were no apparent bake-ovens (pithoi were probably fired individually on platforms), so that bread was still unleavened maza rich in phytic acid, unless it was alkalized by the addition of ashes. Almost certainly this phytate produced enough binding of protein, iron, and zinc to affect growth.[7] Fruits, vegetables, and green herbs were available in Anatolia; grapes and olives, which began to appear in Greece at this time, were not.[8] Hesse and Perkins' study of the animal bones from Karataş shows beef dominant (accounting for at least 75 percent of the meat eaten); pork, mutton, and goat in about equal parts made up the remainder.[9] Perhaps because of the cutting of the woodland, pig bones decline, and cattle bones increase during the Early Bronze Age, and by EB II about two sheep were killed for each goat. Slaughter peaks for sheep-goat were in the first year and at the end of the second year, with a substantial portion surviving into maturity. Likewise, most cattle survived into maturity, past the time of best meat use, with about half slaughtered at 2.5 to 3.0 years old. The older animals were probably kept for milk (and blood?) as well as for producing young. Their existence implies the availability of cheese (and yogurt?) as well as fresh milk for children, with the potential of reinforcing childhood anemia as well as maintaining blood calcium and pro-vitamin D. Deer and wild goat bones occur; occasional use of wild meat may have paralleled that at Lerna.[10] Cattle were larger than in the Levant. As at Lerna in the fourth and third millennia before the considerable size loss which occurred during the later Bronze Age,[11] the presence of large cattle implies that there was no loss in the fertility of flat grassland. Modern cattle around Semayük are rather small. Kalınkaya, on the other hand, has much less extensive grassland, so the people probably ate less meat. There is no evidence for fish. Equus and canis occur, with no evidence that they were eaten.

Wooden artifacts do not survive. Although dirt casts of posts and wattle-and-daub wall construction occur, there is no evidence of yokes for oxen, looms, or hollow log beehives.

Evidence for the spinning of wool fibers and the weaving of clothes consists of spindle-whorls,[12] the notching of upper incisor teeth in people of both sexes,[13] and designs on pottery which may reflect textile patterns. Yet woolen clothes, tailored as in Lycian times,[14] and leather mocassins or boots[15] would be as important for winter warmth as adequate wood fires in houses and plentiful food. Bronze razors found with males in tombs[16] suggest an interest in coolness in the summer heat, although fashion may have been as important as comfort. Stamps may have been used on textiles as well as on skin.

### METHODS

In analyzing skeletal remains for their chemical content in an attempt to "fingerprint" them, Bisel used small (500 mg) samples of dense cortical bone (usually the tibia midshaft) to minimize diagenetic exchange of elements with the surrounding soil and to ensure that the elements present entered the bone during growth or remodeling—that is, come from the diet. She excluded iron and copper from the analysis because their presence in bone is minute, lead because it became an important ingested poison only later, and fluorine because its chemical absorption from ground water is rapid enough to make it usable as a rough dating signal. Cleaned bone was dissolved in 3 ml concentrated hydrochloric acid and diluted in distilled water at appropriate concentrations for analysis in the Mayo Clinic Trace Metal Laboratory (a 303 Perkin-Elmer atomic absorption spectrophotometer using an air-acetylene flame and the following wave lengths; calcium 422.0, strontium 460.7, magnesium

285.2, zinc 213.8). Phosphorus was read at wave length 630 on a Perkin-Elmer Hitachi 200 spectrophotometer, after dilution and addition of 2 ml each of the standard phosphorus reagents amino-naphthol-sulphonic acid and ammonium molybdate to each 1 ml of the sample. Bones of meat animals—preferably sheep-goat—went through the same process. Analysis of soil samples differed only in the preparation of the dilute solutions.[17]

Calcium is vital for nerve transmission; plasma calcium must stay constant to avoid tetany and death, so that hyperparathyroidism draws calcium from the amorphous bone reservoirs and finally from the hydroxyapatite crystalline structure itself! Blood calcium needed for bone growth and repair is further regulated by vitamin D, made in the kidneys from pro-vitamin D in the diet and sterols transformed by skin absorption of ultraviolet rays.[18] Rickets from lack of sunlight is unlikely in Anatolia, and milk products (ignoring the possible nonabsorption of milk from lack of serum lactase) should have provided enough calcium.

Variations in magnesium level probably reflect soil magnesium, since the mineral is easily absorbed from vegetables (except by chronic alcoholics).

Zinc is needed for enzymes essential for growth, of which more than seventy have been identified, and phytate binding of zinc, as well as of iron, calcium, and protein, causes dwarfism, inability to reproduce,[19] anemia, liver and spleen enlargement, and mental lethargy. Zinc is vital for growth in childhood, and during pregnancy, illness, and wound healing. The chief dietary source of zinc is red meat. It also occurs in fish, but there is very little in other foods. Probably high fiber intake (cereal diets) reduces zinc absorption, as do intestinal parasites, and pregnancy. Excess zinc may come from the soil or the fumes of metallurgy.

Strontium has no special physiologic use and resides almost entirely in bone, especially in the apatite crystals. The amount of environmental strontium in the soil controls the amount in plants; the strontium consumed by herbivores is deposited in their bone rather than in muscle. Hence, carnivores, eating only meat, will have much less bone strontium, and omnivores, including humans, will have bone strontium levels which reflect the relative amounts of meat and vegetables consumed.[20] Sea fish and molluscs "breathe" strontium-containing water and hence have strontium in their flesh as well as bone.[21] One must standardize the strontium/calcium ratio of humans by taking it as a proportion of the strontium/calcium ratio of herbivores at each site being compared. This yields the site-corrected strontium/calcium ratio. Low levels of 0.3 to 0.5 indicate a fair amount of meat in the diet; higher levels indicate more vegetable food. Levels above 1.0—that is, with more bone strontium than the herbivores—indicate a diet rich in sea food, especially if zinc levels are above average. Carbon isotopes measured by mass spectroscopy can indicate more about plant versus marine food sources,[22] but bone usually will have lost enough collagen in 5,000 to 6,000 years to make its extraction impractical. Sillen is developing new approaches to deal with the further difficulty of increasing diagenesis from soil with increasing length of burial.

Table 2-1 lists effects of stress on general, nutritional, and social health.

examining longevity we include everyone over 15, since until modern times this was the youngest age at which females married and then conceived. For long bone measurements we use the subadult completion of lower limb growth at age 18 as the start. Porotic hyperostosis is hypertrophy of marrow space in childhood, generally with porosity of the skull vault, persisting into adulthood in either healed (slight to +) or active (++) form and usually signaling anemia.[24] In the eastern Mediterranean it is often a heterozygous expression of one of the abnormal hemoglobins (at least in populations where there are

Table 2.1. Bone concentrations of various elements in people, sheep and cattle, and soil ($\mu$g/g)

| | Karataş | | | | Kalınkaya | | | | United States[a] | |
|---|---|---|---|---|---|---|---|---|---|---|
| | Female (N = 173) | | Male (N = 149) | | Female (N = 23) | | Male (N = 19) | | Both Sexes (N = 40) | |
| | M | σ | M | σ | M | σ | M | σ | M | σ |
| Calcium | 306.8 | 55.1 | 304.9 | 44.9 | 295.3 | 33.4 | 293.1 | 38.1 | 220.4 | 20.7 |
| Phosphorus | 165.3 | 24.6 | 174.1 | 18.9 | 143.4 | 30.0 | 147.9 | 30.0 | 102.5 | — |
| Magnesium | 1.149 | .253 | 7.136 | .344 | 2.25 | 1.30 | 2.68 | .9 | 2.81 | .33 |
| Zinc | 137.0 | 60.7 | 161.0 | 75.4 | 210.6 | 200.0 | 192.4 | 99.2 | 147.1 | 49.8 |
| Strontium | 55.7 | 18.0 | 58.1 | 24.5 | 144.8 | 50.0 | 153.1 | 56.5 | — | — |
| Sr/Ca ratio | .185 | .066 | .196 | .092 | .501 | .216 | .527 | .215 | — | — |
| Site-corrected Sr/Ca ratio | .586 | .203 | .605 | .240 | .751 | .25 | .647 | .30 | — | — |

| | Sheep and Cattle (N = 10) | | | Soil (N = 3) | |
|---|---|---|---|---|---|
| | M | σ | | M | σ |
| Calcium | 277.48 | 21.7 | Calcium | 5.285 | .428 |
| Magnesium | 2.224 | .849 | Magnesium (low) | .205 | .551 |
| Zinc | 98.7 | 22.0 | Zinc (low) | .467 | .358 |
| Strontium | 89.4 | 9.4 | Strontium | 5.470 | 1.152 |
| Sr/Ca ratio | .323 | .037 | Sr/Ca ratio | 1.032 | .169 |

Note: Concentrations measured by S. C. Bisel.
[a] For U.S. data, see Bisel 1980 (n. 7).

Age at death we determine from bony changes at joints, especially at the pubic symphysis, which reflect the gradual increase in cross-bonding of collagen in fibrous tissue; for example, exostoses start to appear at about age 35, and skull sutures close irregularly after that.[23] Since what we read from the skeleton is physiologic age, our closeness to chronological age decreases as age increases; the divergence Angel has discovered in adults is 3.5 years overall, ignoring sign, with an increase from 1 to 5 years in the first four decades of adulthood, and from 5 to 12 years between ages 50 and 90. If we take account of sign, the total "error" is −0.2 years, with overaging of 1 to 2 years up to age 50 and underaging from then on. (These data are based on examination of 140 willed and forensic skeletons of known age.) In

severely anemic dead children), but hookworm or some other cause of blood loss may cause iron-deficiency anemia severe enough to produce or increase porotic hyperostosis. Falciparum malaria is a highly probable factor in hyperostosis in Anatolia. Linear hypoplastic growth arrests of the enamel of permanent teeth are a signal in adulthood of either an illness or an episode of starvation severe enough to stop or interfere with the enamel organs which make the tooth crowns. A spot of hypoplasia may have some other cause.

Once an infant can hold up its own head, its skull base is growing against gravity; after the child has begun to walk and run, its arched pelvis (especially the ilium and sacrum) is growing against the earth's gravitational force. The growing limbs and vertebrae likewise support

Fig. 2-1. Severe porotic hyperostosis in a very young child (61 Ka), probably from homozygous thalassemia. Note marrow infection also. (Labels in photographs measure 2 cm by 3 cm and thus give scale.)

Fig. 2-2. Porotic hyperostosis in a child about six years of age (303 Ka)

Fig. 2-3. Porotic hyperostosis in middle age (461 Ka)

increasing weight. The height of the skull base, the depth of the pelvic brim, and stature, therefore, all measure the effects of nutrition on bone. The first and second factors respond especially to protein and pro-vitamin D plus sunlight; the third responds to caloric intake as well.[25] The skull base and the pelvis oppose steadily increasing weight during childhood and adolescence, as do the long bones and vertebrae, which grow critically during the postpubertal spurt.

The bone thickness needed both to bear weight and to resist bending (due to rickets) in a fast-growing child obviously depends on good nutrition and the absence of disease interrupting growth. Bone shafts respond to muscle pull as well as to gravity, which together largely determine the activity of the periosteum in laying down the bone layers (osteoblastic action) and remodeling

them (osteoclastic action). Bones with scarcely enough calcium tend to resist stress with flanges (e.g., linea aspera) and some degree of flattening: the upper femur, needing transverse stress to balance the body, flattens from back to front (platymeria), whereas the upper tibia expands posteriorly as a result of the pull of the thigh extensor and calf muscles lowering the cnemic index. The robusticity of the femur, determined by the following formula, records general bone thickness:

$$\frac{\text{anteroposterior thickness} + \text{transverse thickness}}{\text{length in natural position}} \times 100$$

The frequency of dental lesions for each individual, standardized to age 40, records two quite contrary things: the adequate development of enamel and dentin and supporting bone in childhood, depending on pro-

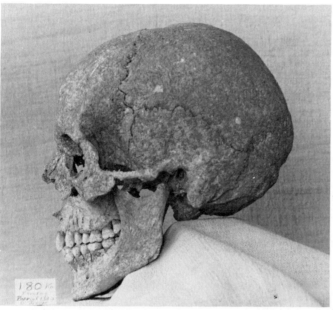

Fig. 2-4. High skull base (180 Ka, female): 30mm

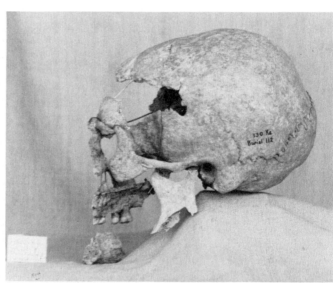

Fig. 2-5. Low skull base (130 Ka, female): 14mm

Fig. 2-6. Average pelvic inlet (406 Ka, male): index 82.6

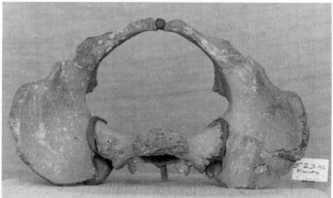

Fig. 2-7. Shallow pelvic inlet (523 Ka, female): index 67.7

*Health and Stress in an Early Bronze Age Population* 17

Fig. 2-8. Femurs (59 Ka): platymeric index 84; pilastric index 126; cnemial index 69; pronounced bowing; pronounced pilaster

tein and minerals, and the richness and acidity of the mouth environment in adolescence and adulthood. The genetic capacity to grow regular caries-resistant enamel and disease-resistant bone is also crucial.

Social health has at least two biological corollaries. The first is the capacity to absorb a variety of strangers and to promote their mixture into the original population, raising the level of variability. The second is the ability to live at peace with neighboring groups (and to fight off attack if inevitable). This latter point we can measure through the frequency and kind of healed injury and also the number of unhealed injuries which apparently caused death.

### RESULTS

Adult longevity (table 2-2), at just under 30 for females and 34 for males, at Karataş as well as at Kalınkaya, continues the general health level of the local Neolithic populations.[26] Only during the second millennium B.C. in Greece does an advance of three to five years occur. The level of marked porotic hyperostosis—that is, anemia—at Karataş is 1 percent for adults and 4 percent for children; 11 percent for each including slight degree. These figures suggest enough continued pressure from falciparum malaria to explain this longevity, in part, at least, since Kalınkaya has only one anemic individual.

Climatic (cold) and work (farming) pressures show up in the occurrence of arthritis at a rate of about 36 percent overall at Karataş and 40 percent at Kalınkaya—medium rates for so young a population, compared with 62 percent in a U.S. sample which is eight years older.

Almost equally important is reproductive health. The number of births per female is 4.1 at Karataş (45) and 3.7 at Kalınkaya (6). Juvenile deaths (0 to 14.9 years) are 2.0 per female at Karataş and at least 1.3 (?) at

Kalınkaya. In this respect Karataş may show an advantage, but the sample size at Kalınkaya is very small.

Nutritional health depends on food actually absorbed, without interference from phytate or roughage from vegetable fibers. Here the site-corrected strontium/calcium ratio is of primary importance. At .595 (322) at Karataş, it indicates a balanced diet with fairly plentiful meat, as one would expect from the environment and animal bone data.[27] The Kalınkaya value of .739 (40) indicates relatively less meat. But the direct bone zinc values are puzzling: 212.5 (40) at Kalınkaya and 148.1 (322) μg/g at Karataş. Diagenesis from the soil in several burials at Kalınkaya might be a factor. It hardly seems possible that fresh-water fish or landsnails could add so much zinc to the diet. The soil zinc level, at Karataş, at least, is not high. A further complication is the statistically significant reduction of zinc in the females of Karataş. Since zinc is important in embryogenesis and carrying a fetus, it seemed possible that this zinc loss might be part of the mild anemia of menstruation and pregnancy; yet in 42 females dying under age 25, the bone zinc level averages 133.4. There is also no difference in the strontium/calcium ratio or stature between these young females and the total group. There is, however, a strikingly significant difference between the bone zinc levels of 12 women who died after only 0–2 births (Zn = 121.8 μg/g) and 12 women who died after many (6–10) births (Zn = 191.4 μg/g). Does a high level of zinc in the diet and bloodstream speed up enzyme production and thus increase fertility? That seems plausible. But what physiologic mechanism raises zinc levels in multiparous mothers? Is it simply the increased bone turnover during each pregnancy? Or is it possible that repeated births and nonstop lactation stimulate some zinc-selecting hormone? There is no age-

Table 2.2. Various indicators of health: general, nutritional, and social

| | Karataş | | | | | | Kalınkaya | | | | | | Modern United States (white) | | | | | |
| | Female | | | Male | | | Female | | | Male | | | Female | | | Male | | |
| | M | σ | N | M | σ | N | M | σ | N | M | σ | N | M | σ | N | M | σ | N |
|---|---|---|---|---|---|---|---|---|---|---|---|---|---|---|---|---|---|---|
| Length of life in adults (yr)[a] | 29.51 | 8.1 | 197 | 33.59 | 8.6 | 159 | 30.11 | 7.3 | 28 | 33.78 | 7.4 | 25 | 78.00 | | | 72.00 | | |
| Porotic hyperostosis[b] | | | | | | | | | | | | | | | | | | |
| In adults[c] | 10%/slight; 1%/medium | | | | | 298[c] | 5%/slight; 0%/medium | | | | | 20[c] | 9%/slight; 0%/medium | | | | | 205[c] |
| In children[c] | 7%/slight; 4%/medium | | | | | 150[c] | 0%/slight; 0% medium | | | | | | 6%/slight; 0%/medium | | | | | 33[c] |
| Growth arrests in tooth enamel: continuous scale | 1.09 | | 45 | 1.15 | | 61 | 1.43 | .53 | 7 | 1.33 | | 6 | 1.51 | | 59 | 1.64 | | 61[d] |
| Skull base height (mm) | 19.7 | 4.2 | 25 | 21.6 | 3.3 | 46 | (20.5) | 4.7 | 6 | (22.0) | 4.1 | 5 | 20.8 | 3.0 | 73 | 21.5 | 4.0 | 89[d] |
| Pelvic inlet depth index | 85.6 | 9.4 | 13 | 84.4 | 7.7 | 14 | 80.0 | 5.1 | 6 | — | — | 0 | 93.5 | 6.8 | 55 | 93.09 | 6.4 | 58[d] |
| Stature (cm)[e] | 153.1 | 4.3 | 68 | 166.5 | 3.8 | 78 | 153.1 | 4.9 | 9 | 164.2 | 4.3 | 70 | 162.4 | 5.1 | 70 | 175.0 | 5.9 | 88[d] |
| Platymeric index | 73.5 | 6.1 | 153 | 76.8 | 6.3 | 126 | 73.6 | 6.3 | 18 | 72.8 | 6.0 | 14 | 86.3 | 6.3 | 72 | 88.2 | 6.4 | 87 |
| Cnemic index | 67.8 | 6.2 | 117 | 66.8 | 6.0 | 104 | 65.7 | 6.7 | 18 | 64.6 | 5.0 | 11 | 70.2 | 5.0 | 65 | 70.3 | 5.3 | 79 |
| Robusticity index | 12.4 | .7 | 47 | 13.2 | .8 | 44 | 12.9? | 1.0 | 13 | 13.5? | 1.3 | 12 | 11.9 | .7 | 63 | 12.7 | .9 | 75 |
| Tooth lesions per mouth | 5.03 | 6.0 | 76 | 5.03 | 6.2 | 99 | 5.00 | 5.5 | 9 | 3.20 | 3.5 | 10 | 12.71 | .4 | 76 | 12.82 | — | 110 |
| Tooth loss in life | 3.38 | 4.3 | 76 | 3.42 | 5.8 | 99 | 1.56 | 2.6 | 9 | 1.70 | 2.7 | 10 | 5.58 | .4 | 76 | 7.44 | — | 110 |
| Caries (number) | 1.38 | 1.8 | 76 | 1.28 | 1.7 | 99 | 2.22 | 3.1 | 9 | .80 | 1.8 | 10 | | | 76 | | | 110 |
| Caries (%) | 8.29 | | 76 | 7.39 | | 99 | 17.84 | | 9 | 5.33 | | 10 | | | 76 | | | 110 |
| Abscesses | .78 | 1.5 | 76 | .84 | 1.5 | 99 | 1.56 | 2.2 | 9 | 1.20 | 1.1 | 10 | | | 76 | | | 110 |
| Periodontal disease[f] | 2.07 | 1.1 | 72 | 2.15 | .8 | 93 | 3.11 | .6 | 7 | 2.70 | 1.0 | 8 | | | 67 | | | 88 |
| Arthritis (%) | 29.7 | | 78 | 43.2 | | 81 | 46.4 | | 15 | 36.0 | | 15 | 55.1 | | 60 | 69.8 | | 75 |
| Healed fractures (per bone or area—%) | 2.7 | | 47 | 3.0 | | 58 | 4.3 | | 10 | 1.0 | | 8 | 3.7 | | 85 | 7.2 | | 86 |
| Parry fractures (%) | 7.7 | | 13 | 7.4 | | 27 | 14.2 | | 7 | 0 | | 5 | 3.3 | | 78 | 5.1 | | 79 |
| Head wounds (%) | 4.4 | | 91 | 11.8 | | 110 | 0 | | 11 | 7.7 | | 13 | 13.2 | | 106 | 11.2 | | 125 |
| Sigma ratio (variability) | 115.4 | 16.2 | (12) | 106.8 | 21.9 | (12) | 81.4? | 19.0 | (12) | 102.4 | 39.8 | 12 | 102.4 | 11.8 | 12 | 106.1 | 10.0 | 12 |

Note: Parentheses indicate a very uncertain measurement; a question mark indicates a slightly uncertain measurement. Modern United States data based on U.S. Census Bureau data, 1975.
[a] Individuals 15 years of age or older.
[b] Measurement = frequency/severity.
[c] Data here are combined male and female.
[d] Figures from a study of individuals born between 1915 and 1965.
[e] Based on Trotter-Gleser formulae.
[f] Measurement is based on a relative scale ranging from 1 = slight to 4 = striking.

and childbirth-related difference in strontium/calcium ratio or stature. (Table 2-3 relates meat consumption to various indicators of health).

Skull base height (table 2-2), just under 21 mm in both Early Bronze Age populations, is about the same as that for modern white Americans (just over 21 mm). The pelvic depth index, on the other hand, at about 85, is 8 percent lower than the average for modern U.S. whites, and about equal to the average figure in late nineteenth-century America. Kalınkaya may have a lower index than Karataş.

Stature is over 5 percent less than the present average for the United States, although over half of this difference is plausibly genetic. With this short stature goes 10 percent greater relative bone thickness than in the United States: there is more sub-periosteal than epiphyseal growth influenced as much by bending stress from running and climbing as by poorer nutrition or less cartilage growth. The same applies to the greater relative flattening of the upper femur (a 10 percent difference) and of the tibia shaft (a 5 percent difference). Economy of bone is a major factor in these differences,

Table 2.3. Correlation of meat consumption indices with growth, fertility, and dental health (Karataş)

| | Site-corrected Sr/Ca ratio | | | | | | | | | Zinc (μg/g) | | | | | | | | |
| | Female | | | Male | | | Both Sexes | | | Female | | | Male | | | Both Sexes | | |
| | M | σ | N | M | σ | N | M | σ | N | M | σ | N | M | σ | N | M | σ | N |
|---|---|---|---|---|---|---|---|---|---|---|---|---|---|---|---|---|---|---|
| **Skull base height** | | | | | | | | | | | | | | | | | | |
| Low (m. < 19 mm; f. < 18 mm) | .741 | .38 | 11 | .689 | .37 | 12 | .714 | .36 | 23 | 125.9 | 30.5 | 11 | 139.9 | 42.1 | 12 | 133.2 | 36.0 | 23 |
| Medium-High (m. = 19+; f. = 18+) | .610 | .19 | 21 | .591 | .23 | 39 | .598 | .22 | 60 | 137.0 | 45.4 | 21 | 167.5 | 93.4 | 39 | 156.8 | 81.2 | 60 |
| Entire group | .661 | .27 | 32 | .604 | .30 | 51 | .626 | .28 | 83 | 133.2 | 40.9 | 32 | 161.0 | 84.8 | 51 | 151.9 | 74.04 | 83 |
| **Pelvic inlet index** | | | | | | | | | | | | | | | | | | |
| Flat (<80) | .595 | | 3 | .582 | | 2 | .598 | | 5 | 141.1 | | 3 | 121.4 | | 2 | 133.3 | | 5 |
| Medium (80–89) | .581 | | 9 | .516 | | 9 | .538 | | 18 | 138.6 | | 9 | 243.0 | | 9 | 190.8 | | 18 |
| Deep (>89) | .829 | | 6 | .446 | | 2 | .733 | | 8 | 137.3 | | 6 | 162.4 | | 2 | 143.6 | | 8 |
| Entire group | .666 | .31 | 18 | .516 | .19 | 13 | .603 | .28 | 31 | 138.6 | | 18 | 211.9 | | 13 | 169.3 | | 31 |
| **Stature** | | | | | | | | | | | | | | | | | | |
| Short (m < 162; f. < 150) | .581 | | 24 | .675 | | 22 | .626 | | 46 | 135.6 | | 24 | 179.5 | | 22 | 156.6 | | 46 |
| Tall (m. > 169; f. > 157) | .608 | | 12 | .585 | | 20 | .594 | | 32 | 131.2 | | 12 | 168.9 | | 20 | 154.8 | | 32 |
| **Births** | | | | | | | | | | | | | | | | | | |
| Few (0–2) | .606 | .21 | 12 | | | | | | | 121.8 | 32.7 | 12 | | | | | | |
| Many (6–10) | .609 | .20 | 12 | | | | | | | *191.4* | *116.1* | 12 | | | | | | |
| **Dental lesions** | | | | | | | | | | | | | | | | | | |
| Few (0–1) | .580 | | 29 | .571 | | 37 | .575 | | 66 | 140.6 | | 30 | 178.7 | | 36 | 161.4 | | 66 |
| Many (10+) | .601 | | 17 | .602 | | 14 | .602 | | 31 | 154.8 | | 17 | 184.5 | | 14 | 168.2 | | 31 |

Note: Measurements in italics indicate a statistically significant difference.

Fig. 2-9. Neck (*left*) and lumbar (*right*) arthritis, severe in middle and old age. This woman of almost fifty (503 Ka), an eastern immigrant, had many births and experienced some bone loss through osteoporosis.

Fig. 2-10. Neck with stress arthritis (545 Ka)

Fig. 2-11. Pubic symphyses (female): 304 Ka (*above*) shows evidence of few births; 381 Ka (*below*) shows slight to moderate birth trauma—about five births

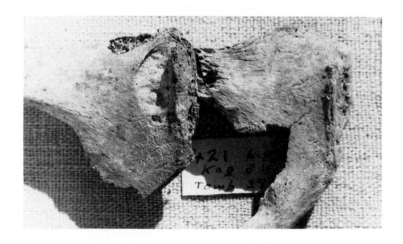

Fig. 2-12. Pubic symphyses: 421 Ka, female (*left*) shows marked scarring (eight to ten births); 422 Ka, male (*right*) shows no scarring and a rim formation typical of the later forties

Fig. 2-13. Symphysis face (545 Ka, male) showing breakdown characteristic of later middle age (just over fifty years)

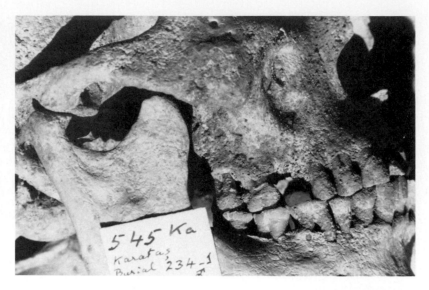

Fig. 2-14. Femurs (94 Ka) with pathological swelling in the lower third and also upper shaft flattening: platymeric index 75

Fig. 2-15. Dental disease (545 Ka): tooth loss, sinus reaction to infection

Fig. 2-16. Healed tibial fracture above right ankle (11 Kk, female): bony union with fibula; bleeding across interosseous membrane

Fig. 2-17. Old fracture of the right clavicle (545 Ka), healed with slight angulation and shortening

Fig. 2-18. Parry fracture of the left ulna with false joint from inadequate splinting: fibrous but not bony union (438 Ka)

Fig. 2-19. Parry fracture of the left ulna during healing (409 Ka). Note bridging callus of woven bone, formed over original blood clot

suggesting that minerals were less easily available in later childhood in the Early Bronze Age populations and that climbing hills placed more frequent stress on the gluteal muscles, especially on the gluteus medius (used in balancing on the great quadriceps during knee-straightening), the soleus, and the arch-supporting muscles used for foot-drive in running and climbing. An important point is that 5 percent shorter bones require a greater circumferential shaft area—hence relatively thicker shafts—for the same mass of muscle fibers. This factor, as well as bending stress resistance, is involved.

It is impossible to guess to what extent the shorter stature at Karataş, at Kalınkaya, in several Neolithic sites, and at Franchthi cave (in contrast to Danubian Mesolithic and Upper Paleolithic sites) is the result of selection (by disease?) for genetic shortness.

The overall picture of nutritional health, therefore, is excellent for the surviving infants and young children both before and after weaning (judging from skull base growth and teeth) and good during middle childhood (pelvic depth, tooth enamel resistance to disease, and lowish strontium/calcium ratio). Phytate may also have played some part then and in later life in reducing protein absorption and zinc level. Phytates, plus some restriction of calories during adolescence, may have limited overall body growth and helped to produce shortness.

The incidence of disease among those children who lived to adulthood is less than in the United States, as

Fig. 2-20. Unhealed occipital gash from axe blow—internal view (287 Ka). Exit wound larger than entry wound

Fig. 2-21. Unsuccessful trephination after skull fracture (522 Ka): note radiating cracks

indicated by the lower degree of lines of growth arrest on tooth enamel in the Karataş populations. Severe childhood epidemics would not be expected with the population density of the Early Bronze Age.

On the other hand, we have to ask what killed the nonsurvivors. Tetanus (from umbilical cord cutting), staphylococcus, malaria, and such domestic-animal-borne diseases as undulant fever may have killed newborn infants and young children; mortality would depend also on the presence of maternal antibodies in milk. As already noted, adults experienced much more overall stress than adults in the modern world and died somewhat younger even than the average for early colonial times in America.

Dental health was in general very good (table 2-2). Bone was slightly healthier, and there were fewer lesions per mouth than in the United States today, when corrected to ages at death in Karataş. The modern threefold increase in caries is especially striking. Since the doubling of Upper Paleolithic dental disease at Karataş indicates some effect of the increased ingestion of unrefined carbohydrates (grain products), the immensely high rate of carious teeth in the United States must be mainly the result of our immense consumption of sugars and refined carbohydrates, which feed mouth bacteria and maintain plaque. We have fewer abscesses, however, probably because of the nature of current dental treatment.

Social health is not bad, at least so far as bone evi-

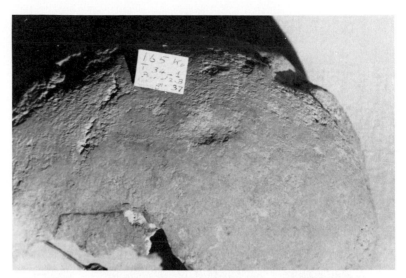

Fig. 2-22. Healed gashes on top of head (165 Ka)

Fig. 2-23. Perforation in front of the helix of the right ear (545 Ka)

dence can show. The overall incidence of healed fractures is not high (approximately the average for a U.S. sample about eight years older than the Karataş sample). The incidence of ulnar parry fractures is proportionately much higher,[28] reflecting hand-to-hand fighting; and healed trauma to the head, excluding fractures, is relatively high in males, but not in females. This fits the evidence at Karataş for male war deaths from head wounds (the torn axe-gash in the occiput of 287 Ka[29] and the unhealed neat circular trephination centered on radiating breaks in 522 Ka).[30] We cannot compare the U.S. data on this point, since almost half of the forensic sample died violently and exhibit many fresh, unhealed head injuries.

We cannot estimate the frequency of fighting. It might have occurred once in a generation, or less, between adjacent settlements in the valley. The original settlers buried around the built tomb of the "chieftain" (himself perhaps ceremonially reburied?) may have entered the area after some fighting. Since the chieftain's group in Trench 98 includes the Iranian horse-faced lady (503 Ka), whom one of us[31] compared to the Pagnık Öreni warrior from the Keban (who had huge healed right parietal trephination and forearm fractures), excavated by Richard Harper, and other possibly eastern people, it is possible that the first steppe-country immigrants came early in the third millennium B.C. It would be rash to assume that they spoke Proto-Lycian, but it is not impossible. Burial 56 contains two males (72 and 73 Ka) with occipital deformation; they also may be immigrants from the east or from Cyprus, where deformation occurs in the Neolithic as well as the Bronze Age.[32] The postvertex flattened type, or true Cypriot deformation,[33]

Fig. 2-24. Skull profiles: 440 Ka (*left*) and 441 Ka (*center*) are male family members from pithos 303. Both show a complete metopic suture (although it is fainter in 440). They are not far from the Karataş average. The horse-faced lady (503 Ka: right) is from the single pithos 349. She resembles Bronze Age people from Keban and from North Iran and differs strikingly from the Karataş average

Fig. 2-25. Skull front views of the trio in fig. 2-24, showing intrafamily variation and similarities (left, center) and the heterogeneity which immigrants can produce, disturbing the Hardy-Weinberg genetic balance (right)

occurs in a subadult (16 to 20 year old) female (549 Ka) and a young adult male with left ulnar parry fracture (555 Ka) from Burials 369 and 373 in Trench 125.

Neither these nor others who may be settlers born elsewhere have consistently different bone chemistries. We cannot be certain of birthplaces of individuals showing slight differences from the majority of the sample.

The level of variability is high at Karataş (table 2-2), again pointing to successful biological mixture, which also acted as a social stimulus.[34] It is to be linked with the intermediate position of the cranial measurements of the sample (table 2-4) and the healthy, normal selection pressure exercised by differential fertility (table 2-5).

Table 2-4 shows that the Anatolians have slightly smaller braincases than modern Americans, as one might expect, given their smaller body size, but about the same mass of face and mouth. The striking difference here is in our lessened muscle development: the breadth of the jaw ramus is 3 to 4 percent less in the United States than in Karataş, and jaw angles are less strongly developed. In proportions both Karataş and Kalınkaya people are surprisingly like us, differing only in slightly broader jaws,

as already noted, relatively wider noses (a 10 percent difference), and relatively lower orbits (2 to 3 percent). Karataş people may differ a little from those at Kalınkaya (higher orbits, longer palate, etc.), but sample size prevents certainty. On the other hand, both groups are much less linear in vault and longer in face than northwestern or central Anatolians of the early third millennium B.C. and the early populations of the Near East river valleys generally.[35] Cyprus departs from this linear trend.

Table 2-5 shows twelve women aged 38.5 producing 7.5 children each, or about one quarter of the mothers producing one half of the next generation. This happened at least in part because these women had the strength and energy to live eight years longer than the group average. These twelve women have a much higher level of bone zinc (191.4 $\mu$g/g), as noted earlier, perhaps because they could resist zinc depletion (by phytate?). They may also have deeper pelves. But they are not taller than average (153.6 cm), do not show lower strontium values, and do not seem to differ from the others in any consistent way, such as lessened linearity or better teeth.

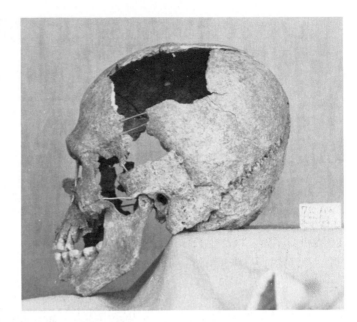

Fig. 2-26. One of two people from pithos 56 who also show occipital flattening as a result of head-binding in early infancy (72 Ka, male). The nearest source of this custom known to us at present is south-central and eastern Cyprus

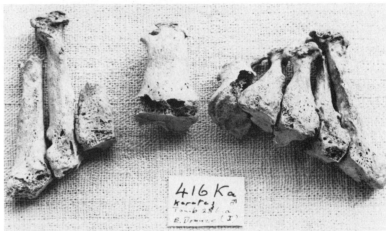

Fig. 2-27. Necrotic bone loss and shortening (416 Ka): spindling disease of medial metatarsals, perhaps from leprosy

The extra fecundity seems related only to better general health. Thus, differential fecundity selects, apparently, for greater energy and maintenance of variety.

To get a true picture of fertility we must take account of the survival of offspring to breeding age (15 years = adulthood). Table 2-6 lists the distribution of age at death for infants and children as related to the number of adult females and males. The number of skeletons is supplemented by empty pithos remains,[36] and the number of stillborn infants is estimated using the basic 3.5−5.0:1.0 ratio of stillbirths to infant deaths in the United States, decreased to 3x in well-preserved cemeteries and increased to 6x in cemeteries much damaged by plowing.[37] The infant:child:adult death ratio is then 5.7:5.1:10.0 overall. But in one of the two early cemetery areas, Trench 37, it is 14:10:10, suggesting that child survival and health improved during the Early Bronze Age. We cannot, however, get a close estimate of each woman's fertility. As shown in table 2-7, at Karataş, where there are more females than males, the infant deaths are then 1.06(?) per female and the child deaths 0.95 per female. In relation to average number of births (fecundity)—4.13 per female (N = 45)—there are 2.12 survivors, enough for a fair rate of increase. Kalınkaya, with 3.67(?) births per female (N = 6), 0.57(?) infant deaths, and 0.71 child deaths, has 2.4 survivors. We think, however, that even the corrected number of infant deaths is an underestimate—0.8 or more per female is

Table 2.4. Skull size measurements and proportions or shape indicators relative to U.S. sample (adults)

| | Karataş | | | | | | Kalınkaya | | | | | | Modern United States[a] | | | | | |
| | Female | | | Male | | | Female | | | Male | | | Female | | | Male | | |
| | M | σ | N | M | σ | N | M | σ | N | M | σ | N | M | σ | N | M | σ | N |
|---|---|---|---|---|---|---|---|---|---|---|---|---|---|---|---|---|---|---|
| Horizontal circumference | 498.6 | 16.7 | 37 | 513.0 | 11.9 | 56 | 495.7 | 13.9 | 7 | 531.1 | 7.6 | 7 | 502.9 | 14.6 | 77 | 552.9 | 15.1 | 104 |
| Skull vault module[b] | 141.9 | — | 39 | 147.1 | — | 64 | 142.4 | — | 5 | 150.7? | — | 9 | 143.5 | — | 77 | 149.8 | — | 104 |
| Bizygomatic br. | 121.7 | 7.3 | 29 | 130.6 | 4.3 | 44 | 113.9? | 4.0 | 9 | 133.9? | 6.2 | 7 | 121.2 | 4.3 | 75 | 131.1 | 5.5 | 99 |
| Palate br. | 60.5 | 3.6 | 15 | 63.6 | 3.3 | 30 | 58.0? | 4.6 | 5 | 66.5? | 4.3 | 6 | 59.2 | 3.0 | 53 | 63.5 | 4.5 | 66 |
| Chin ht. | 30.9 | 2.7 | 76 | 34.5 | 2.8 | 78 | 30.9? | 1.4 | 10 | 33.4? | 2.0 | 9 | 29.9 | 2.6 | 56 | 34.1 | 3.0 | 65 |
| Minimum ramus br. | 29.3 | 2.4 | 62 | 31.1 | 4.4 | 75 | 29.5? | 2.9 | 10 | 29.8? | 3.3 | 10 | 27.9 | 3.0 | 65 | 30.2 | 2.9 | 83 |
| Indices | | | | | | | | | | | | | | | | | | |
| Cranial br./l. | 78.1 | 3.7 | 43 | 76.6 | 3.7 | 62 | 78.8? | 3.2 | 9 | 76.7 | 5.9 | 9 | 77.0 | 3.6 | 77 | 76.5 | 3.9 | 107 |
| Auricular ht./l. + br. | 72.3 | 2.6 | 39 | 73.4 | 3.0 | 59 | 74.7 | 2.2 | 8 | 71.2 | 3.4 | 8 | 72.8 | 2.5 | 77 | 72.4 | 2.4 | 104 |
| Fronto-parietal br. | 69.3 | 3.0 | 36 | 68.4 | 3.9 | 62 | 68.2 | 3.4 | 9 | 69.4 | 4.3 | 8 | 68.4 | 2.7 | 77 | 67.8 | 3.4 | 107 |
| Crano-facial br. | 88.9 | 4.3 | 28 | 93.2 | 3.7 | 41 | 84.0 | 5.2 | 7 | 93.0 | 3.2 | 8 | 88.5 | 2.8 | 75 | 91.8 | 3.8 | 100 |
| Fronto-gonial br. | 98.6 | 7.2 | 16 | 106.4 | 7.1 | 34 | 101.0 | 4.4 | 6 | 102.4 | 6.5 | 7 | 96.7 | 5.9 | 63 | 103.0 | 6.6 | 69 |
| Facial ht./br. | 93.9 | 5.8 | 18 | 89.8 | 4.8 | 31 | 93.7 | 3.4 | 5 | 89.3 | 6.1 | 7 | 92.1 | 5.7 | 50 | 92.8 | 5.4 | 55 |
| Upper facial (upper ht./br. | 55.7 | 3.8 | 20 | 53.5 | 2.8 | 36 | 55.8 | 1.7 | 5 | 54.0 | 4.2 | 7 | 55.7 | 3.4 | 56 | 55.5 | 3.3 | 72 |
| Nasal br./ht. | 49.6 | 5.8 | 18 | 50.1 | 4.6 | 36 | 49.0 | 3.3 | 5 | 48.7 | 3.1 | 7 | 45.2 | 4.2 | 70 | 45.7 | 4.4 | 93 |
| Orbital ht./br. | 83.9 | 5.9 | 25 | 80.6 | 5.0 | 45 | 82.8 | 3.2 | 5 | 79.0 | 5.9 | 7 | 86.2 | 6.4 | 69 | 83.4 | 6.2 | 93 |
| Alveolo-palatal br./l. | 120.6 | 9.9 | 15 | 117.3 | 5.1 | 25 | 121.5 | 9.6 | 5 | 125.5 | 6.9 | 6 | 115.6 | 8.7 | 51 | 120.4 | 8.1 | 63 |
| Gnathic face proj./ skullbase | 93.3 | 5.1 | 15 | 93.0 | 4.4 | 34 | 93.7 | 6.5 | 3 | 92.2 | 3.5 | 4 | 93.0 | 3.4 | 54 | 92.2 | 3.6 | 66 |
| Facial angle relative to Frankfort horizontal plane | 86.4 | 3.5 | 20 | 87.0 | 3.9 | 39 | 88.0 | 2.0 | 3 | 88.5 | 4.2 | 4 | 86.2 | 2.7 | 58 | 87.5 | 2.8 | 70 |
| Index deviations (sexes combined) | | | | | | | | | | | | | | | | | | |
| from Kalınkaya | | | | 1.0 | | | | | | — | | | 1.5 | | | | | |
| from USA | | | | 1.2 | | | | | | 1.5 | | | | | | — | | |

Note: Skull size is in part environmentally determined; proportion and shape are largely genetic. A question mark indicates a slightly uncertain measurement.
[a] The modern U.S. sample consisted of white adults.
[b] This measurement is the average of the sum of the length, breadth, and height of the skull.

likely. The number of child deaths seems high, but it does not exceed the ratio of 8 : 5 : 10 found at Middle Bronze Lerna.[38] In colonial America several juvenile deaths per family were normal. This does not mean that the dead children produced little grief or memory of love. The damage to social health from child deaths was greater than the damage to physical health.

There is another effect of child deaths: the survivors may be better nourished as well as being lucky. It is also conceivable that child deaths have a genetically selective effect, although we can find no evidence for this at Karataş. The relative lack of males (table 2-6) at Karataş seems greater than could be accounted for by war deaths with burial elsewhere. In part it reflects better male health.

Finally, with respect to population increase and its pressure on food supply and social system,[39] the steady rate of increase in a town at the center of a rather long

Table 2.5. Number of births (fecundity) and age at death in Karataş female sample

| | No. Births | | | | | | | | | | | | | Total Births | No. Mothers | Mean No. Births |
|---|---|---|---|---|---|---|---|---|---|---|---|---|---|---|---|---|
| | 0 | 1 | 2 | 3 | 4 | 5 | 6 | 7 | 8 | 9 | 10 | 11 | 12 | | | |
| Maternal age | | | | | | | | | | | | | | | | |
| 15–19 | | 5 | 1 | | | | | | | | | | | 7 | 6 | 1.17 |
| 20–24 | | 1 | 3 | 1 | | | | | | | | | | 10 | 5 | 2.00 |
| 25–29 | | | 1 | 1 | 3 | | | | | | | | | 17 | 5 | 3.40 |
| 30–34 | 1 | | 2 | 1 | 5 | 1 | | 4 | | 1 | | | | 70 | 15 | 3.40 |
| 35–39 | | | 1 | | 2 | 2 | 2 | | 1 | | | | | 41 | 8 | 5.13 |
| 40–44 | | | 1 | | | 1 | | | | 1 | | | | 16 | 3 | 5.33 |
| 45–49 | | | | | | | 1 | 1 | | | | | 1 | 25 | 3 | 8.33 |
| No. births | 0 | 6 | 16 | 12 | 40 | 20 | 18 | 35 | 8 | 9 | 10 | 0 | 12 | 186 | | 4.13 |
| No. mothers | 1 | 6 | 8 | 4 | 10 | 4 | 3 | 5 | 1 | 1 | 1 | 0 | 1 | | 45 | |
| Maternal age at death | 32 | 18 | 28 | 30 | 32 | 38 | 41 | 36 | 38 | 42 | 32 | — | 48 | | 31.4 yrs. | |

| | | |
|---|---|---|
| Age | 28.9 | 38.4 |
| No. births | 94 | 92 |
| No. mothers | 33 | 12 |
| Mean no. births | 2.85 | 7.50 |
| Stature | 153.8 cm | 153.6 cm |

Table 2.6. Age distribution in two Bronze Age populations

| | Age | | | | Adult | | |
|---|---|---|---|---|---|---|---|
| | 0–1 | 1–4 | 5–9 | 10–14 | Female | Male | Total |
| Karataş | (246) | 95 | 66 | 60 | 233 | 197 | 897 |
| Kalınkaya | 20?[a] | 6?[a] | 6 | 4 | 28 | 26 | 90 |

Note: Parentheses indicate a very uncertain measurement; a question mark indicates a slightly uncertain measurement.
[a] These figures are estimates based on an actual find of 4 infants in the 0–1 age group and 2 infants in the 1–4 age group.

Table 2.7. Birth rate and mortality: Two Bronze Age populations and the United States

| | Karataş | Kalınkaya | United States[a] |
|---|---|---|---|
| Births per female | 4.13; N = 45 | 3.67?; N = 6 | 2.4 |
| Infant deaths per female | 1.06?; N = 233 | .57?; N = 28 | .2 |
| Child deaths per female | .95 | .71 | .1 |
| Survivors to age 15 | 2.12 | (2.41) | 2.1 |

Note: Parentheses indicate a very uncertain measurement; a question mark indicates a slightly uncertain measurement.
[a] Based on U.S. Census Bureau data, 1975.

and very fertile valley would provoke no crisis as long as some emigration was possible.

## CONCLUSIONS

The Early Bronze Age people of Karataş were notably healthy for their time. In nutritional health they surpassed contemporary and Middle Bronze samples. They were also a little better off in child health and in resistance to disease. They had enough protein, as shown by bone strontium and zinc levels.

Longevity and dental disease were about the same as in other prehistoric groups. We find above-average female longevity in those women who had many births. This group also has very high bone zinc levels (as do a few women in the Kalınkaya population), a result of better nutrition and of a physiologic interaction favoring the absorption of zinc, needed for enzymes and embryos.

Diseases apparently included malaria.

Population variability was high at Karataş, largely as a result of mixture with migrants from the east and the southeast. The population at Kalınkaya appears to be less mixed. Both share the Anatolian culture, with gabled houses and pithos burial.

Fighting is reflected in healed fractures and wounds (less frequent than in the United States) and fresh injuries. Bronze weapons and stone clubs were used. Much of the fighting may have been intravalley.

Fertility was adequate for population increase and may have had some selective effect favoring genotypes for longevity and energy.

NOTES

In addition to Professor Machteld J. Mellink and her staff at Elmalı, we owe thanks to many others. J. L. A. repaired and studied the people of Karataş in the laboratory of the excavation house at Elmalı in 1965 and 1967 with the help of Sally Harris (Todd) and Beyhan Sezer; in 1969, 1972, 1975, and 1977, with the help of his wife, Peggy Angel; in 1975, with the help of David C. Fredenburg; and in 1977, with the help of S. C. B. S. C. B. did bone chemistry analyses on the human and animal samples collected in 1977 and 1979. In July 1978 J. L. A. and S. C. B. mended and studied the people from Kalınkaya in the preparation laboratory of the Museum of Anatolian Civilizations. We are both grateful to all these people for their assistance in recording, mending, measuring, and photographing.

For the opportunity to study these ancient populations, we thank the excavators, the successive directors of the Turkish Antiquities and Museums Department—Mehmet Önder, Hikmet Gurçay, and Aykut Özet—and their staffs, David French, and the British Institute, where we stayed in Ankara.

Special thanks are due Theresa Lovell for general statistics, Jennifer Olsen Kelley for analysis of statistics on bone chemistry, and Katharine Holland for typing.

1 J. L. Angel, "Early Bronze Age Karataş People and Their Cemeteries," *AJA* 80 (1976) 385–91.

2 J. L. Angel, *The People of Lerna: Analysis of a Prehistoric Aegean Population* (Princeton and Washington, D.C., 1971) 63–65, pls. 16–17, fig. 5, tables 15 and 19.

3 J. L. Angel, "Physical Anthropology: Determining Sex, Age and Individual Features," in T. A. and E. Cockburn eds., *Mummies, Disease and Ancient Cultures* (Cambridge 1980) 241–57.

4 M. J. Mellink, "Excavations at Karataş-Semayük in Lycia, 1964," *AJA* 69 (1965) 245–49.

5 K. Bittel, *Guide to Boğazköy* (Ankara 1969) 1–3, 40–41, map 1.

6 H. Helbaek, "The Paleoethnobotany of the Near East and Europe," in R. J. Braidwood and B. Howe eds., *Prehistoric Investigations in Iraqi Kurdistan* (SAOC 31, Chicago 1960) 99–118; K. W. Butzer, *CAH³* 1.2, 35–69, esp. fig. 4.

7 S. L. C. Bisel, *A Pilot Study in Aspects of Human Nutrition in the Ancient East Mediterranean* (Ph.D. diss., University of Minnesota, 1980) 14, 115; J. G. Reinhold, "Phytate Concentrations of Leavened and Unleavened Iranian Breads," *Ecology of Food Nutrition* 1 (1972) 187–92.

8 M. Hopf, "Nutzpflanzen von lernäischen Gulf," *RGZM* 9 (1962) 1–19.

9 B. Hesse and D. Perkins, Jr., "Faunal Remains from Karataş-Semayük in Southwest Anatolia: An Interim Report," *JFA* 1 (1974) 152–56.

10 N.-G. Gejvall, *Lerna 1. The Fauna* (Princeton 1969) 11–12, tables 7–8.

11 Gejvall (supra n. 10) 51–52.

12 See, e.g., M. J. Mellink's reports on excavations at Karataş-Semayük: *AJA* 69 (1965) 244; *AJA* 70 (1966) pl. 62; *AJA* 72 (1968) 252; *AJA* 73 (1969) 323, 328.

13 J. L. Angel, "Human Remains at Karataş," *AJA* 72 (1968) 260–63, pl. 86 lower.

14 M. J. Mellink, "Excavations at Karataş-Semayük and Elmalı, 1972," *AJA* 77 (1973) 297–98, 302.

15 M. J. Mellink, "Excavations at Karataş-Semayük and Elmalı, Lycia, 1969," *AJA* 74 (1970) pl. 58, fig. 21.

16 See, e.g., M. J. Mellink, "Excavations at Karataş-Semayük in Lycia, 1966," *AJA* 71 (1967) 257.

17 Bisel, (supra n. 7) 10–12; S. C. Bisel, "Human Bone Mineral and Nutrition," in W. A. McDonald, W. D. E. Coulson, and J. Rosser eds., *Excavations at Nichoria* 3 (Minneapolis 1983) 264–65.

18 H. F. DeLuca, "The Control of Calcium and Phosphorus Metabolism by the Vitamin D Endocrine System," *ANYAS* 355 (1980) 1–17.

19 Reinhold (supra n. 7) 187–92.

20 A. Sillen, "Strontium and Diet at Hayonim Cave," *AJPA* 56 (1981) 131–39.

21 H. L. Rosenthal, "Uptake, Turnover and Transfer of Bone-Seeking Elements in Fishes," *ANYAS* 109 (1963) 278–93.

22 M. J. Schoeninger, M. J. De Niro, and H. Tauber, "Stable Nitrogen Isotope Ratios of Bone Collagen Reflected Marine and Terrestrial Components of Prehistoric Human Diet," *Science* 220 (1983) 1381–83.

23 Cf. J. L. Angel, "The Bases of Paleodemography," *AJPA* 30 (1969) 427–35, esp. 428 and bibliography quoting Todd, Krogman, and others; T. D. Stewart, *Essentials of Forensic Anthropology* (Springfield, Ill., 1979) 147–84.

24 J. L. Angel, "Porotic Hyperostosis, Anemias, Malarias and Marshes in the Prehistoric Eastern Mediterranean," *Science* 153 (1966) 760–63 (reprinted in P. Reining and I. Tinker eds., *Population Dynamics, Ethics, and Policy* [Washington, D.C., 1975] 96–98); "Porotic Hyperostosis in the Eastern Mediterranean," *Medical College of Virginia Quarterly* 14 (1978) 10–16; and J. L. Angel, "Health as a Crucial Factor in the Change from Hunting to Developed Farming in the Eastern Mediterranean," in M. N. Cohen and G. J. Armelagos eds., *Paleopathology at the Origins of Agriculture* (San Diego, in press).

25 W. W. Greulich and H. Thoms, "The Dimensions of the Pelvic Inlet of 789 White Females," *Anatomical Record* 72 (1938) 45–51; G. Nicholson, "The Two Main Diameters of the Brim of the Female Pelvis," *Journal of Anatomy* 79 (1945) 131–35; J. L. Angel, "Pelvic Inlet Form: A Neglected Index of Nutritional Status," *AJPA* 48 (1978), 378; J. L. Angel, "A New Measure of Growth Efficiency: Skull Base Height," *AJPA* 58 (1982) 297–305, esp. 299–301, 303–4; J. L. Angel and J. O. Kelley, "Experiment in Human Growth Response to Improving Diet and Disease Control," *AJPA* 63 (1984) 197.

26 Angel, in press (supra n. 24).

27 Hesse and Perkins (supra n. 9).

28 J. L. Angel, "Human Skeletal Remains at Karataş," *AJA* 74 (1970) 253–59, pl. 62.

29 Angel (supra n. 13) 262, pl. 86, fig. 1, upper.

30 Angel (supra n. 1) 385.

31 Angel (supra n. 28) pl. 62.

32 J. L. Angel, "Neolithic Crania from Sotira," in P. Dikaios, *Sotira* (Philadelphia 1961) appendix 1, pp. 223–29.

33 C. M. Fürst, "Zur Kenntnis der Anthropologie der prähistorischen Bevölkerung der Insel Cypern," *Lunds Universitets Årsskrift* 29.6 (1933) 91–100; J. L. Angel, "Late Bronze Age Cypriotes from Bamboula," in J. L. Benson, *Bamboula at Kourion* (Philadelphia 1973) 148–65.

34 F. H. Hulse, "Ethnic, Caste and Genetic Miscegenation," *Journal of Biosocial Science*, Suppl. 1 (1969) 31–41; see also Angel, in press (supra n. 24).

35 J. L. Angel, *Troy. The Human Remains* (Suppl. Monograph 1, Princeton 1951) table 2 (foldout), pls. 4–5.

36 Angel (supra n. 1) 386–87.

37 Angel (supra n. 1) 390, table 6.

38 Angel (supra n. 2) esp. table 4.

39 M. N. Cohen, *The Food Crisis in Prehistory* (New Haven 1977) 42–50, 128–51.

# New Observations on the Relationship of Kültepe with Southeast Anatolia and North Syria during the Third Millennium B.C.

TAHSIN ÖZGÜÇ

## 3

For many years I have followed the invaluable publications of my friend and colleague Machteld Mellink, as well as her excavations and surveys of the progress of Anatolian archaeology. I have always been impressed by her deep insight. Each year the Anatolian plateau has produced new material for us to share and discuss. Her boundless energy has been concentrated on Anatolia for many years, and her devotion to Turkey has inspired the development of archaeology there. Her admirable scholarly digests of annual work have been most influential in all parts of the field.

All her Turkish colleagues are indebted to her for her love of Turkey and its people; above all, we admire her warmth and kindness. She has provided a great link among institutions and fellow scholars throughout the world. This paper is offered to her as an inadequate token of thanks from one who has been privileged to collaborate with her for more than thirty-seven years.

New evidence from Kültepe (ancient Kaneš) shows that interaction between Southeast Anatolia and North Syria intensified during the second half of the third millennium B.C. It is a subject which has long interested Machteld Mellink, who long ago pointed out that the legends of later times which tell of early Mesopotamian kings coming to Anatolia may on archaeological grounds reflect historical reality (see below).

The occurrence of Ubaid material at Fraktin[1] means that the southern part of central Anatolia had access to Syria and Mesopotamia from early times. The relevant finds from Kültepe are contemporary with the Early Dynastic III, the Akkadian, and the post-Akkadian periods.

The early period at Kültepe is characterized by unusual features: monumental architecture in several building levels; a significant number of imported items; and a well-developed style of polychrome pottery painting, alabaster statuettes of deities, and disc-shaped idols.

Here I deal with finds dating to the middle and late periods of the Early Bronze Age in Kültepe.

## ARCHITECTURE

At Kültepe, EB III is subdivided into three secondary periods (c = Level 13, b = Level 12, a = Level 11);[2] and excavations in one area of the mound show that Level 11 consists of two different phases (11a–b). Our investigations of the later phase of Level 11 (11a) are still in progress, but we have unearthed a large structure of the earlier phase (11b) in squares N–R/36–38. The plan of the building is almost square (preserved length: 22.5 m; width: 24.0 m). The foundations are built of small stones, and the walls of large mudbricks (length of bricks: 0.70 m; width: 0.50 m; thickness: 0.12 m). The width of the north and west walls is 0.9 m; that of the east and south walls, 1.2 m (ills. 3-1 and 3-2). The partition walls are also thick (figs. 3-1–3-3), and one section of the dividing wall in squares O–P/37 is 3 m wide. Although the northwest and northeast corners of the building have been destroyed, two wall fragments in P–R/38 show that the building continued to the south.

The large interior hall is 10.5 m wide and 17.0 m long (ill. 3-1). Near the center was a large hearth (no. 1—diameter: 4.3 m). The south wall of the hall has three rectangular mudbrick pilasters, or half-pillars (length: 0.9 m; width: 0.4 m) on the inside and three on the outside, exactly opposite one another and at the same level (fig. 3-4). The north and south walls have such pilasters only on the interior. The pilasters were evidently designed to help carry the roof or the ceiling of the hall.

Fig. 3-1. Kültepe, Level 11b, large building

Fig. 3-2. Kültepe, Level 11b, large building

Fig. 3-3. Kültepe, Level 11b, large building

Fig. 3-4. Kültepe, Level 11b, large building, interior pilasters

Large pine beams supported the roof; they fell to the floor when the building burned down (fig. 3-3). The floor is of hard, tightly packed earth. On the north and east walls (squares O–P/37) are rather high mudbrick benches, 2.3 and 2.1 m long respectively and 0.7 m wide; they must have been comfortable to sit on. A third bench on the west wall extends around the corner into the passage from the entrance into the central hall (in

O/37). In squares N–P/36 are two rooms, one of which is divided into three chambers by two spur walls (ill. 3-1, no. 8). A doorway 1.2 m wide (no. 7) leads from the subdivided room into a long and narrow (1 m wide) passage (no. 5). At the eastern end of the passageway (P/37) is another room (no. 6; 4.5 by 2.8 m). The western part of the corridor (no. 4) widens to form a short passage (no. 9; 3.5 m wide) into a part of the building which is

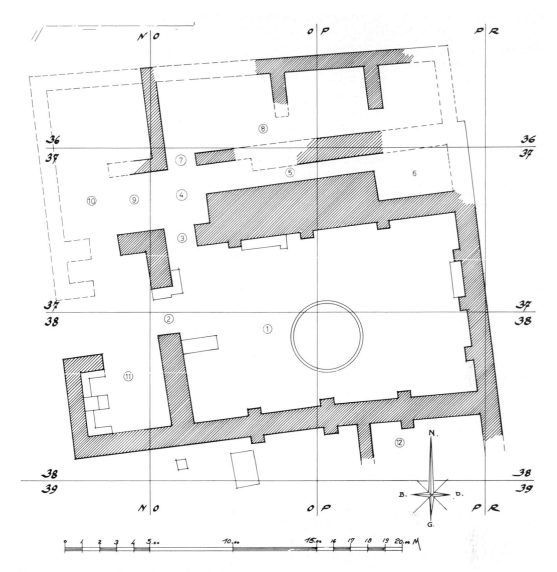

Ill. 3-1. Kültepe, Level 11b, plan of large building

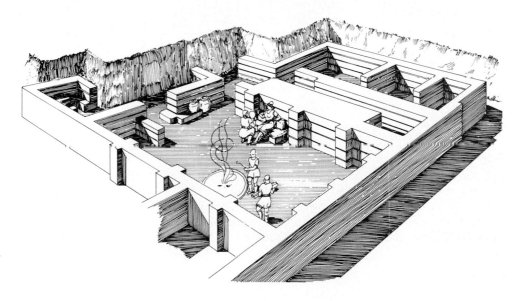

Ill. 3-2. Kültepe, Level 11b, iso-
metric reconstruction of large
building

completely destroyed (no. 10). From the western part of the corridor another door (no. 3; 1.8 m wide) opens into the great hall.

The main entranceway to the central hall consists of a long chamber (no. 11; 5.0 by 3.8 m) of which only the southern part was preserved (N–O/38). The north wall of this chamber was intentionally built to only one-half the height of the rest of the walls, so that this side was always open. The benches built along the west and north walls and part of the south wall are quite well preserved. The long bench on the west wall is divided into two parts by a short mudbrick partition.

The opening into the central hall (no. 2; 2.8 m wide) had no door leaves; it was either left open or was closed with some perishable material, such as reed mats. The mudbrick walls of the entranceway were covered with several layers of mud plaster and then carefully coated with lime plaster on all sides (fig. 3-5); a similar plaster covers the floor. At a height of 0.7 m the walls bore a wooden molding, as indicated by vertical slots (fig. 3-4) which sometimes contained charcoal. The wooden molding may have been placed there in order to facilitate the hanging of objects.

The building must have been destroyed by intense fire, since the charcoal remnants of beams and posts occur throughout. Because only a few intact vessels and sherds were found on the floor, it is assumed that the building was emptied before the fire. The function of the structure is not known (temple, palace?), but it is clearly not a private dwelling.

Although the complete plan is not known, we can still see that this building differs from the modest architecture of contemporary central Anatolia, both in dimensions and in the presence of half-pillars and benches. No buildings of such a size can be found during the Early Bronze Age in Alişar, Alaca Höyük, or Karaoğlan. The building seems to be unique to Kültepe and is in an area where, in each phase of the Early Bronze Age, large structures existed. Because of the extensive destruction, it is hard to establish whether it was in some way a product of foreign influence. I am inclined to think that we see here signs of ideas originating in Mesopotamia.

An older building of Level 12, a temple destroyed by a severe fire, was unearthed directly below the structure in Level 11b.[3] The 11b building was erected on its remains. Little time must have elapsed between the destruction of the old temple and the construction of the new building, judging from finds on the floor dating to Level 12.

Below building phase 12, in Level 13, was an older building on stone foundations. It has not yet been completely excavated. Thus, in Kültepe during the last phases of the Early Bronze Age there were three large buildings constructed on top of each other, each destroyed by fire.

IMPORTED MATERIAL

Numerous imported objects have been found in the houses, the large buildings, and the graves at Kültepe. These include pottery, luxury items made of gold and precious stones, and cylinder seals.

Pottery

*Flasks.* A flask of alabastron shape was imported into Kültepe from North Syria or southeastern Anatolia (ill. 3-3); it was found in Level 12.[4] Two similar vases are represented by neck sherds in Level 13;[5] these sherds have the double-ring rim (figs. 3-6 and 3-7; ills. 3-4 and 3-5) which we reconstruct for the Level 12 bottle. In Level 11b, however, are neck sherds with both everted

Fig. 3-5. Kültepe, Level 11b, large building, entranceway

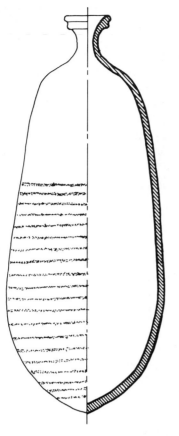

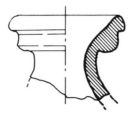

Ill. 3-4. Kültepe, Level 13, neck sherd from flask

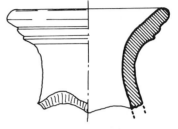

Ill. 3-5. Kültepe, Level 13, neck sherd from flask

Ill. 3-3. Kültepe, Level 12, flask

Fig. 3-6. Kültepe, Level 11b, neck sherd

Fig. 3-7. Kültepe, Level 11b, neck sherd

and angular rims (ills 3-6 and 3-7).[6] In a pot grave of Level 11b was a similar flask with a double-ring rim and rounded base (fig. 3-8).[7] This vessel is of considerable interest because it is decorated with grooves around the base of the neck, three on the shoulders and three on the lower part of the body; zigzag incisions run between the grooves of the shoulder and those on the lower body. Two lug handles appear on the shoulder. It is a local imitation of a Syrian bottle of alabastron shape.[8]

Pots with the same shape and made by the same technique have been found at Gözlü Kule (Tarsus) in the EB III stratum[9] and in the burials at Amarna.[10] Examples

*The Relationship of Kültepe with Southeast Anatolia and North Syria*    35

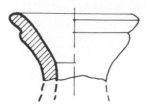

Ill. 3-6. Kültepe, Level 11b, neck sherd

Ill. 3-7. Kültepe, Level 11b, neck sherd

Fig. 3-8. Kültepe, Level 11b pot grave, flask

Fig. 3-9. Eskiyapar, silver flask

with more rounded bodies occur at Germayir,[11] Tilmen Höyük in Level III D,[12] and Tell Chuera in Early Dynastic levels.[13] The rich collection of Syrian flasks in the museum at Gaziantep has not yet been published, but the Anatolian evidence should help refine their chronology.

The hoard at Eskiyapar contained a silver flask in a typical alabastron shape (fig. 3-9).[14] Its presence allows us to date this rich hoard more easily, since the shape of the flask and other objects in the hoard have parallels in Early Dynastic III contexts. The silver flask is the first of its kind to be found in the Near East and suggests that similar ceramic flasks are based on metal prototypes. The importance of Syrian flasks in establishing the chronology and nature of east-west contacts was clearly

shown by Machteld Mellink,[15] and H. Kühne has recently made detailed comparative studies of these flasks among the "metallische Ware" of Tell Chuera,[16] a site which must form a link in the chain of communication between Mesopotamia, Syria, and Anatolia.

The flasks from Level 13 at Kültepe, as well as the Eskiyapar flask, are contemporary with the latest phase of the Early Dynastic III period; the flasks from Level 12b are contemporary with the Akkadian and post-Akkadian phases. This dating is confirmed by other finds from these levels.

The EB II period at Kültepe consists of four building levels (14–17). Level 14 is representative of the last phase of EB II, Levels 15–16 of the middle phase, and

Fig. 3-10. Kültepe, Level 15 cist grave, flask

Fig. 3-11. Kültepe, Level 15 cist grave, flask

Fig. 3-12. Kültepe, Level 15, flask sherd

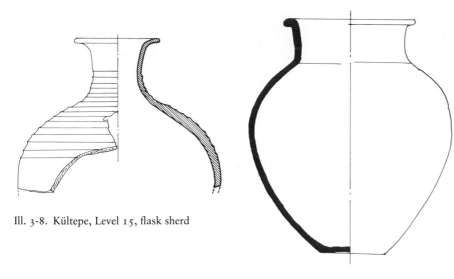

Ill. 3-8. Kültepe, Level 15, flask sherd

Ill. 3-9. Kültepe, Level 14, flask

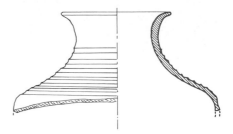

Ill. 3-10. Kültepe, Level 14, flask sherd

Fig. 3-13. Kültepe, Level 14, local imitation of Syrian flask

Level 17 of the earliest. During the last and middle phases there is an increase, over the early phase, in the amount of pottery imported from the area of the Upper Euphrates, a demonstration of the continuous connection between the two areas during the Early Bronze Age.

Two flasks found in the stone cist grave of Level 15 belong to type F2 of Kühne's classification.[17] As are all comparable finds, these two flasks (figs. 3-10 and 3-11) are wheelmade.[18] A sherd from a flask was also found in situ on the floor of a building of Level 15 (fig. 3-12; ill. 3-8).[19] These three pieces look exactly like their "metallische Ware" counterparts found in sites in northern Syria and southeastern Anatolia,[20] and are precisely paralleled in Tarsus, Tell Brak, Tel Tainat, and Tell Chuera. Detailed studies of their distribution and chronological correlations have been made by Machteld Mellink[21] and by Kühne.[22]

These ceramic linkages indicate the existence of relations between North Syria and Cilicia, from central Anatolia to southern Mesopotamia (Ur and Fara). Of three flasks found at Alişar—one in a grave of Level 13T,[23] another in Level 7M,[24] and the third one without context[25]—two are local imitations of ware imported from Syria.[26] A flask found at Kültepe in Level 14 (fig. 3-13) is also a local imitation of a Syrian import;[27] another flask from the same grave is of Kühne's F3 type (fig. 3-14; ill. 3-9).[28] From Level 15 come two smaller flasks (figs. 3-15 and 3-16),[29] and a piece of a similar flask from Level 14 (fig. 3-17; ill. 3-10).[30]

The examples of "metallische Ware" found at Kültepe are among the most splendid of the group, which was distributed from the Upper Euphrates, the Habur and Balikh regions into Anatolia and Mesopotamia. Levels

Fig. 3-14. Kültepe, Level 14, flask

Fig. 3-15. Kültepe, Level 15, flask

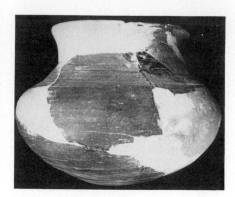

Fig. 3-16. Kültepe, Level 15, flask

Fig. 3-17. Kültepe, Level 14, flask sherd

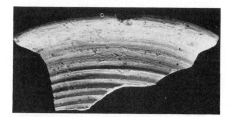

Fig. 3-18. Kültepe, Level 15, flask sherd

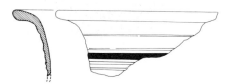

Ill. 3-11. Kültepe, Level 15, flask sherd

Fig. 3-19. Kültepe, Level 14, beaker

15 and 14 at Kültepe should be contemporary with Early Dynastic II in Mesopotamia, as should Tarsus EB II and Tell Chuera.[31] A further confirmation of this correlation is offered by a piece of a flask from Kültepe Level 15, of the type called "metallische Ware mit Streifenbemalung" (fig 3-18; ill. 3-11).[32] The third corrugation on the neck of this flask is in the form of a painted band. The distribution of this type is extensive, ranging from Kültepe to Ur.[33]

*Beakers.* Two beakers found in Level 14 constitute the second type of imported ceramic wares (figs. 3-19 and 3-20; ills. 3-12 and 3-13).[34] Found in the same cist grave as the beakers was a handmade beak-spouted pitcher in a shape foreign to central Anatolia (fig. 3-21).[35] It finds its closest parallel at EB II Tarsus.[36]

*Bowls.* A matter of continuing scholarly concern has been the extent of commercial relations between western Anatolia and North Syria and southern Mesopotamia.[37] Recent finds establish that southerners carried on trade not only with western Anatolia, but also with central Anatolia and northern Cappadocia. Kaneš was at all times part of this commerce, which was conducted by both land and sea. It is therefore not surprising that we find objects at Kaneš from Mesopotamia and North Syria on the one hand, and from western Anatolia and Troy on the other. Some discoveries at Kültepe illustrate the complex involvement of Kaneš in these farflung ventures.

In Levels 11b and 12 at Kültepe there occur, together with monochrome and polychrome local wares, ceramic bowls[38] whose exact equivalents we find in Troy II b–c, d, f, g, and in Level III a–d,[39] as well as in Tarsus EB III.[40] All are wheelmade and thick-walled. Most have a plain, unslipped surface, although some are coated with a pale, reddish, or light brown wash. They exhibit great variety in size (figs. 3-22 to 3-24; ills. 3-14 and 3-15). A small number of these vessels occur at Kültepe for the first

Fig. 3-20. Kültepe, Level 14, beaker

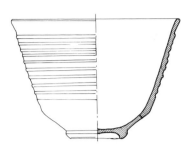

Ill. 3-12. Kültepe, Level 14, beaker

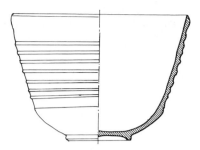

Ill. 3-13. Kültepe, Level 14, beaker

Fig. 3-21. Kültepe, Level 14, beak-spouted pitcher

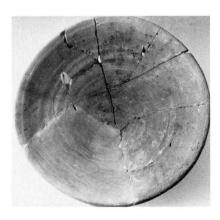

Fig. 3-22. Kültepe, Levels 11b–12, bowl

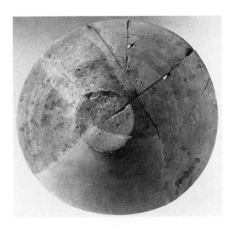

Fig. 3-23. Kültepe, Levels 11b–12, bowl

Fig. 3-24. Kültepe, Level 13, bowl

Fig. 3-25. Kültepe, Levels 11b–12, bowl

time in Level 13 (fig. 3-25), and none were found in EB II levels. All of them must have been imported from western Anatolia (Troy).

*Two-Handled Vessels.* The two-handled cups found at Kültepe in EB III levels are most significant in illuminating the continuing exchange between Kaneš and Troy. They are found not only in central Anatolia and Tarsus,[41] but also at Tilmen Höyük, Gedikli,[42] and Tel Selenkahiye.[43] Two-handled cups at Kültepe in Levels 11b and 12 (i.e., EB II 2–3)[44] are numerous and of various types. Those from Level 12 have a light brown slip and are decorated with dark red bands extending from rim to rim around the base, crossing at the bottom another band which covers each handle (fig. 3-26; ills. 3-16 and 3-17). Similar vessels are known from previous excavations at Kültepe[45] and Alişar.[46] All were manufactured in central Anatolian workshops.

A *depas amphikypellon* with light brown slip (fig. 3-27) documents connections between Troy II d and g[47] and Kültepe Level 12.[48] The decoration of this *depas*—with

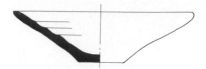

Ill. 3-14. Kültepe, Levels 11b–12, bowl

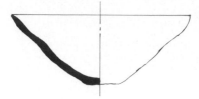

Ill. 3-15. Kültepe, Levels 11b–12, bowl

Fig. 3-26. Kültepe, Level 12, two-handled cup

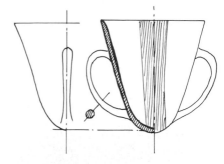

Ill. 3-16. Kültepe, Level 12, two-handled cup

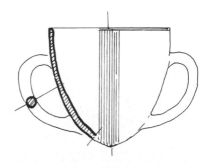

Ill. 3-17. Kültepe, Level 12, two-handled cup

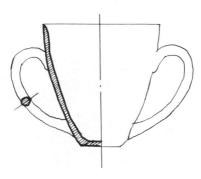

Ill. 3-18. Kültepe, Levels 11b–12, two-handled goblet

Fig. 3-27. Kültepe, Level 12, *depas*

Fig. 3-28. Kültepe, Levels 11b–12, two-handled goblet

Fig. 3-29. Kültepe, Levels 11b–12, two-handled goblet

Fig. 3-30. Kültepe, Levels 11b–12, two-handled goblet

brown slip and vertical red bands—is similar to that of the two-handled cups found in Kültepe Level 12.

The third group of two-handled goblets is wheelmade. They were also found in Levels 11b and 12 (fig. 3-28) and are of the type most widely distributed in Southeast Anatolia and North Syria (figs. 3-29 and 3-30; ill. 3-18).[49]

The fourth group is represented by the two-handled tankards in Level 12 (fig. 3-31).[50] Machteld Mellink correctly identified as being of Anatolian origin the two-handled goblets carried by the leader in the lowest register of the Nasiriyah stele—an Akkadian representation of soldiers bringing home booty.[51] This ware was brought to Kültepe from western Anatolia or Troy, where silver counterparts were found.[52] The two-handled tankard from an EB III level at Karaoğlan must also have been obtained via the main route connecting Troy with Kaneš.[53] The two short-necked, round-bodied varieties of tankards come from the earliest phase of EB III, building phase 13 (figs. 3-32 and 3-33).[54] A similar two-handled tankard found at Acemhöyük in a pot grave is wheelmade (fig. 3-34).[55] These last tankards resemble most closely a group of round-bodied vessels from Karataş-Semayük, Tarsus, Gedikli Höyük, and Troy with round bases and longer necks.[56] In addition, they demonstrate the great similarity between the local polychrome and monochrome wares of Kültepe and those of Acemhöyük—and, as Nimet Özgüç has shown, disc-bodied idols were found outside of Kültepe for the first time at Acemhöyük.[57] It is most likely that the tankards in the central Anatolian sites were imported from the same workshop.

From the same pot grave at Acemhöyük in which the two-handled tankard was found comes a one-handled cup (fig. 3-35).[58] It has a counterpart in EB III Tarsus,[59]

Fig. 3-31. Kültepe, Level 12, two-handled tankard

Fig. 3-32. Kültepe, Level 13, tankard

Fig. 3-33. Kültepe, Level 13, tankard

Fig. 3-34. Acemhöyük pot grave, tankard

Fig. 3-35. Acemhöyük pot grave, one-handled cup

Fig. 3-36. Kültepe, EB II grave, gold pendant

Fig. 3-37. Kültepe, Level 12 pot grave, electrum spirals

and similar ware was found at Alişar, where a unique pitcher occurred on the western edge of Level I. Schmidt states: "Though period I remains were frequent around its find-spot, the pitcher certainly belongs to the Alishar II fine, red ware."[60] He may be incorrect in assigning the vessel to Alişar II, since this ware has never been found in Hittite levels. It clearly was found in Level I together with Early Bronze Age pottery, and it does not have a Hittite shape or other characteristics. On the basis of these facts, the Alişar cup must be dated to EB III.

### Jewelry in Precious Metals
At Kültepe jewelry made of gold, electrum, and precious stones was found in the graves of Levels 11b and 12–13,

all, as we have seen, Early Bronze Age in date. The jewelry has connections with Early Bronze Age pieces found in western Anatolia, North Syria, and Mesopotamia. Some of the jewelry is published here for the first time.

Already published are an earring and a circular gold pendant of Mesopotamian type,[61] found in a grave of Level 13. The earring is 3.6 cm long and 2.3 cm wide. The gold pendant (D. 2.7 cm, H. 4.3 cm; central stone or gold disc missing), with filigree and granular decoration, is a counterpart of a small pendant with gold filigree found at Ur in the Royal Cemetery.[62] Both earring and pendant are made in gold-working techniques typical of Mesopotamia and thus show that easily transportable small objects were imported into Anatolia from the Early Dynastic III and Akkadian periods on.[63]

An earth grave below the floor of Level 13 was destroyed by a deep Roman bothros built above it. At the base of the bothros in the preserved part of the grave were found the bones of an adult with Early Bronze II ceramics and a circular gold pendant. In the center of the pendant is a small gold disc (fig. 3-36). Arranged around the circle are four concentric coils of twisted gold wire joined together by tight winding (and in places by gold solder). There is a suspension loop in the shape of a wide, rolled band (D. 1.8 cm). Maxwell-Hyslop[64] correctly compared our piece to the circular pendants with suspension strips and a mold for such ornaments from Tell Brak,[65] Mari,[66] and Tell Asmar (silver).[67] The Mari treasure may be dated to Early Dynastic III, whereas the hoards from Tell Asmar and Tell Brak belong to the Akkadian period. On the basis of the level in which it was found, I date the Kültepe pendant not later than the Early Dynastic III or the Akkadian period. It could have been imported to Kültepe from northern Mesopotamia.

In a pot grave of Level 12 were a pair of spirally curled hair rings (D. 1.4 and 1.1 cm), made of solid electrum (fig. 3-37a–c) with deeply ribbed decoration on the surface. They differ from the gold lock rings of Alaca Höyük[68] and invite comparison with the curled silver hair rings of Tell Brak which Mallowan dated between 2300 and 2200 B.C.[69] Kültepe Level 12 is contemporary with the Akkadian period.

A strip of thin silver plate, oval, pierced at each end, was found in a stone cist grave of Level 13 (L. 2.55 cm, W. 1.6 cm). This strip (ill. 3-19) is the earliest yet found at Kültepe, but the type is documented in southern

Ill. 3-19. Kültepe, Level 13 cist grave, silver strip

Fig. 3-38. Kültepe, Level 11b, gold bead

Fig. 3-39. Kültepe, Level 13.1 grave, gold beads: (a-b), globular beads; (c-d), flat-winged discs; (e), double conoid bead

Fig. 3-40. Kültepe, Level 12 pot grave, electrum pendant

Mesopotamia beginning in the Akkadian period.[70] During the Old Assyrian Colony period at Kültepe (Levels 11.1 a and b), gold and silver frontlets occur in most graves. These oval and rectangular objects have never appeared in the relatively poor graves of the Old Hittite period or the Imperial Hittite period.[71] They are of Mesopotamian type and have close connections with that area.

A double conoid gold bead with a well-marked ribbed collar at each end (L. 1.6 cm, W. 1.0 cm; fig. 3-38) was found in Level 11b. It is unique at the city mound of Kültepe and is a rare form in Anatolia during the second half of the third millennium B.C.

Five gold beads come from a tomb of Level 13.1. Two of them are distinctive, flat-winged discs with a central tube (fig. 3-39 c–d) made of two folded gold sheets (L. 7 and 6 mm respectively). A convex rib (a tubular string hole) runs across the face of the bead. This type of ornament occurs in a steatite mold found at Mari[72] in the Early Dynastic III level. Beads made by this technique and in this shape are common during the Third Dynasty of Ur as well. They have a wide distribution, with examples found at Karataş, Troy IIg, Poliochni, Alaca Höyük, Eskiyapar, at Ur in Early Dynastic and Akkadian levels, and at Tepe Hissar IIIB and Mohenjo Daro.[73]

Also worth mentioning are a double conoid gold bead with flat end (fig. 3-39e) and two globular gold beads, one of them slightly flattened at one end (fig. 3-39 a–b).

In the same grave with the spirally curled hair-rings, a flat pendant of electrum was found. The upper end is narrow and pierced; the lower is wider and rounder

(L. 5.1 cm, W. 1.4 cm; fig. 3-40). It is a very rare type of pendant with no parallels in the graves of Alaca Höyük or the hoard of Eskiyapar. Reminiscent of pendants found at Troy,[74] it must have been imported to Kültepe.

In a grave of Level 13 were found 71 ring-shaped beads of gold and 56 of carnelian (55 of which are globular), and 1 double conoid and 3 cylindrical beads of lapis lazuli (fig. 3-41). Round, cylindrical, and ring-shaped beads occur at all periods.

Objects manufactured of lapis lazuli were imported from Mesopotamia into Anatolia during all periods. The immediate source of the three lapis lazuli beads mentioned above must also be Mesopotamia, as the trans-shipment point from the geological source in Afghanistan.

Artifacts from Alaca Höyük and some found more recently at Kültepe and Eskiyapar show that during the second half of the third millennium, central Anatolia had strong commercial links with northwestern Anatolia (Troy) as well as with Syria and Mesopotamia. The finds from Kültepe and Eskiyapar show that this lively interchange started during the Early Dynastic III period, increased significantly during the Akkadian period, and continued during the Third Dynasty of Ur.

Several of the jewelry items presented here[75] are imports from Mesopotamia; other pieces were made by artisans in Anatolia well acquainted with Mesopotamian types. Trade—in particular the demand for metals—not only opened Anatolia to the outside world, but contributed considerably to its riches. It seems clear that the choice of Kültepe as the center of the Assyrian Trade Colonies in the second millennium was predetermined

Fig. 3-41. Kültepe, Level 13 grave, gold, carnelian, and lapis beads
(see fig. 3-41b for detail)

Fig. 3-42. Kültepe, surface find, lapis lazuli cylinder seal
(impression)

Fig. 3-43. Kültepe, surface find, lapis
lazuli cylinder seal (impression)

by earlier interaction. The evidence of the archaeological finds suggests that the later traditions about Sargon's and Naramsin's expeditions into Anatolia, and about the latter's war against a coalition of seventeen Anatolian kings, partly legendary as they are, might reflect historical reality.[76]

### Cylinder Seals

A lapis lazuli cylinder seal found at Kültepe in Level 11a[77] can be dated to the last quarter of the third millennium, but was reused, as indicated by later additions, in the post-Akkadian period (Level 11a). Two lapis lazuli cylinder seals in the Archaeological Museum at Kayseri were found by villagers on the city mound at Kültepe (figs. 3-42 and 3-43).[78] They also belong to the post-Akkadian period and bear typical presentation scenes. Another cylinder seal from Kültepe, of the Akkadian period, also found by villagers, has been published by Bittel.[79]

All these foreign, imported objects were found alongside items of local manufacture. The co-occurrence of material with such different characteristics again demonstrates the continuity and strength of the connection between the two areas.

### NOTES

1 T. Özgüç, "Das prähistorische Haus beim Felsrelief von Fraktin," *Anadolu* 1 (1956) 65–70.
2 T. Özgüç, "Early Anatolian Archaeology in the Light of Recent Research," *Anadolu* 7 (1963) 12–14.
3 T. Özgüç (supra n. 2) 12.
4 H. 24 cm, D. 9 cm. Wheelmade, ring-burnished; narrow oval body; slightly pointed base. Uniform dark gray clay with traces of mica. Rim and part of neck missing. N. Özgüç, "Marble Idols and Statuettes from the Excavations at Kültepe," *Belleten* 81 (1957) 78, 80, fig. 27.
5 Fig. 3-6, ill. 3-4—H. 2.5 cm, D. 3.5 cm. Wheelmade rim with double-ring edge. Fine clay, slightly micaceous; gray inner and outer surfaces, carefully polished.
Fig. 3-7, ill. 3-5—H. 4.5 cm, D. 4.8 cm. Wheelmade ring-edged rim. Fine clay, traces of mica; dark gray inner and outer surfaces. Irregular horizontal burnishing strokes on exterior.
6 All wheelmade, of buff to yellow clay containing traces of mica.
7 H. 16.7 cm, W. 7.5 cm. Wheelmade, uniformly dark clay. Ovoid body, double-ring rim, round base. Part of lower body missing.
8 M. J. Mellink, "Archaeology in Asia Minor," *AJA* 69 (1965) 135. For vertically pierced rectangular lugs, see also H. Goldman, *Excavations at Gözlü Kule, Tarsus* 2. *From the Neolithic Through the Bronze Age* (Princeton 1956) 119, fig. 250.23; A. Öktü, *Die Intermediate-Keramik in Kleinasien* (Ph.D. diss., Munich 1973) 105, pl. 58, I/ko2.
9 Goldman (supra n. 8) 131, 154; figs. 268, 614–67.
10 L. Woolley, "Hittite Burial Customs," *AnnLiv* 6 (1914) 92, pl. 33.12.
11 M. E. L. Mallowan, "The Excavations at Tell Chagar Bazar and an Archaeological Survey of the Habur Region," *Iraq* 4 (1937) 105, pl. 19.5.

12 U. B. Alkım, "Archaeological Activities in Turkey, 1962," *Orientalia* 33 (1964) 505, pl. 56.9, and "Excavations at Gedikli," *Belleten* 30 (1966) 45.
13 A. Moortgat, *Tell Chuēra in Nordost-Syrien: Vorläufiger Bericht über die zweite Grabungskampagne 1950* (Wiesbaden 1960) 6, fig. 6; also *Tell Chuēra in Nordost-Syrien: Bericht über die vierte Grabungskampagne 1963* (Cologne and Opladen 1965) 15, 47; H. Kühne, *Die Keramik vom Tell Chuēra und ihre Beziehungen zu Funden aus Syrien-Palästina, der Türkei und dem Iraq* (Berlin 1976) 33–72. See also: on Tell Djidle, M. E. L. Mallowan, "Excavations in the Balih Valley, 1938," *Iraq* 8 (1946) 153, fig. 12.6; on Tell Habuba Kabira, E. Strommenger, "Keramik," in E. Heinrich et al., "Habuba Kabira, 1969," *MDOG* 102 (1970) 50, fig. 12d; on Mari, A. Parrot, *Le temple d'Ishtar* 1 (Mission Archéologique de Mari, 1, BAH 65, Paris 1956) 209, figs. 100–101, 106–7; on Kish, L. C. Watelin, *Excavations at Kish* (Paris 1934) 16, pl. 16.3, and W. Orthmann, *Halawa 1977 bis 1979* (Bonn 1981) 57–59, pl. 59, 28–30 (I. Kampschulte).
14 Narrow oval body, short flaring neck with grooves at base, everted rim, rounded base. See M. J. Mellink, "Archaeology in Asia Minor," *AJA* 73 (1969) 206–7; *AJA* 74 (1970) 161; *AJA* 81 (1977) 293. I am grateful to Raci Temizer, former director of the Museum of Anatolian Civilizations, Ankara, for permission to publish the Eskiyapar flask.
15 M. J. Mellink, "The Prehistory of Syro-Cilicia," *BibOr* 19.5–6 (1962) 225–26, and "Anatolian Chronology," in R. W. Ehrich ed., *Chronologies in Old World Archaeology* (Chicago 1965) 111.
16 Kühne (supra n. 13) 33–72.
17 Kühne (supra n. 13) 38, figs. 66–67, 70.
18 H. 7.8, 7.5 cm, D. 6, 6.2 cm. Ovoid bodies, round bases, short cylindrical necks with thickened rims. Clay fine, hard, uniform buff; buff slipped; well fired. Spiral burnished.
19 Uniform cream clay, cream slipped, thin wall. Decorated with regularly spaced grooves around upper body.
20 Tell Kara Hasan—Amarna: Woolley (supra n. 10) 89, pl. 19. b/2; 91, pl. 33. 13–14. Tell Brak: M. E. L. Mallowan, "Excavations at Braq and Chagar Bazar," *Iraq* 9 (1947) 226, pls. 68. 4, 9; 71. 1–3. Tell Girmahir: Mallowan (supra n. 11), pl. 19.5; fig. 17.6. Tell Djidle: Mallowan (supra n. 13) 46, fig. 19.12. Til Barsip, hypogaeum (oval and round bodies, ring bases): L. Thureau Dangin and M. Dunand, *Til Barsip* (Paris 1936) pl. 23. 1–4. Tel Tainat: R. and L. Braidwood, *Excavations in the Plain of Antioch* 1. *The Earlier Assemblages, Phases A–J* (OIP 61, Chicago 1960) 450, fig. 348 (Level J). Mari: Parrot (supra n. 13) 218–19, fig. 106.690–93. Orthmann (supra n. 13) 54–57, pottery from tombs H-70 and H-119. Lidar: Mellink, "Archaeology in Asia Minor" *AJA* 86 (1982) 563, and *AJA* 87 (1983) 433, pl. 58.8.
21 Mellink 1962 (supra n. 15) 225–26, and 1965 (supra n. 15) 110–11.
22 Kühne (supra n. 13) 38–67.
23 E. Schmidt, *The Alishar Hüyük, Seasons of 1928 and 1929* 1 (OIP 19, Chicago 1932) 147, 176, fig. 168.d 2762 (dx46); W. Orthmann, *Die Keramik der frühen Bronzezeit aus Inneranatolien* (Berlin 1963) 84, 86, 112, pl. 11.2/70; Mellink 1965 (supra n. 15) 112.
24 H. H. von der Osten, *The Alishar Hüyük, Seasons of 1930–32* 1 (OIP 28, Chicago 1937) 43, fig. 45.b 130, pl. 8.
25 Von der Osten (supra n. 24) 43, fig. 46.d 2683, pl. 8.
26 Mellink 1962 (supra n. 15) 225; Orthmann (supra n. 23) 86.
27 H. 7.6 cm, D. 6.4 cm. Thick walls, pointed base, grooved neck and body. Pale red slip.
28 H. 16 cm, D. 15.5 cm. Wheelmade, uniform brick-red clay. Wide round body, short cylindrical neck with strongly everted

rim, flat base. Neck and upper part of body spiral-burnished. Kühne (supra n. 13) 38.

29 H. 8.8, 9.1 cm, D. 8.9, 9.0 cm. Wheelmade, reddish buff clay, well fired. Biconoid bodies, cylindrical necks with overhanging everted rims. Spiral-burnished.

30 Wheelmade, uniform brown clay. Spiral-burnished.

31 Mellink 1965 (supra n. 15) 110–11; Kühne (supra n. 13) 58–67.

32 Kühne (supra n. 13) 67–70.

33 Mellink 1965 (supra n. 15) 110; Kühne (supra n. 13) 68, figs. 89–90, D.1–9, pls. 8, 42.7.

34 H. 7.0, 6.0 cm, D. 8.5, 8.0 cm. Wheelmade. Fine, uniform greenish yellow clay, self-slip. Slightly burnished inside and out. Offset concave disc base. Horizontal corrugations from rim to just above base.

35 H. 5.5 cm, D. 4.3 cm. Handmade. Coarse, uniformly brown clay, wet-smoothed. Irregular ovoid body; short, thick neck with beaked spout; pierced lug handles at base of spout; vertical loop handle from shoulder to rim.

36 Goldman (supra n. 8) 118–89, fig. 247.

37 K. Bittel, *Grundzüge der Vor- und Frühgeschichte Kleinasiens*[2] (Tübingen 1950) 38–39; M. J. Mellink, "The Royal Tombs at Alaca Hüyük and the Aegean World," in S. S. Weinberg ed., *The Aegean and the Near East. Studies Presented to Hetty Goldman* (Locust Valley 1956) 47–48, 52–54; T. Özgüç (supra n. 2) 13; M. J. Mellink, "Archaeology in Asia Minor," *AJA* 62 (1958) 93, and *AJA* 67 (1963) 175; M. J. Mellink, "An Akkadian Illustration of a Campaign in Cilicia?" *Anadolu* 7 (1963) 101–15; J. V. Canby, "Early Bronze 'Trinket' Moulds," *Iraq* 27 (1965) 42–61; K. Bittel, "Bemerkungen über einige in Kleinasien gefundene Siegel," *AfO* 13 (1939–1941) 299–307; G. F. Bass, "Troy and Ur, Links Between the Two Capitals," *Expedition* 8.4 (1966) 26–39; K. R. Maxwell-Hyslop, *Western Asiatic Jewellery* (London 1971) 18, 29, 38–42; M. J. Mellink, "Anatolia: Old and New Perspectives," *PPS* 110 (1966) 120.

38 T. Özgüç (supra n. 2) 12–13.

39 C. W. Blegen, *Troy* 1 (Princeton 1950) 225–26, figs. 372–74; *Troy* 2 (Princeton 1951) figs. 62–63.

40 Goldman (supra n. 8) 134, 136, figs. 265, 412–18. See also M. J. Mellink, "Archaeology in Asia Minor," *AJA* 62 (1958) 94, pl. 16.4.

41 P. Z. Spanos, *Untersuchung über den bei Homer "depas amphikypellon" gennanten Gefässtypus*, IstMitt-BH 6 (1972) 73–75 and passim; Goldman (supra n. 8) figs. 265, nos. 472, 480, 483–84; 266, nos. 494, 507; 356, nos. 484, 491, 495; 357, no. 497.

42 U. B. Alkim, *Anatolien* 1 (Munich 1968) 95–96, fig. 40; *Anatolica* 2 (1968) pl. 1.4.

43 M. van Loon, "New Evidence from Inland Syria for the Chronology of the Middle Bronze Age," *AJA* 73 (1969) 276.

44 T. Özgüç (supra n. 2) 12.

45 H. de Genouillac, *Céramique cappadocienne* 2 (Paris 1926) 43, pl. 30.111 (A. 09450); N. Özgüç (supra n. 4) 79, fig. 29.48; Öktü (supra n. 8) pls. 15–16.

46 Schmidt (supra n. 23) 41, fig. 43, pl. 1.139; and E. Schmidt, *Anatolia Through the Ages. Discoveries at the Alishar Mound 1927–29* (OIC 11, Chicago 1931) 59, fig. 90.

47 Blegen, *Troy* 1 (supra n. 39) figs. 381–82.

48 H. 21.4 cm, rim d. 8.6 cm. Elongated body, rounded base, flaring rim, two vertical handles on body from just below neck to just above base. See de Genouillac (supra n. 45) pl. 49.112; Öktü (supra n. 8) pl. 16, I-C/06.

49 H. 8.0 cm, 8.7, 11.0 cm; rim d. 7.5 cm, 4.8, 8.0 cm. Profile spreading to small, flat base, slightly inverted rim, two vertical handles from base to shoulder. Uniform buff clay, slightly

micaceous. Buff slip, burnished exterior. See Öktü (supra n. 8) pl. 54.

50 H. 19.4 cm, rim d. 12.6 cm. Wheelmade. Ovoid body, flaring rim, two vertical handles from below rim to shoulder. Clay buff to light brown; abundant fine sand in fabric, surface smoothed. See T. Özgüç (supra n. 2) pl. 10.3; Goldman (supra n. 8) 141, fig. 356 N2.471; Blegen, *Troy* 1 (supra n. 39) 345; vol. 1.2, fig. 380. 35.415, 35.558.

51 Mellink, 1963, "An Akkadian Illustration" (supra n. 37) 106.

52 Schmidt (supra n. 46).

53 T. Özgüç (supra n. 2) 4, pl. 10.2.

54 H. 8.0, 8.5 cm, rim d. 7.4, 9.0 cm. Wheelmade. Flaring rim, flat base, handles from below rim to shoulder. Light buff clay, surface smoothed. See Öktü (supra n. 8) pl. 57, l-h/02.

55 H. 14.5 cm, body d. 14.0 cm. Round body, flat base, splayed rim and neck, two vertical handles from rim to body. Uniform reddish buff clay with traces of mica. Burnished buff slip on exterior.

56 Cf. H. Schmidt, *Heinrich Schliemann's Sammlung trojanischer Altertümer* (Berlin 1902) no. 5873; Mellink (supra n. 8) pl. 65.36; Mellink in Goldman (supra n. 8) fig. 356, no. 471.

57 N. Özgüç, "Acemhöyük Kazısı 1979 Çalış maları," *Belleten* 175 (1980) 621.

58 H. 9.5 cm, rim d. 10.1 cm. Handmade, spherical body, high splaying rim and neck, flat base, single vertical handle. Reddish brown clay. Exterior slipped reddish brown and burnished.

59 Goldman (supra n. 8) vol. 1, 141, figs. 266, no. 467; 356, no. 470. M. J. Mellink, "Excavations at Karataş-Semayük in Lycia, 1963," *AJA* 68 (1964) pls. 80.14, 81.18 (from Karataş-Semayük).

60 Schmidt (supra n. 23) 114, fig. b 2536.

61 T. Özgüç (supra n. 2) 13, pl. 7. 1–2; Maxwell-Hyslop (supra n. 37) 47–48.

62 C. L. Woolley, *Ur Excavations* 2. *The Royal Cemetery* (London 1934) 167, pl. 138, U. 11806 A–B.

63 H.-J. Nissen, *Beiträge zur ur- und frühgeschichtlichen Archäologie des Mittelmeer-Kulturraumes* 3 (1966) 180.

64 Maxwell-Hyslop (supra n. 37) 15, 29, pl. 38.

65 Mallowan (supra n. 20) 177, pl. 25. For stone molds for circular pendants, see also Canby (supra n. 37) 45, pl. 10b; and K. Emre, *Anatolian Lead Figurines and Their Stone Moulds* (Ankara 1971) 112, 125, pl. 1.8, fig. 11.

66 A. Parrot, *Mission archéologique de Mari* 4. *Le "trésor d'Ur"* (Paris 1968) 28, pl. 15.1–2.

67 H. Frankfort, *Iraq Excavations of the Oriental Institute, 1932/33, Third Preliminary Report of the Iraq Expedition* (OIC 17, Chicago 1934) 35–36, fig. 29: "Jewelry hoard from the Akkadian palace."

68 R. O. Arık, *Les fouilles d'Alaca Höyük 1935* (Ankara 1937) 176–77, nos. A1.254–55; 230–31, nos. A1.998–99; H. Z. Koşay, *Les fouilles d'Alaca Höyük, 1937–1939* (Ankara 1951) pl. 186, A1.D. 47K.

69 Mallowan (supra n. 20) 176, pl. 33.4–9.

70 Woolley (supra n. 62) pl. 219, type 1–3; see also Maxwell-Hyslop (supra n. 37) 22, 67, fig. 13, pl. 23.46a–47.

71 M. J. Mellink, *A Hittite Cemetery at Gordion* (Philadelphia 1956) esp. 49–50.

72 A. Parrot, *Les temples d'Ishtarat et de Ninni-Zaza* 3 (Paris 1967) 198, figs. 245–46; Maxwell-Hyslop (supra n. 37) 10 n. 1.

73 M. J. Mellink, "Excavations at Karataş-Semayük in Lycia, 1968," *AJA* 73 (1969) 323 and n. 7; Maxwell-Hyslop (supra n. 37) 8, 20–21, 58, 79, pl. 15b, 55; L. Bernabò Brea, *Poliochni* 2.1–2 (Rome 1976) pls. 247, 252.14–16.

74 Schmidt (supra n. 56) 236, fig. e.

75 Including T. Özgüç (supra n. 2) pl. 7.1–2, and here, figs. 3-36, 3-41, and ill. 3-19.

76 H. G. Güterbock, "Sargon of Akkad Mentioned by Hattušili I of Hatti," *JCS* 18 (1964) 1–16; C. J. Gadd, "The Dynasty of Agade and the Gutian Invasion," *CAH*³ 1.2 (1971) 427–30; Mellink 1963, "An Akkadian Illustration" (supra n. 51) 113.

77 K. Balkan, *A Letter of King Anum-Hirbi of Mama to King Warshama of Kanish* (Ankara 1957) 2 n. 5, fig. 12.

78 Fig. 3-42—L. 1.9 cm, D. 1.1 cm. Worshiper led by god, with left hand raised toward seated deity; star above offering stand. Fig. 3-43—L. 1.9 cm, D. 1.2 cm. God seated on low-backed throne; goddess holding plant and leading female worshiper by hand; suppliant holding an object in the other hand, crescent above offering stand.

79 K. Bittel 1939–1941 (supra n. 37) 302, fig. 5.

# Seals of the Old Assyrian Colony Period and Some Observations on the Seal Impressions

## 4

NIMET ÖZGÜÇ

I would like to dedicate the following five notes on second-millennium Anatolian glyptic to Machteld Mellink in hopes that she will find them of interest.

## I

At Acemhöyük in the so-called Bullae Depot (Room 6) of the Sarıkaya palace, twenty-nine bullae were unearthed which bore fifty-six mostly fragmentary impressions of the same cylinder seal. All are of the irregular pyramidal ("muska") shape and, because of the fire which destroyed the building, they are of various colors: black, gray, mottled gray and red, brick red, light brown, white, and yellow. The cylinder was impressed on the broader facets of the bullae, and the narrow sides were inscribed with the names of the seal owner, his father, and the person who was to receive the goods to which the bullae were attached: *Kunuk I-bi-eš me-ra I-din-Aššur, a-na Šu-ki-ma*—"Seal of I-bi-eš, son of I-din-Aššur to Šu-ki-ma" (Ac. i 1029; Ac. i 1031; Ac. i 1038; Ac. i 1086; fig. 4-1).

A study of the impressions shows that the seal contained a contest frieze depicting the struggle between animals and heroes, a theme rarely used in the Old Babylonian style of the early second millennium B.C., although frequently seen in the Akkadian style of third-millennium Mesopotamia. There are three groups of figures: a bull-man grasping a lion by the chest and right front paw; a naked hero dangling a bull by its tail and hind leg while stepping on its neck; and a winged lion-dragon with open jaws standing on its hind legs, about to bite an antelope, which is seated on a small hill with its head turned back.

At the Karum at the site of Kültepe, a large fragment of an envelope probably belonging to a letter was discov-ered in a house of Level I b within Trenches bb/18–19 (fig. 4-2).[1] The inscribed section above the seal impression is broken off except for a small piece. The only well-preserved impression on the envelope is from the seal used for the Acemhöyük impressions just described. On the Kültepe sealing the scene is complete, thus providing us with the evidence needed to restore the scene of the Acemhöyük impressions, whereas the bullae from Acemhöyük give us the name of the seal owner.

The relatively rare Old Babylonian seal friezes depicting hero, bull-man, lion, lion-dragon, and bulls form an interesting group.[2] Specimens with winged lion-dragons attacking antelopes[3] or trying to swallow a hero[4] are numerous. Bullae of Mesopotamian origin are of "muska" shape and are beige, as are some of the unburnt Acemhöyük specimens. The majority of friezes showing the struggle between heroes and animals on the seal impressions of the Old Assyrian Colony Period are in the Old Babylonian style. Some specimens from Kültepe have already been published.[5] A lapis lazuli seal discovered in a building of Level III within the area 1 DB–HB/27–30 at Acemhöyük[6] can also be placed in this group (Ac. a 1; H. 2.4 cm, W. 1.2 cm). Its style, especially the rendering of the beards of the bull-men, and the elixir vase indicate that the seal is contemporary with the level in which it was found, contrary to the opinion of H. Kühne, who dated this seal to the third millennium B.C.[7]

Since seals in the Old Babylonian style were used in Assyria and North Syria in the eighteenth century B.C.—as we know from the seals of Šamši-adad and the daughter of Iahdum-lim[8]—it seems likely that our bullae as well as the envelope from Kültepe originated in those lands.

Figs. 4-1a–4-1e. Acemhöyük, Sarıkaya palace, bullae of I-bi-eš. Fig. 4-1a. Ac. i 1029

Fig. 4-1b. Ac. i 1031

Fig. 4-1e. Ac. i 1029

Fig. 4-1c. Ac. i 1086

Fig. 4-1d. Ac. i 1038

Fig. 4-2. Envelope from Kültepe

II

At Acemhöyük nineteen bullae (one of them of "muska" shape) bearing the impressions of the same seal have been discovered in rooms 3, 6, 7, and 10 of the Sarıkaya palace. They too turned different colors when the palace burned: mottled brick red, shades of brick red, gray, beige, and black and beige. The majority of impressions are clear. The design is a braid which encircles a rope pattern looped seven times with dots in the middle (ill. 4-1; fig. 4-3).[9] A bulla discovered in the palace at Kültepe (Kt.u/t 1) displays an almost identical impres-

sion, except that the loops are set farther apart (fig. 4-4). At Acemhöyük a very interesting object was found in Room 7 (Ac. i 24). It is an irregular disc with a string hole (1.9 × 2.0 × 1.2 cm) containing a negative impression of the type we are discussing. It may be that the seal owner lent this item to members of his family or to his partner while keeping the original for himself.

III

In discussing the seals of the Old Assyrian period, M. Trolle Larsen pointed out that despite the existence

Ill. 4-1. Drawing of bulla in fig. 4-3

Fig. 4-3. Acemhöyük, Sarıkaya palace, bulla with impression

Fig. 4-4. Kültepe, bulla with impression

of numerous seal impressions, none of the seals which produced them have been recovered.[10] I believe I have been able to identify two seals which were used to make impressions found on envelopes. One is a slightly damaged hematite seal of Old Babylonian style now in the collection of the Pierpont Morgan Library in New York (fig. 4-5).[11] It shows two human-headed bulls struggling with two bull-men. A lion-headed scepter separates the groups. A vase and an elixir vase are placed between the individual combatants. A framed cuneiform inscription which mentions the god Šamaš and the goddess Aia is to be seen above a rampant lion facing to the left. One of the impressions on an envelope of a loan deed published by B. Hrozný[12] may well have been made from this seal. The juncture of the heads and necks of the human-headed bulls is not clear in the drawing of the impression; however, the lion-headed scepter, which is broken in the original seal, can be reconstructed with the help of the impression. An examination of the pieces side by side could determine whether they are in fact identical.

The second example is an Anatolian seal reflecting Syrian influence, now in the collection of Mrs. William H. Moore.[13] It is made of quartzite and is complete, measuring 2.2 cm by 1.5 cm (fig. 4-6). The seal shows an adoration scene of a type seldom encountered in the Anatolian group of cylinders. Here the adorant is led by a bearded interceding god to another god, who wears a long tunic and a skullcap. The latter carries an axe on his left shoulder and has a drinking cup in his right hand. Between the heads of the gods is a bull-altar with a conical top. The garments of the adorant and the gods are clearly distinguished. Many figures of varying sizes complement the main composition, a treatment which,

Fig. 4-5. New York, Pierpont Morgan Library, seal no. 347 (courtesy Pierpont Morgan Library)

again, is rare among the seals of the Anatolian group. The first group, rendered horizontally, depicts a struggle between a lion and a hero and between a bull and a hero. The heroes wear skullcaps, and the hems of their tunics are curved and fringed like the tunic of the adorant. Other figures include a seated monkey, animal heads with and without horns, and heads of humans and gods. A stool with bulls' hoofs stands in front of the god. The large vessel resting on it is of a different shape from the ones on local impressions. Stylistically, this seal, which displays both Anatolian and Syrian elements, may be compared to a seal impression in which the god carrying an axe, a struggle between a lion and an antelope, and animal heads are depicted in a lion-hunting scene.[14]

Almost all the scenes of the Moore seal occur in seven impressions on an uninscribed tablet from Kültepe, drawn by Marie Matoušova, and on a strange object in Brussels.[15] A close study of the original seal permits the following corrections to the drawing. First, the vaselike object next to the bird behind the adorant is a hare's

Fig. 4-6. Moore Collection, on loan to the Metropolitan Museum of Art, New York, seal no. L55.49.50 (courtesy Metropolitan Museum)

Ill. 4-2. Drawing of stamp seal in fig. 4-9

head, whereas the object of unclear shape beside it is a bull's head. Second, it is very clear on the seal that one of the opponents of the heroes is a lion and the other is an antelope. Finally, Matoušova thought that there were three human and two gods' heads on the impression; however, the horned crowns on the original show that three heads are those of gods.

IV

An interesting stamp seal of good workmanship was purchased by the Museum of Anatolian Civilizations in 1976 (ill. 4-2; figs. 4-7 to 4-9; inv. no. 70-3-76; black stone; H. 2.8 cm, W. 2.1 cm). The seal has a disc base with a tall stem decorated by seven grooves and a rounded, conical pierced top. The design carefully carved on the base of the seal shows a goddess seated on a recumbent mountain sheep. She faces right and holds her clenched left hand in front of her chest. In her raised right hand she holds a cup. She is dressed in a long tunic with short sleeves and a round neckline, a wide-brimmed cap, and shoes with upward curved tips. Her cheeks are full, her nose is large, her lips are fleshy, and her chin is pronounced. Above her raised hand are a crescent and disc

Fig. 4-7. Ankara Museum of Anatolian Civilizations, stamp seal no. 70-3-76

Fig. 4-8. Impression of seal in fig. 4-7.

Fig. 4-9. Photograph of base of seal in fig. 4-7.

flanked by two stars. In front of her another figure in a long tunic and tall pointed cap offers a beak-spouted pitcher to the goddess while raising his right hand in a gesture of benediction. Behind him is an eagle and before him an S-spiral. The scene is arranged above a horizontal line, below which are a lion crouching with tail raised and an undistinguishable sign.

Elsewhere I have discussed the importance of the goddess with a mountain sheep on the local seals of the Old Assyrian Colony period and pointed out that this figure represents a type which continued to be used during the Hittite Empire period.[16] Adoration scenes in honor of this goddess are frequently encountered on the bullae from Acemhöyük. On these the goddess is shown wearing a scaled garment, whereas the vase bearers are dressed in a long tunic which leaves one shoulder free. Their heads are covered with a slightly pointed cap. In contrast to the seal under discussion, the caps of the goddesses from Acemhöyük are narrow-brimmed and their bodies more softly modeled. The crown of the goddess on our seal recalls those of later goddesses, such as the figurine from Alaca Höyük,[17] the sculpture at Eflatunpinar,[18] and the gold pendant in the Norbert Schimmel Collection.[19] Furthermore, the beak-spouted pitchers on the Acemhöyük bullae reflect a shape current during the eighteenth century B.C.,[20] whereas the one on our seal has a less pronounced belly, shorter beak, and wider bottom, thus resembling those found in Level III at Boğazköy.[21] Although the seal is shaped like the Kültepe Karum I b seals, the figures and other details are closer stylistically to the Empire than to the Colony age. The stylistic features of the scene on the seal in the Museum of Anatolian Civilizations, therefore, suggest that it should be dated to the period of the figurine from Alaca Höyük[22] and the "madonna" pendant in the Schimmel collection[23]—that is, to the fifteenth or fourteenth century B.C. in my opinion.

V

At Acemhöyük a cylinder seal made of green serpentine was brought to light in Level III of Trench B of the lower city in 1972 (ill. 4-3; figs. 4-10 and 4-11; Ac. k 84; 1.3 × 1.8 cm). Although it is slightly cracked at the lower edge, the figures, which are rendered in an archaic style, are complete. A god is seated on a four-legged chair. The details of his garment are not clear; an elixir vase and another vase are visible behind him. He is drinking from a double-handled vase by means of a tall straw. A figure in a short kilt is tipping toward the god a large beak-spouted vessel which rests on the floor. Three gazellelike animals walk below this group. Behind the god is a tall object, probably a fruit stand, which is flanked by two seated lionlike creatures.

Ill. 4-3. Drawing of seal in fig. 4-11

Fig. 4-10. Acemhöyük, Level III, cylinder seal ac. k 84

Fig. 4-11 Impression of seal in fig. 4-10

Although this seal, with its drinking scene, seems at first sight to belong in the third millennium, it is obvious from the vessels that it belongs to the eighteenth century B.C.—that is, to the level contemporary with the Acemhöyük palaces. The vase with the drinking straw and the large beak-spouted vessel carried by the adorant are of the types found at the Hatipler and Sarıkaya palaces and contemporary private houses at Acemhöyük. The small vase and the elixir vase also support this date.

NOTES

I thank Dr. Ilknur Özgen for translating this article, Rüştü Çetinkaya and Metin Akyurt for the drawings, and Veysel Dombaz for reading the inscriptions on the bullae. I am also indebted to Osman Aksoy, director of the Museum of Anatolian Civilizations, Ankara, for permission to publish the stamp seal, and to Cem Karasu for his constant help during my research in the museum.

1 N. Özgüç, *Kaniş Karumu Ib Katı Mühürleri ve Mühür Baskıları. Seals and Seal Impressions of Level Ib from Karum Kanish* (Ankara 1968) 30, 69, pls. 16.2, 26.2.
2 E. Porada, *Corpus of Ancient Near Eastern Seals in North American Collections. The Collection of the Pierpont Morgan Library* (New York 1948) 43–46, pls. 51–53; B. Buchanan,

*Catalogue of Ancient Near Eastern Seals in the Ashmolean Museum* (Oxford 1966), pl. 36, nos. 531–37, and *Early Near Eastern Seals in the Yale Babylonian Collection* (New Haven and London 1981) pls. 967–82; A. Moortgat, *Vorderasiatische Rollsiegel* (Berlin 1940) pls. 56, 57.

3 Porada (supra n. 2), figs. 359, 361.

4 Porada (supra n. 2), figs. 360, 362.

5 T. and N. Özgüç, *Kültepe Kazısı Raporu, 1949* (Ankara 1953) 671–72, pl. 60.

6 N. Özgüç, "Acemhöyük Kazıları," *Anadolu* 10 (1966) 11, 38, pl. 14.1.

7 H. Kühne, *Die Keramik vom Tell Chuēra und ihre Beziehungen zu Funden aus Syria-Palästina, der Türkey und dem Iraq* (Berlin 1976) 118, n. 1037.

8 N. Özgüç, "Seal Impressions from the Palaces at Acemhöyük," in E. Porada ed., *Ancient Art in Seals* (Princeton 1980) 81, figs. 3.1 a–c, 3.3 a, b.

9 Özgüç (supra n. 8) fig. 3.54.

10 M. Trolle Larsen, "Seal Use in the Old Assyrian Period," in *Seals and Sealing in the Ancient Near East* (BibMes 6, Malibu 1977) 89.

11 Porada (supra n. 2) pl. 51.347.

12 B. Hrozný, *Inscriptions cunéiformes du Kultépé 1* (Monografie Archivu Orientaniho 14, Prague 1952) pl. 73, Kültepe 50a, seal B.

13 G. A. Eisen, *Ancient Oriental Cylinders and Other Seals with a Description of the Collection of Mrs. William H. Moore* (OIP 47, Chicago 1940) pl. 13.128; E. W. Forte, *Ancient Near Eastern Seals: A Selection of Stamp and Cylinder Seals from the Collection of Mrs. William H. Moore* (Metropolitan Museum of Art, New York, n.d.).

14 N. Özgüç, *Kültepe Mühür Baskılarında Anadolu Grubu. The Anatolian Group of Cylinder Seal Impressions from Kültepe* (Ankara 1965) pl. 23.68.

15 L. Matouš and M. Matoušova, *Inscriptions cunéiformes du Kultépé 2* (Prague 1962) 53, pl. 129 Ka 662; and L. Speleers, *Catalogue des intailles et empreintes orientales des Musées Royaux d'Art et d'Histoire. Supplément* (Brussels 1943) 169–70, no. 660; these are probably modern impressions of the Moore seal.

16 N. Özgüç (supra n. 14) 27, 69; and (supra n. 8) 73.

17 K. Bittel, *Die Hethiter* (Munich 1976) fig. 172.

18 Bittel (supra n. 17) fig. 257.

19 Bittel (supra n. 17) fig. 173.

20 N. Özgüç (supra n. 6) pl. 8.1.

21 F. Fischer, *Die hethitische Keramik von Boğazköy* (Berlin 1963) pls. 23.260–62, 29.260–62.

22 Bittel (supra n. 17) fig. 172.

23 Bittel (supra n. 17) fig. 173.

# The Child in Hittite Iconography

JEANNY VORYS CANBY

The following material, if not all the conclusions, will have few surprises for Machteld Mellink, since most of it has been discussed with her. Like all of her students, I am indebted to the warm generosity with which she has lent her time, vast knowledge, and encouragement and especially to those penetrating, so gently phrased questions which bring scattered thoughts into focus and suddenly open up new and exciting avenues of approach.

In the Walters Art Gallery, Baltimore, there is a rock crystal figurine which, because of its strange appearance, lay for many years off view (figs. 5-1 and 5-2).[1] It had been tentatively classified as "Hittite" by Dorothy Kent

Fig. 5-1. Rock crystal infant, Hittite, ca. 1400–1200 B.C., H. 6.9 cm. (Courtesy Walters Art Gallery)

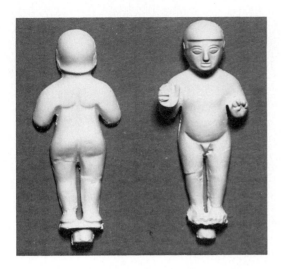

Fig. 5-2. Casts of rock crystal infant. (Courtesy Walters Art Gallery)

Hill, former curator of the collection, on the basis of a generic resemblance to a rock crystal figure excavated in 1935 at Tarsus (fig. 5-3).[2] But when it was shown to visiting Anatolian experts, they shook their heads in puzzlement, and the piece was returned to the vault. The Hittite "madonna" pendant now in the Schimmel collection (fig. 5-4)[3] finally provided an explanation for the peculiar figure of the Walters piece. It is a Hittite craftsman's version of an infant. The next question was, whom does it represent? That turned out to be a difficult question,

not because there are so few parallels, but rather because there are so many important children in Hittite art.

Mr. Walters acquired the figure in 1926 from Dikran Kelekian, the knowledgeable dealer who guided him in the formation of his ancient Near Eastern collection. The piece is 7 cm high and made of highly polished rock crystal. The little figure has a very large head and almost no neck. It stands with right arm bent tautly up to shoulder level, large hand turned forward, fist clenched. The thumb is held stiff, as it usually is in Hittite representations of adults making this gesture. The left hand, which is much smaller, is shown balled up like a baby's fist, with the thumb tucked under the fingers.[4]

The head of the figure is very well preserved. The sharp facial features are delineated by grooves rather than modeling. The wide eyes are treated in typically Hittite manner, with the bony structure of the top edge of the eye socket represented, but not the brows. The figure has a long narrow nose, wide flat cheeks, short thin lips, and a square jaw. The ears lie flat against the head. The lobes are indicated, but the interior is merely indented. A smooth head covering, which falls straight across the forehead, bends out just above the shoulders. A curl in front of the right ear suggests that this covering represents hair rather than a cap or helmet. In contrast to the rather bland unmodeled head, the undulating surfaces of the body have been sensitively treated. The chest rises softly at the nipples, sinks at the navel, and swells out again to the belly. Soft grooves delineate the shoulder blades, spinal furrow, buttocks, and groin. Sharp grooves

Fig. 5-3a. Cast of rock crystal figure from Tarsus, Hittite, ca. 1400–1200 B.C., H. 6 cm. (Courtesy Bryn Mawr College)

Fig. 5-3b. Cast of rock crystal figure from Tarsus (detail). (Courtesy Bryn Mawr College)

Fig. 5-3c. Rock crystal figure from Tarsus (detail). (Courtesy Adana Museum)

*The Child in Hittite Iconography* 55

Fig. 5-4. Gold pendant, Hittite, ca. 1600 B.C. (?),
H. 4.3 cm. (Courtesy Norbert Schimmel Collection)

are used only for the details of fingers, toes, and pubic area, the last feature represented by a narrow, unarticulated triangle set off by grooves. In view of the observant representation of the rest of the body, it is striking that the sex of the figure is not made more explicit.

The carver of the figure has gone to some pains to represent a baby. The muscleless feet are spread out, and baby fat masks the bony structure of the back and legs. The child does not have the firm, hyperextended stance typical of grown Hittites.[5] It stands as babies do, hesitantly, knees slightly bent, buttocks protruding. If we can judge by scientific standards (ill. 5-1), the relative proportions of the parts of the body (i.e., large head, narrow chest, and short legs) and the ability to stand alone suggest that the child is approximately one year old.

The Walters figurine shares enough technical and stylistic features with the Hittite figurine made of rock crystal from Tarsus (fig. 5-3) to support the hypothesis that the piece is of Hittite manufacture. Both have character-istic Hittite faces, with broad, low foreheads, thin lips, and strong chins. The eye and mouth are treated in almost identical fashion. The Tarsus figure's broad nose, separated from fat cheeks by a crease, is, however, like those of the sphinx and the warrior god on the gate sculptures at Hattuša,[6] whereas the narrow nose of the Walters figure is more like that of Hittite bronzes.[7] The uneven carving, in which simple grooves and indentations appear in combination with real modeling, is similar on both pieces. In both cases the artist treated the part of the body in which he was interested with more care than he gave to the other parts. In the case of the Tarsus piece, where the subject is an adult Hittite clothed in a long robe, it is the face which is carefully modeled.

There are few clues to the identity of the child in the Walters Gallery. It bears no attributes. Even its sex is uncertain. It is clear, however, that this is no ordinary infant. The baby stands unsupported and makes the ges-

Fig. 5-5. Pharaoh Pepi II on his mother's lap, ca.
2200 B.C., H. 39 cm. (Courtesy Brooklyn Museum)

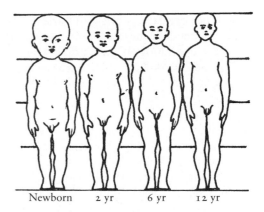

Ill. 5-1. Growth chart. (Adapted by Catalina Davis
from L. E. Holt, Jr., and R. McIntosh, *Holt's Diseases of Infancy and Childhood. A Textbook for
the Use of Students and Practitioners*[11] [New York
1940] 26, fig. 9)

ture of homage, blessing, or greeting made by kings and
gods in Hittite art.[8] In this precocious dignity the Walters child resembles the other Hittite infant represented
in the pendant mentioned above, which is in the collection of Norbert Schimmel (fig. 5-4). This child is shown
perched almost upright on the edge of a woman's lap.
Like the Walters child, it makes a formal adult gesture,
in this case raising its clasped hands.[9] This unusual pendant makes a clear statement as to the relationship of
woman and child. The woman, seated on a throne, does
not hold the child or even touch it. Her left hand merely
hovers near, as if ready to catch her charge should it lose
its precarious balance. This woman is not a nourishing,
life-giving, mothering figure like the earlier Anatolian
bronze figure from Horoztepe who holds a sprawling in-

Fig. 5-6. Alaca Höyük, orthostat block, Hittite,
ca. 1500–1400 B.C. (?). (Courtesy Museum of
Anatolian Civilizations, Ankara)

fant at her breast,[10] but more a nursemaid for a very special, independent infant. The focus here, it seems to me, is on the child, not on the woman who attends it.

The unusual relationship between woman and child seen on the Schimmel pendant is paralleled in a 6th Dynasty Egyptian group in the Brooklyn Museum (fig. 5-5).[11] It represents the six-year-old pharaoh, Pepi II, on his mother's lap. The miniature king, dressed in royal regalia, sits with dignity at a right angle to his mother, almost as if the queen were his throne. He expresses his relationship to her only by laying his hand on hers. The queen supports Pepi lightly with her left arm across his shoulders, her right hand over his legs. The dignified

Fig. 5-7. Alaca Höyük, orthostat block, Hittite, ca. 1500–1400 B.C. (?). (Courtesy Museum of Anatolian Civilizations, Ankara)

posture of the child-king and the restrained gesture of his mother contrast markedly with the more familiar Egyptian mother-child group which shows the goddess Isis offering her breast to the child Harpocrates.[12] Harpocrates, although old enough to sit up straight, is usually shown somewhat limp and helpless, supported in his mother's arms. The status of the children in these two Egyptian compositions is as different as the status of the infant of the Schimmel pendant is from that of the Horoztepe baby.

It may be useful in the present context to look more closely into these contrasting Egyptian mother-child types because in Egypt the reason for the distinction is known. Harpocrates, Horus-the-child, is on the one hand one of the miraculous child-gods; he has extraordinary power over many dangerous animals and is often shown standing on a crocodile brandishing a scorpion, lion, serpent, and antelope. When, however, he is shown as a child, still sucking his thumb, helpless at his mother

Isis' breast, he is used to suggest the goddess's role as the embodiment of motherly love.[13] The composition of the Brooklyn statuette expresses quite a different concept. It reflects an unusual moment in Egyptian history at which a six-year-old boy actually did become king.[14] Pepi II was the son of his father's old age, the child of his third queen. Since the chief queen had been put aside under suspicious circumstances, Pepi II's mother had some need to promulgate her claim as queen mother, as she does so well in this statuette. The iconography of the Brooklyn statuette is a piece of political propaganda. Later, in the 18th Dynasty, a child is again used to imply the status of its custodian in a famous group of statuettes—those showing Hatshepsut's vizier Sen-en-mut holding the young royal princess.[15] In this instance the political message was not as urgent as it was at the time of Pepi II's ascension. All that Sen-en-mut needed to suggest was his intimacy with the royal family. The little princess is not given the extraordinary prominence of the boy-king in these compositions. The "status flow" is reversed in scenes which show the king, as a grown man, being nursed by a goddess in the form of a divine cow.[16]

There is little to be gained by further surveying the numerous meanings surrounding representations of miraculous children or adult-child groups.[17] The broad range of meanings cautions that the specific identification of our child must come from the imperial Hittite world.[18] Unfortunately, the Schimmel pendant gives few clues as to the identity of the figures it represents. The child bears no attributes, and the woman's headdress is found worn by both goddesses and queens over a long period of time.[19] Still, the pendant does prove that the Hittites knew of an extraordinary infant like the one represented in the Walters rock crystal piece—one who is clearly not a normal, helpless babe.

### ROYAL CHILDREN

Hittite kings, like other Near Eastern monarchs, sometimes called themselves children of deities.[20] Kings and queens and even a prince speak of being "reared" by gods.[21] An extraordinary statement of a childlike relationship to a deity is made in the great bilingual text of Hattušili I.[22] While the king was campaigning in Arzawa, the enemy from Hanigalbat in the east came into the country. The lands fell away from him, and only the capital, Hattuša, was left. At this juncture, the king tells us, the sun goddess placed him on her lap, took his hand, and helped him in battle. Somehow by being taken on the lap of a deity the king magically received the power to win battles.

Unfortunately, the two versions of the bilingual text do not agree on the gender of the solar deity. The Hittite text, which is damaged, refers to the sun deity of Arinna, who is known to be feminine. The Akkadian text says that the sun deity (no epithet) put the king "on his lap," implying that the deity is masculine. The "his" in the Akkadian version has generally been explained as a grammatical error made by the Hittite scribe copying the Akkadian text. An alternative explanation has been offered by C. Melchert. The text which we have is a copy of an original written in the Old Hittite period, a period in which the sun goddess of Arinna is not so far attested. It may be, then, that in the original text it was, indeed, a male sun god who took the king on his lap. The scribe who copied the Hittite text in the thirteenth century B.C. changed the gender of the sun deity, for by that time the sun goddess of Arinna was the main solar deity. The Akkadian scribe, unconcerned with current Hittite theology, merely copied the original text. Recently O. R. Gurney has expressed the opinion that this Hattušili I text may actually contain the earliest reference to the sun goddess.[23]

Since the gender of the deity in this passage is in question, it is difficult to say whether sitting on the deity's lap symbolized relegitimization of the king, as it would were the deity male—that is, the king's spiritual father. The custom of placing a child on the father's lap so that the man might acknowledge the child as his son is well attested in the Hittite world.[24] If a goddess took the king on her lap, one would suppose that the act symbolized her capacity to provide security, nourishment, and encouragement as his spiritual mother. The protective power of a goddess's lap was known in Mesopotamia, where, for instance, the goddess Nanše is said to "shelter the fugitive in her lap."[25] The question in the present context is whether such a metaphor would have been used in art as well as literature. If it were, it seems more likely that the king would have been represented in full royal regalia, rather than as a naked babe.

There is some evidence for the heir apparent's having been shown as a very young child in Hittite art. Two figures on the reliefs at Alaca Höyük are smaller than the surrounding figures, barefoot, and completely nude (figs. 5-6 and 5-7). They have plump buttocks and thick waists. Since the figures have no voluptuous features, they cannot represent the goddess Ištar-Šaušga, the only unclothed figure known in Hittite art. They must be children, shown at an age when, according to Hittite custom, children could properly appear without clothes. One of these figures (fig. 5-6) occupies a prominent position in the layout of the Alaca Höyük reliefs. It appears immediately around the corner from the scene of the king and queen worshiping the divine bull which climaxes the ceremonial procession of the left front façade; that is, the figure occurs on the short wall decorating the left side of the gate entry.[26] This child stands erect, its small figure elevated in some manner to the level of the adult figure it faces to the right. The child's head and lower left arm are missing. The angle at which this arm is bent suggests that it was held up before the face. Since the child's right arm hangs down and masks the pubic area, its gender cannot be determined.

The figure facing the child, dressed in the long robe of the attendants or dignitaries in the ceremonial procession,[27] presents a staff with a loop or ring attached in the center. Behind the child two slender male figures, dressed in short, tight-fitting skirts, face each other supporting an upright pole. Since the figures on the reliefs of Alaca Höyük are usually integrated into scenes, it seems probable that the pole bearers have some relationship to the child. Machteld Mellink has suggested that the pole was crowned with the winged sun disc which appears under the feet of the crouching lion on a block found at the site.[28] If her reconstruction is correct, the symbol raised beside the child might have been used to

Fig. 5-8. The "Royal Buttress" at Carchemish. (Courtesy British Museum)

Fig. 5-9. Ivory girl, Hittite, ca. 1400–1200 B.C., H. 12 cm. (Courtesy British Museum)

suggest that the child is a royal figure, presumably the heir apparent. The winged disc is used in Hittite art to refer to the king, one of whose titles was "My Sun." It is also used with the sun god,[29] but, as far as we know, the sun god is represented as a fully clothed adult in Hittite art.[30] Further support for reading the sun disc as a royal symbol here is the fact that the standard bearers are human. Elsewhere in the ancient Near East, standards with winged discs are held by fantastic beings and presumably allude to deities.[31]

Regardless of whether the winged disc belonged atop the pole, other elements indicate that this must be a special, royal, child. First is the proximity of the royal parents, who appear immediately around the corner. Second is the character of the figures which in all probability were placed immediately to the right of the child and its attendants (fig. 5-7). They occur on a block which was found fallen into the gate.[32] It has the proper length to fill the gap between the scene just described and the great sphinx. On this block six children march toward the sphinx. They are thus going in the same direction as the specially honored child. These figures are barefoot, and their heads are shaven except for a topknot gathered into a pigtail at the crown—a hair style which, at least in contemporary Egypt, indicates a child. All figures except the third from the left are shown clad in short skirts. The curve of the buttocks and upper left leg and the indication of male genitalia on this third figure make it clear that this child is nude. He is presumably younger than the others. The children are shown divided into two groups of three, in each of which the figures diminish in size. The heads are at the same level, but the legs are shown as progressively shorter. It is true that the sculptors at Alaca Höyük do not seem to have been much concerned about maintaining a consistent ground level. Here, however, the repeated pattern of progressively shorter legs seems deliberate. I would think that the different sizes of the figures were intended to show their different ages. The fact that the smallest child is shown nude tends to confirm this hypothesis.

The persons represented at Alaca Höyük on the projection in front of the gate are, then, the royal sons, divided into two groups, and the very young heir apparent, clearly distinguished from them by special honors. Fortunately, a ready explanation for this extraordinary scene exists in the archives of the Hittite capital. The famous text of Hattušili I comes immediately to mind.[33] In this poignant document the ailing king, lamenting the treachery of his own children, appoints his grandson to the throne. Muršili must have been very young at the time, for Hattušili gives instructions that he is not even to go on a campaign for three years and adds an admonition: "If you take him [while still a child] with you on a campaign, bring him back safely." The question of whether Hattušili's brother served as regent during Muršili's minority is undecided. This text of the Old Hittite period, which, Gurney points out, is unique in cuneiform literature, is known only from late copies. This means that the story of Muršili I's appointment to the throne while he was still a child must have been long remembered. It would therefore be difficult to insist that the relief with the royal children at Alaca Höyük was contemporary with the situation described in the text of Hattušili I. The scene could be a later reference to a famous event, or, given the several occasions on which succession to the throne was in dispute in the Hittite kingdom,[34] it could represent another, similar situation for which no details have been preserved.

A striking parallel for both the scene at Alaca Höyük and the historical circumstance which has been proposed to explain it is offered by a much later monument, the so-called Royal Buttress at Carchemish (fig. 5-8).[35] The scenes here—a procession led by a young man escorted by an adult, two registers of children, and, finally, a woman carrying a baby and leading a goat—are accompanied by inscriptions which tell us who is represented.[36] The inscription over the figures at left states: "This is Yariris and this is Kamanas. These following are his brothers. I took him by the hand and set him over the temples when he was a child." Further details are given by the long text in front of the figures. We know that Yariris was the ruler of Carchemish in the early eighth century B.C. and that he was followed by Kamanas. Despite all this information the Royal Buttress has remained a puzzle until recently. The monument is unique in the ancient Near Eastern world in the degree of interest focused in both texts and reliefs on children: on

Kamanas, the young heir apparent, on whom, the long text in front of him says, honors were heaped even though (we are several times told) he was a child; on the brothers of Kamanas, seen on the second slab, all but one identified by name;[37] and even on the infant still nestled in its mother's arms on the third slab.

Although archaeologists have been content to take this unique scene as representing the usurper Yariris, introducing his son and family, philologists have long sought some historical explanation for it. The problem was that Yariris' relationship to both his predecessor and his successor was imperfectly understood. Recently, J. D. Hawkins has reexamined the texts and concluded that Yariris was neither a usurper nor the father of Kamanas.[38] He was acting as regent while the children of the former king were minors. This makes the focus on the children understandable. The Royal Buttress is a public proclamation by the regent in which he names the heir apparent and specifies the order of succession should anything befall that child.

The monument itself explains why such an elaborate proclamation was necessary. The repeated statement that Kamanas was a child informs us that his father, the king, died before his children had reached an age to rule, thus explaining why a regent was necessary. The youth of the boy and his dependence on the regent are clearly pictured on the reliefs. The status of the regent is skillfully represented on the first slab. The child Kamanas may lead the procession, indeed hold the royal staff, but he is obviously being guided by the towering, dignified figure of Yariris behind him. Yariris reaches forward and grasps the boy supportively by the wrist in an inversion of the typical Near Eastern introduction scene. This is not the famous composition of Imperial Hittite times in which the king is shown under the arm of the god, who grasps him by the wrist, but it is close to it in spirit.[39] The composition of these figures, like the phrasing of the long text, is designed to convey the great power of the regent without diminishing the status of the royal prince and heir apparent.

The following scene, in which two sets of children are clearly differentiated, suggests that the family situation at the time of the king's death was somewhat complicated. The text tells us that these are the brothers of Kamanas. In the upper register the children, although still clutching their toys, are clearly taking part in the procession behind Yariris. The children in the lower register are idly playing games. As P. Meriggi long ago noted,[40] the distinction made here is between those who may take part in the official ceremonies of government and those "playboys" who may not, a distinction he believed was also made in the text. The distinction was not a matter of age, for a nude toddler brings up the rear of

Fig. 5-10. Nuzi figure. (Courtesy Baghdad Museum)

the procession in the upper register and the tallest, oldest boys squat playing dice in the lower. The political status of the children was determined on some other basis. Bossert must have been right when he suggested that we see here two different families of the deceased king—that is, children by two different queens.[41] The composition is designed to make it quite clear which set of children was in line to the throne should anything happen to Kamanas. To make it even clearer, all but one of these children were identified by name. The fact that the status of the two sets of children is so clearly differentiated on the reliefs suggests that the issue needed public clarification and that the question as to which set of children was in line for the throne had been in serious dispute.

The nature of the dispute is suggested by the woman who ends the procession. She must be the queen who won the harem intrigue.[42] She must be the heir apparent's mother and the mother of the other children in the procession. They are younger than the "playboys" below, and that fact, added to the infant the queen carries, shows that she was the mother of the king's younger children. She must have been the dead king's second queen, one whose status was likely to have been disputed by an older or former queen if the king had left the matter of succession unclear at the time of his early death.

Thus, the reliefs on the Royal Buttress are not intimate scenes of royal family life, for which there would be no parallel in ancient Near Eastern art. The monument is, rather, a strongly stated political document in which Yariris, who undoubtedly aided the young queen in overthrowing the claims of her predecessor, proclaims himself regent for her child, Kamanas. He seeks to protect the child and the state from further harem intrigue by going on to show that the other children of the second queen are in line for the throne, but that the children of the former queen are relegated to idle pursuits.

The purpose of the Royal Buttress and the Alaca Höyük reliefs discussed above appears to be virtually identical. A sculptured monument placed in a prominent position publicly designates one child as heir apparent in the presence of his peers. It would be difficult not to believe that Yariris, who was, by his own account, both learned and well traveled,[43] was aware of the scenes at Alaca Höyük and their meaning when he planned his monument at Carchemish. The location of the Royal Buttress would confirm this suggestion. Yariris had a number of choices as to where to put his monument.

Most of the reliefs we know from the site were already standing when the Royal Buttress was built. It is significant that he chose the façade of the "Processional Entry," where the reliefs preserve the strongest flavor of Imperial Hittite art. Here two processions converged at a ceremonial entrance.[44] Soldiers came from the left.[45] From the right, men bearing sacrificial animals, preceded by the "priestesses," approached the back of the throne of a seated goddess.[46] Lining the right side of the entrance, around the corner from the goddess, were a trumpeter, two men playing a giant drum,[47] and, finally, a sphinx in relief.[48] Opposite these figures on the left side of the entryway was an earlier scene of musicians and dancers,[49] which was probably covered up by the time the Royal Buttress was built as a support for a ramp leading up to the old, now abandoned, ceremonial entry. The general similarity of this layout to that of the Alaca Höyük reliefs is striking. At both sites, along entrance-ways in which there were sphinxes, and opposite scenes in which a seated goddess was worshiped, were scenes representing the designation of one young prince as crown prince. At both sites the processions were accompanied by music and included sacrificial animals.

### FEMALE CHILDREN

Richard Barnett long ago recognized as Hittite a fine ivory figurine of a girl in the British Museum (fig. 5-9).[50] The girl is nude except for ear studs. She stands stiffly, hands at her side, shoulders hunched slightly, and head protruding. Her hair, gathered into a single tress, falls over her back to her shoulder blades. Her figure is unusual. She has a heavy chest, with little indication of breasts, and a thick torso. She has flat hips, but her plump buttocks are sensitively modeled. A small pubic triangle has been cut out for inlay. This is not the anatomy of a full-grown woman, which, we know, Hittites represented in as shapely a form as other ancient artists.[51] The nude figure represents neither fertility goddess nor courtesan. The ivory carver must have been attempting to portray a young girl. The relative proportions of legs, torso, and head would by clinical standards suggest that she is about six years old (see ill. 5-1). The length of the hair and the well-developed legs confirm this estimate. Stylistically, this figure, with her large head, flat cheeks, heavy chin, and short neck, compares well with the rock crystal child in the Walters Gallery. The sensitive modeling of the soft body forms, the groove down the back, and the demarcation of the shoulder blades are also very similar. The British Museum piece represents a child who is older than the Walters figure and clearly female. Like the Walters piece and the baby of the Schimmel pendant, the figure has no attributes or special characteristics which would help to

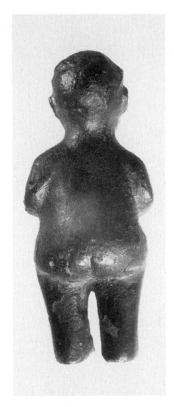

Fig. 5-11. Bronze infant, Alaca Höyük, Tomb H, late third millennium B.C., H. 8.8 cm. (Courtesy Museum of Anatolian Civilizations, Ankara)

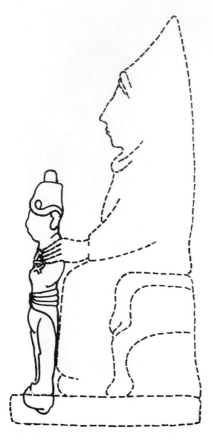

Ill. 5-2. Reconstruction of attendant with ivory child from Nuzi, Baghdad Museum. (Drawing by Iduna Hanel)

something while the upper part, which is modeled, stood free. The most natural support for a child of this age would be an adult figure—father, mother, nurse, or guardian (ill. 5-2). The figure wears a blouse, a strange skirt which leaves the lower part of the body exposed, and one shoe. This costume, the axe which the figure carries, and the ambiguous representation of gender led Machteld Mellink to identify it with the bisexual Hurrian deity Ištar-Šaušga. She, however, recognized the juvenile features of the figure and admitted the difficulty of interpreting the revealing skirt as a seductive feature when it exposes an unseductive body.[53]

If we are right in classifying the peculiarities of the Nuzi figure as characteristics of a very young child, there may be a better explanation for the figurine. One of the Hittite cult inventories may refer to a child.[54] In a 1976 letter to me, H. Güterbock kindly provided the following translation of the passage: "image of stone, of a woman standing; on the knees of a/the divinity it stands; of Anzili." Although the text mentions a woman, not a child, the position she takes on the lap of the divinity is that of a child, unless this is some sort of acrobatic scene. Unfortunately, the phrase "of Anzili" is ambiguous. It is impossible to tell whether it refers to the woman, the deity, or the whole group.

A goddess Anzili is known.[55] She and her counterpart Zukki belong to a group of deities who, like the popular Hattic deity, Telipinu,[56] fly into a rage, disappear, and are eventually found, after several futile attempts by the great gods, by bees sent out by the mother goddesses. When the bee stung Telipinu as it had been instructed, the god flew into another rage shouting, "How dare ye arouse me from my sleep? How dare ye force me to talk when enraged?" Finally, "the rage, anger, malice, and fury" are "taken off" by the eagle's wing. The description of the effect of anger on these deities is of interest in the present context. Telipinu becomes so distraught that he puts his shoes on the wrong feet. Anzili, in her anger, puts on backward not only her shoes, but also her dress, her blouse, and her *hubiki*, a two-part garment which Laroche explains as a veil.[57] Otten remarked on the clear, lively style of the Telipinu passage.[58] Indeed, if adult deities are being described, the text sounds more like farce. The idea of a grown god stumbling off in anger with his shoes on the wrong feet would surely have seemed as ridiculous in ancient times as it does today. It is true that gods in Hittite texts often react with human weakness when they become upset. Fear of the monstrous Ullikummi causes them to weep or faint and gives them shaky knees and diarrhea.[59] But these physical reactions can occur in terrified adults. Confusion over the simple action of getting dressed seems to me a different matter. It is the reaction of a child to whom getting

identify it. But again, the very existence of the statuette, finely carved in a precious material, is proof that a young girl had some special importance in Hittite thought.

Two other important female children known from the Hittite world may have some connection with the British Museum figure. The most intriguing Hittite representation of what appears to be a divine child is an ivory figurine found in the fifteenth-century B.C. levels at Nuzi (fig. 5-10).[52] The horned crown makes it clear that this child is a deity, but, as in the case of the Walters Gallery figure and the Schimmel pendant, the gender of the figure is not made clear. The peculiarly shaped body, the narrow, flat chest, short, chubby legs, and plump belly must again be taken as a Hittite attempt to represent a very young child. The relative proportions of the large head, long torso, and short legs, judged by clinical standards, suggest that the child is about two years old (see ill. 5-1). It was still young enough to need a nurse, and there is some evidence that it once had one. The back of the piece is flat and unworked from the waist down. The lower part of the body must have been placed against dressed is not yet a matter of routine. It is more logical to assume that these passages describe the gods as children, rather than that they are examples of ancient humor. The idea that Telipinu was a child-god is not new.[60] The *pinu* (meaning "child") in his name[61] and the association with the mother goddesses and bees would tend to confirm this suggestion.

The unusual wardrobe of the ivory figurine from Nuzi comes to mind when one reads of Anzili's disarrayed costume. It has "one shoe off and one shoe on," as in the English nursery rhyme, and the strange skimpy skirt which leaves the lower part of the body exposed. Can this be a kind of apron designed for children who are not yet toilet-trained which the goddess, in a fit of anger, has put on backward? The extreme youth of the figure might make this a more logical alternative to taking the skirt as the voluptuous garment of Ištar. It may be, then, that in this figurine from Nuzi we have a representation of Anzili, one which might roughly correspond to the description of her in the cult inventory on the knees of a goddess.

Thanks to the careful recording of the early excavators of Alaca Höyük, we have good evidence for the worship of a female child[62] in third-millennium Anatolia. In a group of bronze figurines found in Tomb H, a plump baby girl lay between two female figures. One of the latter has her arms outstretched as if carrying something over them. The other is holding a jug. Four clear photographs of the figures as they were discovered make it possible to see how they must once have been arranged. They were lying in a row, faces turned in the same direction. The baby was found resting rather awkwardly on the woman with the jug, its buttocks level with her shoulders (ill. 5-3). It is unlikely that the figures were put into the tomb in this position. They must originally have been upright. The baby is shown in a seated position,[63] implying that it had been placed on a chair made of some perishable material. It may be that the slow decay of the chair gradually lowered the figures into the position in which they were found. Their alignment does not suggest a sudden fall. The child's head was completely above that of the woman with a jug and slightly above that of the woman with arms extended. The group should thus be reconstructed with the infant placed high on a chair in a position of honor between two female attendants (ill. 5-4).

The baby is on a larger scale than the attendants and is quite different in style (fig. 5-11). The enormous head shows that this is a very young child. The oval ears are clearly marked by ridges. The large, almond-shaped eyes are cut out for inlay. The nose is long and thin but projects very little. The mouth is slightly pinched, with a tiny groove marking the lips. The infant rests long thin

Ill. 5-3. Alaca Höyük figures from Tomb H as found. (Drawing by Catalina Davis)

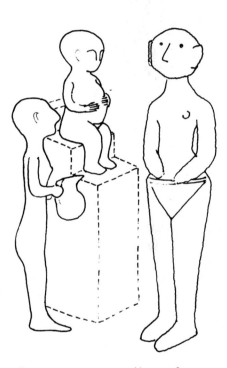

Ill. 5-4. Reconstruction of bronze figures from Tomb H, Alaca Höyük, late third millennium B.C., Ankara Museum. (Drawing by Iduna Hanel)

fingers on a very fat stomach, has chubby legs, well-defined buttocks, and a sizable cut-out pubic triangle. Its large, well-rounded, clearly articulated forms are in marked contrast to the idollike quality of the attendants. These have flat disc-shaped faces, tiny round eyes, and very large protruding noses. They also have flat, narrow chests with button breasts. Their hips swell out in a sharp diagonal line, and a giant pubic triangle, indicated by incision, covers the lower half of their bodies. Only the buttocks are naturalistically curved. In her right ear the taller figure has a gold ear stud shaped like a maltese cross. Her close-fitting, complicated hairdo is indicated by incised lines on the back of her head. Stylistically the two attendants resemble female idols found in other tombs.[64] The exaggeration and abstraction of natural forms are in the tradition of numerous animal figures from the site.

The infant figure clearly belongs to a different artistic tradition. The more naturally shaped forms are closer to early Hittite art of the Old Assyrian Colony period[65] than to anything from the Alaca Höyük tombs. The figure likewise has very little in common with the spider-like baby of the Horoztepe "mother goddess" group, which is dated somewhat later than the Alaca Höyük material.[66] The difference between the baby and its attendants in style as well as scale strongly suggests that the figurines found arranged together in Tomb H were not originally made as a group. The attendants were locally made. The exalted child was not. The fact that the figurines were nevertheless grouped into a meaningful composition in the grave requires some explanation. If differences in style can be taken as reflecting different cultural backgrounds, certain historical conclusions can be drawn.

For many years it has been thought that the distinct culture revealed in the tombs at Alaca Höyük was that of the native Hattic-speaking population which the Indo-European Hittites found when they arrived, a culture for which—as the written record makes clear—the Hittites had much respect and from which they borrowed many cultural and religious elements.[67] The theory fits the archaeological evidence very well. In second-millennium, Hittite, Anatolia, for instance, many "Hattic" pottery forms typical of the third millennium are used with a refreshing new spirit, the exotic pitcher (or *Schnabelkanne*) being the classic example. The more recent theory which holds that the people buried in the Alaca Höyük tombs were early Hittites seems to me to contradict this archaeological evidence.[68] It also disregards the fundamental stylistic and iconographic difference between Hittite art and that revealed in the tombs. This is not to argue against the now widely held view that the Hittites were already in Anatolia in the third millennium.[69] On the contrary, I would suggest that the baby from Tomb H, who looks so exotic at Alaca Höyük and so Hittite, is actually a very early Hittite piece. It was imported to Alaca Höyük, perhaps as a royal gift. At least it was treated very respectfully and provided with "Hattic" nursemaids.

## DIVINE AND MYTHOLOGICAL CHILDREN

The best-known children in Hittite art are those who stand behind the chief goddess, Hepat, at the main Hittite sanctuary, Yazılıkaya, where they are represented as merely small versions of the adult figures.[70] The boy, number 44, who stands directly behind Hepat is Šarruma, tutelary deity of Tuthaliya IV, ca. 1250–1220 B.C. Laroche has shown that Šarruma, originally a Kizzuwatnan god, was introduced to the capital in late Imperial times.[71] The theological stratagem used to incorporate him into the established Hittite pantheon was to present him as a son of the chief deities. Šarruma's position directly behind the great goddess Hepat on the reliefs at Yazılıkaya emphasizes his relationship to her and thereby proclaims his right to be considered a major deity. On the rock relief he is shown as a young adult, but some of the texts imply that he was not always envisioned as fully grown. They mention an entity "Hepat-Šarruma," sometimes written with only one divine determinative. In these cases, Laroche explains, Šarruma is an attribute of his mother, a concept comparable to the "Madonne à l'Enfant" in Christian iconography.[72] To be considered a sort of attribute of his mother, the god must have been envisioned as an infant, still at an age when he would have been inseparable from her. If, as Laroche suggests, the introduction of Šarruma as a child of the well-established goddess Hepat was a somewhat forced affair, it could well have been accompanied by the creation of propagandistic statues or statuettes of Hepat and baby.

Another important child is found in the mythological world of the Hittites. The story about the Hurrian Ullikummi contains a long episode in which the stone monster, while still an infant, is set on the knees of his father, Kumarbi.[73] Kumarbi fondles the child while he thinks over what name to give him. With the child still on his knees, Kumarbi speculates on Ullikummi's future and worries about how to protect him until he is grown. He then summons the Irsirra deities to take the child and place him on the shoulders of the Atlas-like creature Ubelluri. Before doing so, however, the Irsirras take the baby to the ancient Mesopotamian god Enlil. They place him on Enlil's lap, and the great god exclaims about the trouble he realizes the child will cause.

The presentation of an infant to his father is a familiar theme in Hittite texts. As mentioned above, it appears to be a legitimization ceremony.[74] The scene was an important part of the myth as it takes up about one-ninth of the preserved text. It seems entirely possible that the scene may also have been a subject for Hittite art. We know that it was depicted shortly after the fall of the Hittite empire on the famous gold bowl from Hasanlu, Iran, dated to the twelfth–eleventh centuries B.C. There, in the lower register, a woman presents an infant to a seated male figure. The close relationship of this scene (and others on the bowl) to the myth of Ullikummi was long ago pointed out by E. Porada.[75] Other links between the bowl and Hittite art have been discussed by Machteld Mellink, who suggests that artists in both areas shared a common, largely Hurrian, iconographic heritage.[76] The episode in which the infant Ullikummi is set on his father's lap may have been a subject for Hittite narrative relief, but it seems doubtful that it would have been represented as a sculptural group in the round.

The Walters figure is probably not Ullikummi, nor Ḫattušili I in distress, nor Muršili I or another heir apparent. The child could represent one of the young disappearing deities or an infant Šarruma. What it does not represent, in my opinion, is a normal, childlike child such as those in the family groups which are known both in lead and from molds for lead figurines of the Old Assyrian Colony period; nor is it connected with alabaster idols of a slightly earlier period.[77] It is, rather, a Hittite expression of the miraculous child concept which is known from so many other mythologies.

#### NOTES

1 Catalogue no. 42.360; see J. V. Canby, *The Ancient Near East in the Walters Art Gallery* (Baltimore 1974) no. 36. The extremities had been reattached in modern times with a glue containing gold flecks. Terry Weisser of the gallery's conservation laboratory, who took the old joins apart and reglued them, found that the irregular breaks joined perfectly—that is, nothing has been reconstructed. The piece is so transparent that it is difficult to photograph. For that reason, photographs of casts made from the piece are included here as fig. 5-2.

2 Adana Museum 2823, H. Goldman et al., *Excavations at Gözlü Kule, Tarsus 2. From the Neolithic through the Bronze Age* (Princeton 1956) 342–44, fig. 456a–d; E. Akurgal and M. Hirmer, *The Art of the Hittites* (New York 1962) pl. 53, bottom right; K. Bittel, *Les Hittites* (L'univers des formes, Paris 1976) 164, fig. 176.

3 O. W. Muscarella, "Seated Goddess," in O. W. Muscarella ed., *Ancient Art in the Norbert Schimmel Collection* (Mainz 1974) no. 125; Bittel (supra n. 2) 162, fig. 193; W. Orthmann, *Der alte Orient* (PK 14, Berlin 1975) pl. 370.b–c.

4 The shortness of the lower left arm and the size of the left hand strongly suggest that the arm broke off and was recarved. The grooves used to delineate the new fingers, seen under a strong microscope, are the same as those on the other hand, suggesting that the repair was done by the original carver.

5 This characteristic adult stance is exaggerated in small figures in the round; see Bittel (supra n. 2) 159, fig. 168.

6 Akurgal and Hirmer (supra n. 2) pls. 64, 65, 68, 69; Bittel (supra n. 2) 229, fig. 265; 230, fig. 267; 298, fig. 339.

7 Bittel (supra n. 2) 147, fig. 148; 227, figs. 262–63; Akurgal and Hirmer (supra n. 2) pls. 50, 51; S. Alp, "Eine hethitische Bronzestatuette und andere Funde aus Zara bei Amasya," *Anadolu* 6 (1962) 217–43, pls. 23–26.

8 See the statue base, in Akurgal and Hirmer (supra n. 2) pl. 71; Tuthaliya at Yazılıkaya, pl. 85; the king and priests at Alaca Höyük, pl. 92; at Atchana, Bittel (supra n. 2) 202, fig. 231.

9 For the gesture, see the ivory figure of a mountain god: Akurgal and Hirmer (supra n. 2) pl. 53, below; and a priest at Alaca Höyük, pl. 93, below.

10 Akurgal and Hirmer (supra n. 2) pl. 23; Bittel (supra n. 2) 24, fig. 7; 49, fig. 32. Muscarella (supra n. 3) disagrees; he thinks the woman of the Schimmel pendant may reflect a revival of the old mother goddess theme. He is followed by Orthmann (supra n. 3) 435.

11 Brooklyn Museum 39.119. See B. Bothmer and J. Keith, *A Brief Guide to the Ancient Art in the Brooklyn Museum* (Brooklyn 1970) 31, and C. Vandersleyen, *Das alte Ägypten* (PK 15, Berlin 1975) 228, pl. 144.

12 See the early example in the Schimmel collection: J. Cooney, "Isis and Horus," in Muscarella ed. (supra n. 3) no. 209.

13 George Steindorff, *Catalogue of the Egyptian Sculpture in the Walters Art Gallery* (Baltimore 1946) 101, 102.

14 W. Stevenson Smith, *CAH*[3] 1.2, 191–92; see J. Cooney, cited in J. Vandier, *Manuel d'archéologie égyptiennes* 3 (Paris 1958) 38 on the propagandistic nature of the statue.

15 See C. Aldred, *New Kingdom Art in Ancient Egypt* (London 1961) pls. 31–34.

16 E.g., Steindorff (supra n. 13) 72, no. 236, pl. 53; see also W. S. Smith, *A History of Egyptian Sculpture and Painting in the Old Kingdom* (London 1946) figs. 124, 125, and p. 283. For a new version of the grown king as child, see the recently discovered statues of Seti I in J. Kamil, "Ancient Memphis," *Archaeology* 38 (1985) 27 photograph; see also p. 30.

17 For a recent summary of scenes showing children with adult figures, see H. Kühne, "Das Motiv der nährenden Frau oder Göttin in Vorderasien," in S. Şahin, E. Schwertheim, and J. Wagner eds., *Studien zur Religion und Kultur Kleinasiens, Festschrift für Friedrich Karl Dörner* (Etudes préliminaires aux religions orientales dans l'empire Romain 66, Leiden 1978), vol. 2, 504–15. See also n. 25 below for occurrences in Mesopotamian literature.

Jung's discussion of the bisexual nature of cosmogenic gods is of interest in light of the Hittites' apparent ambiguity in representing the gender of some of these children. See C. Jung, "The Special Phenomenology of the Child Archetype," in V. S. de Laszlo ed., *Psyche and Symbol: A Selection from the Writings of C. G. Jung* (New York 1958) 139–43.

18 In the Neo-Hittite period, children play an important role on some of the so-called *Speiseszenen*, which are apparently connected with the cult of the dead. W. Orthmann, *Untersuchungen zur späthethitischen Kunst* (Saarbrücker Beitrage zur Altertumskunde 8, Bonn 1971) 380–82, has demonstrated rather convincingly that the ideas behind these scenes are not derived from Imperial Hittite art.

19 The headdress of the woman may be worn by queens or goddesses: see the discussion in J. Börker-Klähn and C. Börker, "Eflatun Pinar, zu Rekonstruktion, Deutung und Datierung," *JdI* 90 (1975) 22, figs. 18–19. See p. 52 above.

20 For the storm god as father, see A. Goetze, "Ritual for the Erection of a New Palace," in J. B. Pritchard ed., *Ancient Near Eastern Texts Relating to the Old Testament* (Princeton 1950) 357. Such passages are discussed by S. R. Bin-Nun, *The Tawannana in the Hittite Kingdom* (Texte der Hethiter 5, Heidelberg 1975) 42, 151.

21 E.g., Puduhepa, Goetze (supra n. 20) 393; Muwatalli, ibid., 398; Kantuzili, 400.

22 H. Otten, "Vorläufiger Bericht über die Ausgrabungen in Boğazköy," *MDOG* 91 (1958) 78; F. Imparati and C. Saporetti, *StClOr* 14 (1965) 47, 61, 62.

23 E. Neu, *Der Anitta-Text* (Studien zu den Boğazköy Texten, Wiesbaden 1974) 127; H. C. Melchert, "The Acts of Hattusil I," *JNES* 37 (1978) 8 and 14, n. 25. For this deity as a goddess, see O. R. Gurney, *Some Aspects of Hittite Religion*

(Schweich Lectures of the British Academy 1976, Oxford 1977) 11, 12.

24 A. Goetze in "Critical Reviews," *JCS* 16 (1962) 24; Goetze, review of H. G. Güterbock, *Kumarbi* in *JAOS* 69 (1949) 180; see also E. Laroche, *Les noms des Hittites* (Paris 1966) appendix 1, pp. 369–70; H. A. Hoffner, Jr., "Birth and Name Giving in Hittite Texts," *JNES* 27 (1969) 201 n. 27.

25 Wolfgang Hiempel, "The Nanshe Hymns," *JCS* 32/2 (1981) 83, line 24. Professor Jerrold Cooper has kindly provided this note on lap-sitting in Sumerian and Akkadian sources. The lap or "bosom" (German *Schoss*), Sumerian $du_{10}$, $ur_{10}$, and Akkadian *birku*, *sūnu*, is a place of refuge and protection. For references in Sumerian, see J. Klein, "Šulgi and Gilgameš: Two Brother-Peers (Šulgi O)," *Kramer Anniversary Volume* (Alter Orient und Altes Testament 25, Neu Kirchen-Vluyn 1976) 291; for the Akkadian, see *Chicago Assyrian Dictionary* B (Chicago 1965) s.v. *birku*, and W. von Soden, *Akkadisches Handwörterbuch* (Wiesbaden 1958–1981) s.v. *sunu* I. Cf. also E. Dhorme, *L'emploi métaphorique des noms de parties du corps* (Paris 1923) 108 and 156–57. The classic text describing a king sitting on a divine lap occurs on Eanatum's Stela of the Vultures, iv 24ff. Inana takes the divinely engendered Eanatum, names him, and presents him to the goddess Ninhursag to be nursed. After this divine nourishment, the god Ningirsu measures Eanatum, finds that he has grown to 9 feet 2 inches, and names him king of Lagash. The most recent translations of the passage in question are the following:

T. Jacobsen, *Kramer Anniversary Volume*, 251: "She set him down for Ninhursaĝa on her [i.e., Ninhursaĝa's] right knee, and Ninhursaĝa fed him at her right breast."
H. Steible, *Die altsumerischen Bau- und Weihinschriften* 1 (Freiburger Alt-Orientalische Studien 5, Wiesbaden 1982) 123: "Sie hat (ihn) der Ninhursag auf ihren rechten Schoss gesetzt, (und) Ninhursag hat (ihn) an ihre rechte Brust g[elegt]."
J. Cooper, *Reconstructing History from Ancient Sources: The Lagash-Umma Border Conflict* (Sources from the Ancient Near East, 211, Malibu 1983) 45: "[Inana] set him on the special lap of Ninhursag. Ninhursag [offered him] her special breast."

In Akkadian, note the following examples: Aššurbanipal on the lap of a goddess as a child; an Esarhaddon oracle proclaiming, "Your son and grandson will exercise kingship on the lap of Ninurta" (both from *Chicago Assyrian Dictionary*, s.v. *birku*); a complaint of Esarhaddon's mother that the goddess takes others in her lap but neglects her son Esarhaddon (from *Akkadisches Handwörterbuch*, s.v. *sūnu* I). As for Hiempel's divine child–old man (p. 93, line 176), I know of no parallel. Perhaps the divine determinative, present in one MS and omitted in the other, might be a mistake, and the line just means "Her angel will not let young and old be silent about it." In any case, most of the text is unintelligible or nearly so.

26 Bittel (supra n. 2) 194, fig. 220.

27 See Akurgal and Hirmer (supra n. 2) pl. 92 below. For a view of the second half of the procession, see Bittel (supra n. 2) 190–91, top.

28 M. J. Mellink, "Observations on the Sculpture of Alaca Höyük," *Anadolu* 14 (1970) 20–24, pl. 5 and fig. 2.

29 On the winged sun disc, see E. Laroche, *Les Hiéroglyphes hittites* 1 *L'ecriture* (Paris 1960) 99–100; on no.190, see Börker-Klähn and Börker (supra n. 19) 24.

30 At Yazılıkaya; see Bittel (supra n. 2) pls. 233, 234.

31 See E. Porada, *Seal Impressions of Nuzi* (AASOR 24, New Haven 1947) 115.

32 H. T. Bossert, *Altanatolien* (Berlin 1942) fig. 502; W. R. Ramsay, "On the Early Historical Relations Between Phrygia and Cappadocia," *JRAS* n.s. 15 (1883) 116–17.

33 Oliver Gurney, *CAH*³ 2.1, 246–49.

34 Gurney (supra n. 33) 659–65.

35 D. G. Hogarth, *Carchemish. Report on the Excavations at Djerablis on Behalf of the British Museum*, part 1 (London 1914) pls. B1, B4–8; L. Woolley and R. Barnett, *Carchemish, Report on the Excavations at Jerablus on Behalf of the British Museum*, part 3 (London 1952) 194–200, pls. 42–44.

36 H. T. Bossert, "Zur Geschichte von Karkamis," *StClOr* 1 (1951) 46–47; P. Meriggi, *Manuale* II, 2, 19–33; J. D. Hawkins, cited in M. E. L. Mallowan, "Carchemish," *Iraq* 22 (1972) 75; J. D. Hawkins, "Problems of Hieroglyphic Luwian Transcriptions," *AnatSt* 29 (1979) 157–60. Hawkins translates ". . . and these are his younger brothers." Meriggi's translation is given here.

37 Meriggi, *Manuale* II, 20–22.

38 J. D. Hawkins, "Karkamis," *RLA* 5 (1980) 444, 445; "Problems" (supra n. 36).

39 Akurgal and Hirmer (supra n. 2) pls. 84–85; Bittel (supra n. 2) pls. 252–53.

40 Meriggi, *Manuale* II, 19, 27.

41 Bossert (supra n. 36) 52, 53, 56.

42 Hawkins, "Problems" (supra n. 36) 159 n. 36, takes the infant as Yariris' son.

43 J. D. Hawkins, "The Negatives in Hieroglyphic Luwian," *AnatSt* 25 (1975) 150–51.

44 Woolley's reconstruction of the architecture here is somewhat difficult to understand: Woolley and Barnett, *Carchemish* 3 (supra n. 35) 195–96.

45 Hogarth, *Carchemish* 1, pl. B1–3; *Carchemish* 3, pl. 42 (both supra n. 35).

46 C. L. Woolley, *Carchemish* 2. *The Town Defenses* (London 1921) pls. B17, B19–24.

47 Woolley (supra n. 46) pl. B18b; Bittel (supra n. 2) pl. 290.

48 Woolley (supra n. 46) pl. B18a.

49 Woolley (supra n. 46) pl. B17b.

50 British Museum 38185; R. Barnett, "An Unrecognized Anatolian Ivory," *BMQ* 10 (1935–1936) 121–23, pl. 34.1, 2; R. Barnett, *A Catalogue of the Nimrud Ivories with Other Examples of Ancient Near Eastern Ivories in the British Museum*² (London 1975) pl. 122, VI6 and p. 128.

51 For a poor picture of the shapely goddess from Alalakh (Antakya Museum 6087) see At/46/20 on pl. 69.1 in L. Woolley, *Alalakh. An Account of the Excavations at Tell Atchana in the Hatay, 1937–1949* (London 1955). On the relief at Imankulu, see M. Wäffler, "Zum Felsrelief von Immakulu," *MDOG* 107 (1975) 17–26, pls. 3–4. On a seal in the Louvre: A. Parrot, "Cylindre hittite nouvellement aquis, A.O. 20138," *Syria* 28 (1951) 180–90, pls. 13–14; E. Porada, "Syrian Seal Impressions on Tablets Dated in the Time of Hammurabi and Samsuiluna," *JNES* 16 (1957) 194 n. 12, pl. 30.4. See also the figurine from Karahöyük, Konya, in Bittel (supra n. 2) 101, fig. 91.

52 Baghdad, Iraqi Museum no. 22359; R. F. S. Starr, *Nuzi, Report on the Excavations at Yorgan Tepa near Kirkuk, Iraq, Conducted by Harvard University in Conjunction with the American Schools of Oriental Research and the University Museum of Philadelphia, 1927–1931* (Cambridge 1937) 1: p. 421, 2: pl. 100.I, 1–4; Bittel (supra n. 2) 163, fig. 174; M. J. Mellink, "A Hittite Figurine from Nuzi," in K. Bittel et al. eds., *Vorderasiatische Archäologie. Studien und Aufsätze, Anton Moortgat zum fünfundsechzigsten Geburtstag gewidmet* (Berlin 1964) 155–64, pl. 20.

53 Mellink (supra n. 52) 151, 160.

54 See now H. G. Güterbock, "Hethitische Götterbilder und Kultobjekte," in R. M. Boehmer and H. Hauptmann eds., *Beiträge zur Altertumskunde Kleinasiens. Festschrift für Kurt Bittel* (Mainz am Rhein 1983) 210.

55 E. Laroche, "Recherches sur les noms des dieux hittites," *RHA* 46 (1947) 79; Güterbock (supra n. 54) 210.

56 Goetze, (supra n. 20) 126–27. On Anzili, see H. Otten, "Die Uberlieferungen des Telipinu-Mythus," *MVAG* 46.1 (1942) 55, 68. For another of these angry gods who mix up their shoes, see H. G. Güterbock, "Rituale für die Gottin Huwassanna," *Oriens* 15 (1962) 350–51.

57 E. Laroche, "Notes de linguistique anatolienne, l. Hittite hubiki," *RHA* 68 (1961) 25–26. See Güterbock (supra n. 54) 206.

58 Otten (supra n. 56) 51.

59 Goetze (supra n. 20) 123–25.

60 See M. Riemschneider's concept of Telipinu as "ein ungehorsames Gotterkind" in *Die Welt der Hethiter* (Stuttgart 1954) 73–79. It would be interesting to know more about the baby she publishes on pl. 30. See also pl. 105 below in the same volume.

61 E. von Schuler in H. W. Haussig ed., *Götter und Mythen im Vorderen Orient* (Stuttgart 1965) 201. For the connection of bees with young vegetation gods as well as a proto-Hattic ritual which pictures the missing god asleep on the lap of a goddess, see V. Haas, *Magie und Mythen im Reich der Hethiter, 1. Vegetationskulte und Pflanzenmagie* (Hamburg 1977) 88.

62 Ankara Museum no. 7062; H. Z. Koşay, *Les fouilles d'Alaca Höyük entreprises par la société d'histoire turque. Rapport preliminaire sur les travaux en 1937–39* (TTKY ser. V, 5, Ankara 1951) 157: H. 3; color pl. 139 (opp. p. 160) below; plan on pl. 118, figures in situ; pl. 120 above and below, pls. 123–24. For attendants, see color pl. 138 (opp. p. 144), pl. 129 (opp. p. 160) above; and Akurgal and Hirmer (supra n. 2) pl. 21; the three figures at left.

63 It might be argued that the Horoztepe figure (Akurgal and Hirmer [supra n. 2] pl. 23) has the same protruding buttocks and stands alone, but I wonder whether this Horoztepe figure was not originally semiseated. See the ivory figure from Kültepe, in Bittel (supra n. 2) pl. 35, top right, fig. 33, and the side view in T. Özgüç, "Die Grabungen von 1952 in Kültepe," *Belleten* 18 (1954) fig. 20:b, c.

64 Akurgal and Hirmer (supra n. 2) pl. 21, top and lower right.

65 For example, the ivory figurine from Kültepe; Bittel (supra n. 2) fig. 33, and the Acemhöyük ivories, ibid., figs. 44, 45, 72.

66 Akurgal (supra n. 2) 26, makes the point that the figures from Tomb H are more developed than those of the earlier Tomb L, and he compares the posture of the baby to that of the Horoztepe figure. The attendant figures may be more advanced stylistically than the figurine from Tomb L, but they share none of the naturalism of the baby, who, to my eye, is also more naturally shaped than the Horoztepe figurine.

67 Gurney (supra n. 33) 255.

68 W. F. Albright and T. O. Lambdin, *CAH*³ 1.1 (1970) 140–42; J. G. MacQueen, *The Hittites and Their Contemporaries in Asia Minor* (Ancient Peoples and Places 83, Southhampton 1975) 33–34; see also Bittel (supra n. 2) 54.

69 Gurney (supra n. 33) 255.

70 Nos. 44–46. See Akurgal and Hirmer (supra n. 2) pl. 76 above, pl. 77, below, and Bittel (supra n. 2) 209, fig. 239; K. Bittel et al., *Das hethitische Felsheiligtum Yazılıkaya* (Boğazköy-Hattuša, Ergebnisse der Ausgrabungen 10, Berlin 1975) no. 44, pp. 153–54, pls. 25.1, 26.1, 29, 30, 58. For the female children, see Güterbock in Bittel et al., 171–72 and 187 on nos. 45–46.

71 E. Laroche, "Le dieu anatolien, Sarruma," *Syria* 40 (1963) 275–302.

72 Laroche (supra n. 71) 292, n. 6.

73 Goetze (supra n. 20) 122; H. G. Güterbock, "The Song of Ullikummi, Revised Text of the Hittite Version of a Hurrian Myth," *JCS* 5 (1951) 153–57.

74 See references in n. 24 supra and Jana Siegelova, *Appu-Märchen und Hedammu-Mythus* (Studien zu den Boğazköy-Texten 14, Wiesbaden 1971) 32.

75 E. Porada, *The Art of Ancient Iran. Pre-Islamic Cultures* (Baden-Baden 1965) 99–100; see fig. 64.

76 M. J. Mellink, "The Hasanlu Bowl in Anatolian Perspective," *IrAnt* 6 (1966) 72–87.

77 E.g., Akurgal and Hirmer (supra n. 2) pl. 25, right, pl. 35, bottom; Bittel (supra n. 2) figs. 89–90; Kutlu Emre, *Anatolian Lead Figurines and Their Stone Moulds* (TTKY ser. VI, 14, Ankara 1971) 133, 136, 137, 149.

# "Hittites" at Grinnell

## 6

HANS G. GÜTERBOCK

Recently I learned from my friend Robert L. Alexander of the University of Iowa that Grinnell College, Grinnell, Iowa, has a collection of artifacts from central Anatolia, probably from Boğazköy, which had reached the college many years ago. Some pieces of correspondence pertaining to the acquisition of these objects were also kept at the college.

The objects consist of seven small pottery bull's heads (Spencer Collection nos. 753–759; figs. 6-1 to 6-14), one spout in the shape of a ram's head (no. 760; fig. 6-15 and 6-16), one leg with hoof of a bull statuette of clay (no. 761; fig. 6-17), and one fragment of a Hittite tablet (no. 768; fig. 6-18; ill. 6-1). In themselves these pieces are not important; it is rather the date and story of their acquisition which are of some interest. In presenting them to Machteld Mellink, I hope that she will be amused by a story going back "before Hittitology."

The bull heads are of the kind found as decorations on vases. None of the Grinnell bull heads is a spout. An example of a vessel decorated with such full-plastic heads on the exterior—albeit connected with bodies in relief—is the Old Hittite vase from Eskiyapar;[1] in contrast, the bull heads around the inner rim of the same vase are spouts. Isolated heads of a similar kind were found in the Hittite capital[2] and in Höyük near Alaca.[3]

Among the heads in the Spencer Collection, no. 759 is the finest (figs. 6-1 to 6-3). Whereas the others are unpainted, it has dark red matte paint along the cheeks and the upper part of the forehead, leaving the frontal triangle, the eyes, the snout, and the neck in the original light brown color of the clay. The head is rather elongated, similar to some from Boğazköy.[4] The nostrils are rendered as small holes (made with a pin?) on top of the snout, not in the front of it, as in Grinnell no. 753

(fig. 6-4). The neck is still connected with a fragment of the wall of the vessel.

How such attachments were fixed to the wall of the vessel is not entirely clear, although some of the Grinnell heads give some clues on their underside. In Grinnell no. 756 (fig. 6-5), the circular groove must have served to fix the roughly cylindrical neck to the head. (A similar device on the underside of Grinnell no. 754 [fig. 6-6] does not appear clearly in the photograph.) In Grinnell no. 755 (fig. 6-7), the right side of the neck (seen on the left on the underside) is still connected with the head; it shows that the neck was hollow (see also fig. 6-8). In Grinnell no. 758 (figs. 6-9 and 6-10), the neck was modeled around a peg which must have served to connect the head to the support, probably a vessel. Most of the neck is lost, leaving the rounded end of the peg visible.[5]

Grinnell no. 757 (figs. 6-11 to 6-14) is hollow; inserted in the opening of the neck was a tubular piece made of a different clay. It may have served to connect the head with the rest of the vessel or animal figure. The neck of the bull has a hump; for humped cattle in Hittite art, see the seal of Muwatalli,[6] the bull rhyton in the Norbert Schimmel collection,[7] and the silver statuette from Boğazköy.[8]

In contrast to the bulls' heads, the ram's head (Grinnell no. 760; figs. 6-15 and 6-16) is a spout. Figure 6-16 clearly shows the channel running through it to the mouth. It is made of light gray clay with a yellow-white surface (slip?). Spouts in the form of animal heads are rather common, and among them the ram is the most popular. Examples are known from Boğazköy,[9] Alishar,[10] and Kültepe.[11] The most spectacular pieces with spouts in the form of rams' heads are the rectangular boxes, with or without added figures, from Kültepe.[12]

Fig. 6-1. Grinnell, Spencer Collection, bull no. 759

Fig. 6-2. Grinnell, Spencer Collection, bull no. 759

Fig. 6-3. Grinnell, Spencer Collection, bull no. 759

Fig. 6-4. Grinnell, Spencer Collection, bull no. 753

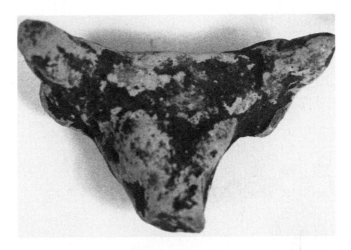

Fig. 6-6. Grinnell, Spencer Collection, bull no. 754

Fig. 6-5. Grinnell, Spencer Collection, bull no. 756

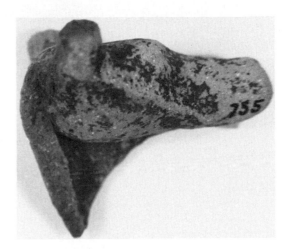

Fig. 6-7. Grinnell, Spencer Collection, bull no. 755

Fig. 6-8. Grinnell, Spencer Collection, bulls no. 756, 755, and 754

Fig. 6-9. Grinnell, Spencer Collection, bull no. 758

Fig. 6-10. Grinnell, Spencer Collection, bull no. 758

Fig. 6-11. Grinnell, Spencer Collection, bull no. 757

Fig. 6-12. Grinnell, Spencer Collection, bull no. 757

Fig. 6-13. Grinnell, Spencer Collection, bull no. 757

Fig. 6-14. Grinnell, Spencer Collection, bulls no. 759 (left) and 757 (right)

Fig. 6-15. Grinnell, Spencer Collection, ram's head spout no. 760

Fig. 6-16. Grinnell, Spencer Collection, ram's head spout no. 760

Grinnell no. 761 (fig. 6-17) is a fragment of one leg of a bull statue, or, rather, a large bull-shaped vessel. The best-known examples are, of course, the two Old Hittite bulls from Büyükkale in Boğazköy.[13] They have close parallels at Inandık.[14] In no. 761 the leg is an unarticulated straight column separated from the cleft hoof by a narrow groove. Above the groove is a row of short vertical incisions, apparently meant to indicate hair. Below the hoof is a remnant of a ground plate. Several single legs with hoof have been found at Boğazköy, of which only two have bases.[15] Such bases or ground plates must be what the Hittites called *palzašḫa-* or *palzaḫa-*.[16] None of the Boğazköy examples have hair above the hoof, although some of them show other anatomical details very well. An isolated example from Kültepe is in Chantre.[17] T. Özgüç has published a leg now in the Asmaya Museum. He also mentions similar legs in the museum of Gümüşhacıköy, said to come from the area of Çankırı (are they perhaps from Inandık?).[18]

In addition to the objects mentioned so far, there are in the collection five heads of human terracotta statuettes, Hellenistic or later, of low quality, which we leave aside here. All these items are said to have been given to the college by the late Rev. Professor G. E. White. A letter of Edgar J. Banks to Professor Spencer, dated 11 December 1939, contains the following information. After listing a tablet, a spindle whorl, the heads of statuettes, and "the heads of the cattle," Banks continues:

> You mention that the objects were presented to the college by a missionary who once lived in Marsavan. You probably refer to Professor White, now I believe dead. Mr. White started an Archaeological Society at Marsevan [*sic*], of which I was made an honorary member, and he spent much of his time in studying the ancient ruins of the vicinity, especially at Boghazkeui and Eyuk. These objects were probably found at Boghazkeui, and before any systematic exploration of that ruin had been made.

Among the objects listed in this letter, the tablet (if it is the same)[19] and the whorl are also mentioned in a letter of G. E. White (to be quoted presently), in which he states that he acquired them in Boğazköy. For the animal heads, however, we only have the passage in Banks's letter stating that all the objects listed by him were presented by this missionary who probably was White. That this person was indeed White is as good as certain, but that the animal heads were acquired by him at Boğazköy does not necessarily follow; they might just as well have been found at Höyük, Kültepe, or any other site. The animal heads are not mentioned in White's own letter, which deserves to be quoted in full:[20]

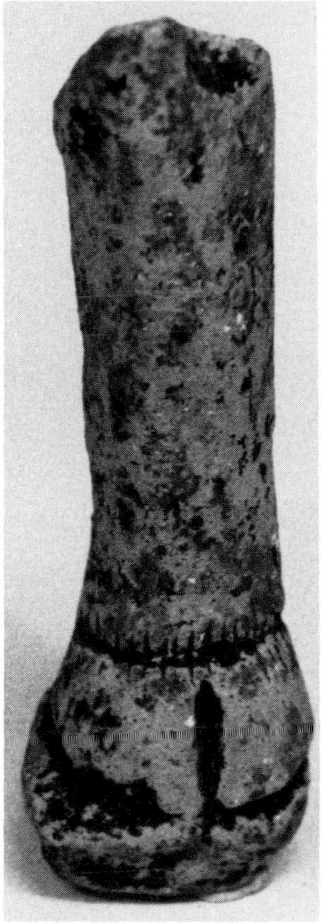

Salem Mass. June 2—'99.

Prof L. F. Parker D. D.
    Grinnel Iowa

    My Dear Prof. Parker. You asked me to write a brief description of the cuneiform tablet, Hittite seal, and whirligig that I placed in your hands for the Alumni alcove of the College.

    Boghaz-Keuy, South of Marsovan in Central Asia Minor, was an ancient Hittite stronghold, and I obtained all these articles there. There are now many ruins of fortifications, walls, castles, and temples, with well-preserved sculptures, to be seen by any traveller. They are the remains of the capital city of a mighty empire, which flourished about the time that Moses led the Israelites out of Egypt. Castle walls are still standing 30 to 50 feet high, and from the top of the surrounding rampart to the outer base in what was a moat, is about 150 feet after the lapse of all these centuries.

    The cuneiform tablet is made of clay written and then baked. It shows that the Hittites had dealings with the dwellers in the Mesopotamian valley, for that was the home of cuneiform script. They could not read this tablet at the British Museum, because, as appears, its language is Hittite, and the Hittite language is lost. It is probably more than 3000 years old.

    The seal (broken) probably had a loop at the back for suspending it from a cord. It is marked with a figure resembling a figure 4, a symbol that the Hittites used. It has "rope work" around the edge. Dr. William Hayes Ward dated it at about 1000 B.C.

    The article which for want of a better name I call a whirligig is exactly like those found by Dr. Schlieman [*sic*] at Troy, and connects the Hittites with the Greeks on the West, as the cuneiform tablet connected them with Mesopotamia on the East. If the siege of Troy took place 1184 B.C., these little toys

Fig. 6-17. Grinnell, Spencer Collection, hoof of bull statuette no. 761

date from that time or before. May we suppose that Hittite boys ever played hookey from school in order to have a game with this whirligig with some Greek boys who lived in Asia Minor? A huge rock in Boghaz-Keuy bears the name of "School-rock," and is roughly carved into a floor with walls where possibly a Hittite school once assembled.

The Hittite language is lost but may be rediscovered, as the Hittite history was lost but is being reconstructed out of fragments old and new. Hittite history is interesting as part of the history of the world, and particularly for the bearing, with that of other archaeological discoveries, upon the present trend of Old Testament studies.

We sail D[eo] V[olente] by the Pavonia to-morrow. Sincerely,
G. E. White

According to this letter, the animal heads were not among the objects given to Grinnell in 1899; or at least they were not among those about which Professor Parker had inquired. This does not, of course, preclude the possibility that they may have been donated by White, perhaps at a later date. But this is all one can say.

Of the three objects which White does mention in this letter, the "whirligig" and the seal have in the meantime disappeared. I was told that at some time in the past objects were given away by a person who had no interest in them. That the seal is lost is regrettable. According to the letter, it seems to have been an Old Hittite stamp seal with a guilloche around a single hieroglyph, a rather common type.[21]

The "whirligig" must have been a normal spindle whorl, as already noted by Mr. Banks in the letter quoted above. For parallels one no longer has to go as far as Troy.[22] The charming idea of little Hittites playing with Greek boys who lived in Asia Minor may have been a projection backward from the Reverend's own time,[23] but it also looks almost like a premonition of our present knowledge about the "Achaean" prince Tawakala-

was, who rode a chariot with the charioteer of the Hittite king![24]

The fragment of a cuneiform tablet, Spencer Collection no. 768 (ill. 6-1; fig. 6-18), finally, is a known text, one of the elusive Merzifon tablets (Merzifon is the present-day name of the place). In the preface to his *Verstreute Boghazköi-Texte*,[25] Albrecht Goetze wrote (in German): "The pieces published by Sayce on different occasions in [the *Journal of the Royal Asiatic Society*] which were in the possession of the Rev. White cannot be found. Perhaps they are in the collection of the American mission at Marzowan, which remained inaccessible to me despite all my efforts." My own efforts were equally unsuccessful. During one of the summers of 1934–1936, when I was on the excavation staff at Boğazköy, we had a visit from some teachers of the American College at Merzifon. In response to my questioning, they confirmed that the college had a few Hittite tablets. I myself visited Merzifon in the summer of 1939 together with my colleague in Ankara Wolfram Eberhard. We found the college in the process of being closed. The teacher in charge, Mr. Blake, told us that the tablets had been sent to the American College in İzmir. Professor Hardy, whom I had recently consulted, wrote that he had visited Merzifon in June of 1938 but that no mention was made of the tablets by Linda and Jack Blake, with whom he was staying. Unfortunately I never had an opportunity to pursue the matter further in İzmir.

The *Journal of the Royal Asiatic Society* in 1907 published an article entitled "Two Hittite Cuneiform Tablets from Boghaz Keui" by the Rev. Professor A. H. Sayce.[26] It begins with the words: "By the courtesy of the Rev. G. E. White, of the American College at Marsovan, I

Fig. 6-18. Grinnell, Spencer Collection, fragment of Hittite tablet no. 768

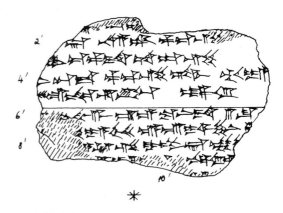

Ill. 6-1. Grinnell, Spencer Collection, fragment of Hittite tablet no. 768

have been permitted to copy a fragment of a Hittite cuneiform tablet which was picked up at Boghaz Keui, the northern capital of the Hittites." This tablet, no. I in that article, has been recognized as part of the *ḫišuwaš* festival.[27] Sayce continues: "Dr. White has also allowed me to publish a copy made by Dr. Pinches of another fragment of a tablet from Boghaz Keui which belongs to himself."[28] This is the fragment now in Grinnell! It is at first puzzling to find Sayce, in Edinburgh, publishing in 1907 a tablet that had been in Grinnell since at least 1899. The explanation is, of course, that Sayce reproduced the copy made by Pinches years earlier when, we may assume, White showed it at the British Museum.

The inscribed side of the fragment is flat, which shows that it is part of the obverse. The other side is smooth. If it is the original surface, then it comes from the uninscribed lower part of the reverse or of the last column. In that case the preserved section of the obverse would be from the upper part. But it is possible that the reverse was originally broken and was later smoothed out for better appearance.

The text is part of a ritual for a royal prince; it is listed in *CTH* under no. 647.14 (as Merzifon 1).

### Transliteration

1′     . . . ]x an-x[   (or ᴰx[ )
2′     . . . ]-kán na-a-wi₅ pa-iz-zi
3′     . . . DUMU].LUGAL^(GIŠ)PA-it ša-ap-zi
4′     . . . pár?]-ni an-da pa-iz-zi ta-aš ti-ia[-zi
5′     . . . . . . . M]EŠ ^(URU)Ne-ri-iq-qa SÌR-RU
_____
6′     . . . ]x ^(LÚ)GUDU₄ ú-e-te-ni-it 3-ŠU [
7′     . . . šu-up-p]í-ia-aḫ-ḫi kal-ú-i-ši-in x[
8′     pa-ra-a ] e-ep-zi DUMU.LUGAL tuḫ^u[^ḫ-ša
9′     . . . ]x x x    x ka-ru-ú[

### Translation

(2′) [. . .] has not yet gone (3′) [The . . .] hits the [pri]nce with a stick. (4′) [. . .] goes into the [ho]use (*or*: temp]le), and he takes a stand. (5′) [The singer]s(? *or*: me]n) of Nerik sing.

_____

(6′–8′) [. . .] the 'anointed' (priest) [pur]ifies [the prince(?)] three times with water. He [pro]ffers the *kalwiši* [to the prince(?)], the prince cut[s (some) off]. (9′) . . . already [. . .

In the *Journal of the Royal Asiatic Society* for 1909, Sayce published nine Boğazköy fragments, of which, however, only nos. 3–5 were in White's possession. Thus, a total of five Boğazköy tablets were published as belonging to him: two in 1907 and three in 1909. One of them is the one at Grinnell College. Will the others also turn up, somewhere, some day?

### NOTES

It was arranged that I could study the Hittite objects at Grinnell College, together with Professor Robert L. Alexander, on 12 December, 1983. Locally, we had the help of Professor Gerald

Lalonde of the Department of Classics, who kindly gave us the use of his office, and of Professor Ralph Luebben, of the Department of Anthropology, who had the objects sent over from the Spencer Collection, which is kept in his department. Professor Alexander took the photographs that accompany this discussion and helped me in many ways. In addition, he made available to me catalogue entries prepared by Christopher Parslow, now a graduate student in classics at Duke University, while he was an undergraduate at Grinnell College. Professor Lalonde gave me photostats of a letter by the Reverend Professor G. E. White and one by Edgar J. Banks, which are kept in the Spencer Collection and pertain to the objects in question. To all these colleagues I wish to express my sincere thanks.

1 T. Özgüç, *Maşat Höyük* 2 (TTKY Ser. V, 38a, Ankara 1982) pl. 87.2 and fig. 164 a–b; R. M. Boehmer, *Die Reliefkeramik von Boğazköy* (*Boğazköy-Ḫattuša* 13, Berlin 1983) 46 fig. 37.
2 F. Fischer, *Die hethitische Keramik von Boğazköy* (*Boğazköy-Ḫattuša* 4 = WVDOG 75, Berlin 1963; hereafter cited as "Fischer" with catalogue number) 156–58, pls. 131–36, esp. nos. 1247 (p. 155, pl. 131), 1265, 1288, 1302.
3 H. Z. Koşay, *Alaca Höyük Kazısı 1937–1939* = *Les fouilles d'Alaca Höyük 1937–1939* (TTKY, Ser. V, 5, Ankara 1951) pls. 68–69.
4 See Fischer nos. 1302, 1320, 1335.
5 I am grateful to Professor Alexander for sharing his observations with me.
6 H. G. Güterbock, *Siegel aus Boğazköy* 2.1 (Berlin 1942) 6, 65, no. 1; the seal is omitted in T. Beran, *Die hethitische Glyptik von Boğazköy* (*Boğazköy-Ḫattuša* 5 = WVDOG 76, Berlin 1967).
7 O. W. Muscarella, *Ancient Art: The Norbert Schimmel Collection* (New York 1974) no. 124; K. Bittel, *Les Hittites* (Paris 1976 = *Die Hethiter*, Munich 1976; hereafter cited as "Bittel" with number) fig. 178.
8 Bittel fig. 179.
9 Fischer nos. 1303, 1315, 1318, 1329, 1335.
10 H. H. von der Osten, *The Alishar Hüyük. Seasons of 1930–32* part 2 (OIP 29, Chicago 1937; hereafter cited as OIP 29) 121–23, figs. 163–65.
11 E. Chantre, *Mission en Cappadoce 1893–1894* (Paris 1898) pls. 15–16, "Tell de Kara Euyuk," i.e., Kültepe; T. Özgüç, *Kültepe Kazısı Raporu 1948* (TTKY, Ser. V, 10, Ankara 1950) pl. 40; fig. 164 (p. 175), pl. 66, fig. 427 (p. 175: Level I).
12 Özgüç (supra n. 11) pl. 67 fig. 433 (p. 188), and T. Özgüç, *Kültepe-Kaniş* (TTKY, ser. V, 19, Ankara 1959) pl. 42 = Bittel fig. 55; and Bittel fig. 71, all Level II.
13 P. Neve, "Die Grabungen auf Büyükkale 1963," *MDOG* 95 (1965) 48–53 and figs. 12–14; Bittel fig. 156.
14 In the Ankara Museum; *The Anatolian Civilizations* I (exhibition catalogue, Ankara 1983) 238–39, nos. A 637–38.
15 Fischer, nos. 1255, 1257, 1266–72, 1287, 1294; the two examples with bases are nos. 1265 and 1287.
16 C.-G. von Brandenstein, *Hethitische Götter nach Bildbeschreibungen in Keilschrifttexten* (MVAG 46.2, 1943) 30–32.
17 Chantre (supra n. 11) pl. 18.14.
18 Özgüç (supra n. 1) pl. 53.2 and p. 110.
19 Banks in his letter writes about a tablet which he calls Assyrian of about 650 B.C. and which includes names of some Assyrian gods. Yet the letter then lists the whorl, the heads of statuettes, and the heads of "cattle." Did he mistake the Hittite cuneiform for Neo-Assyrian, and the *AN* signs of lines 1′ and 4′ for divine determinatives? Or had he another fragment before him?
20 I thank the authorities of Grinnell College for the permission to quote this letter and the passage from the other.
21 Examples are in Beran (supra n. 6) pls. 9 and II.

22 Whorls from Alishar: OIP 29, 450–52, figs. 504–506; from Höyük: Koşay (supra n. 3) pls. 90–93, 113–15.

23 According to information supplied by Robert S. Hardy, formerly of Robert College, Istanbul, White moved to Greece following his congregation, who were part of the transfer of populations under the agreements of the League of Nations.

24 See, most recently, H. G. Güterbock, "The Hittites and the Aegean World: 1. The Ahhiyawa Problem Reconsidered," *AJA* 87 (1983) 136.

25 A. Götze, *Verstreute Boghazköi-Texte* (Marburg and Lahn 1930; hereafter cited as *VBoT*) iv.

26 A. H. Sayce, "Two Hittite Cuneiform Tablets from Boghaz Keui," *JRAS* (1907) 913–21.

27 E. Laroche, *Catalogue des textes hittites* (Paris 1971; hereafter cited as *CTH*) 111, no. 628 II c 8, as "Merzifon 2"; it was edited by A. Dinçol, *JCS* 24 (1971) 29–30. In *JRAS* (1908) 985–95, Sayce published a fragment which had come into his possession. He wrote that it "is shown by its contents to belong to the same tablet as that of which I have published another portion in [*JRAS*] 1907, 919, 920." This observation is correct in that the fragment at least belongs to the same series: cf. Laroche, *CTH*, 111, sub no. 628, where *VBoT* (Götze, supra n. 25) no. 89 is the fragment first published in 1908. Sayce's own tablets from Boğazköy came into the Ashmolean Museum, Oxford, in 1933.

28 Sayce (supra n. 26) 918 under no. II.

# Three Hittite Cylinder Seals in the Istanbul Archaeological Museum

## 7

EDIBE UZUNOĞLU

The three seals which I publish here in tribute to Machteld Mellink are in the Department of the Ancient Orient at the Istanbul Archaeological Museum. Two date to the Hittite Empire period and one to the later, Neo-Hittite period.[1]

The cylindrical sealing device characteristic of Mesopotamia and Syria was dominant in these areas from the end of the fourth millennium B.C. until the second quarter of the first millennium B.C. In Anatolia, however, the stamp seal was the standard type from the beginning. Only in the Old Assyrian Colony period, in the first quarter of the second millennium B.C., was the cylinder seal much used in Anatolia. Very few cylinder seals have been found at the Hittite capital, Hattuša.[2] They were, however, used at Carchemish[3] and other vassal kingdoms of the Hittite empire in Syria. These two new examples of Hittite cylinder seals are therefore an important addition to a rare group of objects which I hope will be of interest to Machteld Mellink.[4]

## I

Our first example is a steatite cylinder seal (inv. no. 12473; purchased), 2.9 cm high and 1.2 cm in diameter (figs. 7-1 and 7-2; ill. 7-1). It has a border consisting of double parallel lines above and below, and a single line separates it into two registers. The top register shows two winged genii flanking an altar topped by a winged sun disc. The conical altar flares slightly at the shoulder and terminates in a point. This type of altar is known from representations on seal impressions, various relief scenes, and actual examples from Emirgazi.[5] Two horn-like appendages protruding from the top of the altar may be branches. Two outward-curving objects (floral elements?) flank the bottom of the altar. Irregular hori-

zontal striations decorate the altar. Basically this object represents a synthesis of the tree of life motif and a typically Anatolian altar.[6] The two winged creatures flanking the altar and supporting the winged sun disc above it wear conical, single-horned headdresses. Their legs and heads are in profile, whereas the bodies are shown frontally. The headdress on the left-hand figure is more clearly depicted.[7] The faces are characteristically Hittite, with a large nose continuing from the forehead and large, almond-shaped eyes. One wing spreads up to the border above, while the other droops down to the ground line.[8] The interior of the wings is filled with horizontal and vertical lines. A bow-shaped curved object (a crook?) with a forked edge is held in the forward hand. The object held by the figure to the left of the altar is clearer.[9] The calf muscles of the legs have been given special emphasis, and their large feet are shod in boots with upturned toes. A crescent appears above each creature near the winged disc, which is depicted as two concentric circles with a cross in the middle.[10] Its wings are represented by two horizontal and three vertical striations. A griffin walking to the right fills the space left in the upper register and at the same time constitutes the end of the scene.[11] It wears a high-peaked headdress,[12] and its upward-turning wing has been rendered like the other wings on the seal. The front legs have the talons of a bird, whereas the rear ones are shaped like lions' claws. The tail is a round, feathery fluff.

The subject of the upper register is characteristic in fourteenth- and thirteenth-century Hittite art and represents the glorification—through worship by composite creatures—of the winged disc.[13] A group of cylinder seals from Alalakh, dating to the fourteenth and thirteenth centuries B.C., resemble this seal in both linear style and subject matter.[14]

Fig. 7-1. Istanbul Archaeological Museum, inv. no. 12473, steatite cylinder seal

The row of animals walking to the right in the bottom register of the Istanbul seal is the second-millennium Syrian version of a common third-millennium Mesopotamian theme.[15] The file begins with a rampant stag, followed by a griffin, a stag and a wild goat, and an eagle with wings akimbo. The fillers include a bird, a scorpion, a fish, and floral motifs. A scorpion and crescent moon appear near the griffin; a plant and an eagle near the wild goat. The file of animals, based on Mesopotamian prototypes, also appears in the Old Syrian,[16] Cappadocian,[17] and Hurro-Mitannian milieux,[18] these styles being the intermediaries through which the motif entered Hittite art.[19] Similar features appear on a North Syrian group of seals which is difficult to date.[20] Our seal exhibits affinities to Mesopotamian, Syrian, and Hurro-Mitannian styles. This fourteenth- or thirteenth-century

Fig. 7-2. Istanbul Archaeological Museum, inv. no. 12473, steatite cylinder seal (impression)

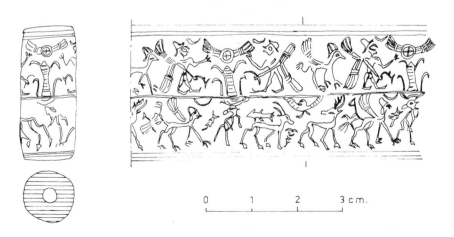

0    1    2    3 cm.

Ill. 7-1. Istanbul Archaeological Museum, inv. no. 12473, steatite cylinder seal

Hittite seal was most likely made in the vicinity of Al-alakh or Carchemish.

## II

Our second example is a dark gray steatite cylinder seal (inv. no. 1955; provenance unknown), 2.5 cm high and 1.1 cm in diameter (figs. 7-3 and 7-4; ill. 7-2). In the middle of the drawing (ill. 7-2) is a sphinx above a lion; the seal is damaged below the lion so that only the body and the tip of the upward-curled tail are visible.[21] There is a sign between the sphinx and the lion. A deity approaches the animals from the left. His legs and face are depicted in profile, and the body is shown frontally. He wears a headdress with two rows of horns.[22] A large nose protrudes, and arms emerge from below a thin neck.

Fig. 7-3. Istanbul Archaeological Museum, inv. no. 1995, steatite cylinder seal

Fig. 7-4. Istanbul Archaeological Museum, inv. no. 1995, steatite cylinder seal (impression)

Ill. 7-2. Istanbul Archaeological Museum, inv. no. 1995, steatite cylinder seal

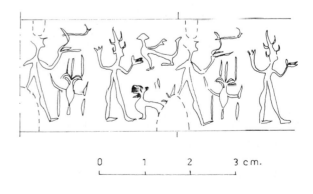

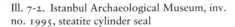
0    1    2    3 cm.

over their heads.[23] Behind the deity appears a double-headed eagle,[24] with three vertical lines protruding from the heads. These lines probably have no relationship to the eagle itself. To the extreme left another figure appears, walking to the right. The damage to the seal in this area has obliterated the right leg and head, but the lower front horn of the headdress is partly visible. Only the nose is evident on the face. The right arm is bent to the chest, while the left is extended toward the sphinx; the left hand, which is empty, has three fingers. The stance resembles Hittite Imperial deities of the thirteenth century who hold a weapon in the hand at waist level and have a symbol over the extended left hand.[25] Although the seal is unfinished, there are enough features typical of the thirteenth century to permit chronological assignment.

### III

Another steatite cylinder seal (inv. no. 6948) is our third example. It was found at Carchemish, and acquired by the museum in 1914; there is no record of the excava-

Fig. 7-5. Istanbul Archaeological Museum, inv. no. 6948, steatite cylinder seal

Fig. 7-6. Istanbul Archaeological Museum, inv. no. 6948, steatite cylinder seal (impression)

The right arm is raised but holds nothing. The left arm is bent at the elbow, and the three fingers are extended toward the sphinx. There is no indication of a garment, but boots with upturned toes are visible. The stance resembles that of Hittite deities normally depicted with a symbol denoting their identity, a mace or an axe, raised

tion find-spot. The dimensions are 3.8 cm by 1.5 cm (figs. 7-5 and 7-6; ill. 7-3).

The seal portrays a bull hunt by chariot, rendered in a linear style. The two-horse chariot has a six-spoked wheel. The front of the chariot is S-shaped and curves upward. A driver and a bowman shooting to the rear ap-

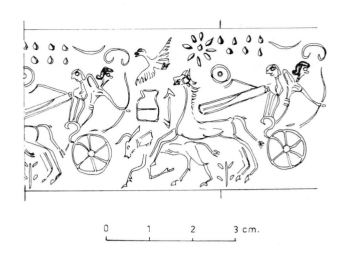

Ill. 7-3. Istanbul Archaeological Museum, inv. no. 6948, steatite cylinder seal

pear in the chariot, which is overtaking a falling bull. The hunters have shoulder-length hair and bangs. The horse trappings are distinctly delineated. A crescent, seven dots (representing seven stars), and an eight-pointed star are above the horse; a bird, probably a hawk, flies behind the chariot. The bull and the outer horse have been expertly distinguished. In the space between the rear legs of the bull and horse is a floral motif. Hittite hieroglyphs appear above and in front of the horse; they are discussed in the appendix to this article.

The seal has characteristics of the Neo-Assyrian style of the time of Assurnasirpal II in the ninth century B.C. The six-spoked wheel occurs in ninth-century B.C. Neo-Assyrian[26] and Neo-Hittite[27] art, and the motif of a hunting bowman is typical of Neo-Assyrian reliefs and seals.[28] The astral symbols and the filler motifs are also characteristic of this style.[29] The hairstyle of the hunters is, however, better paralleled in the long wall reliefs at Carchemish depicting battle and hunting scenes with chariots.[30] These reliefs have recently been dated to the period of King Suhis II and Katuwas—that is, to before 870 B.C.[31] The reliefs of the lion gate at Malatya are also of about the same date. With the help of parallels with the art of Carchemish and other Late Hittite sites, as well as Neo-Assyrian glyptic and reliefs, we can date this seal to a time span ranging from the second half of the tenth century B.C. to the first half of the ninth century B.C. An unprovenanced cylinder in the Moore Collection, on loan to the Metropolitan Museum of Art, (fig. 7-7),[32] can now be classified as coming from Carchemish, like our seal.[33]

### NOTES

I wish to thank Ali and Belkıs Dinçol for writing the appendix to this paper, Ayşe Haznedar Özkan for the drawings, Turhan Birgili

Fig. 7-7. Assyrian cylinder seal (collection of Mrs. William H. Moore. Lent to the Metropolitan Museum of Art by Rt. Rev. Paul Moore, Jr.)

for the photographs, and Aslıhan Yener for translating my text into English.

1 For a seal impression with the same subject, see E. Uzunoğlu, "Die Abrollung eines hethitischen Siegels auf einem Pithos," *IstMitt* 29 (1979) 65–75, pls. 8–9.
2 T. Beran, "Hethitische Rollsiegel der Grossreichzeit," *IstMitt* 8 (1958) 137–41, pl. 35; H. G. Güterbock, *Siegel aus Boğazköy* 2 (*AfO*-BH 7, Berlin 1942) 78–79, pl. 7.122, no. 235.
3 C. F. A. Schaeffer et al., *Ugaritica* 3 (Mission de Ras Shamra 7, Paris 1956) 23–30, 46–52; figs. 30–37, 63–73. For the use of both seal types by the kings of Carchemish, see Beran (supra n. 2) 137–38.
4 E. Porada, "The Cylinder Seals Found at Thebes in Boeotia," *AfO* 28 (1981–1982) 46–49, no. 25; G. Beckman, "A Hittite Cylinder Seal in the Yale Babylonian Collection," *AnatSt* 31 (1981) 129–35, pl. 20; D. Beyer, "Notes préliminaires sur les empreintes de sceaux de Meskéné," in J. C. Margueron ed., *Le moyen Euphrate. Zone de contacts et d'échanges. Actes du Colloque de Strasbourg, 10–12 Mars 1977* (Leiden 1980) 265–83, and "Les empreintes de sceaux," in D. Beyer ed., *Meskéné-Emar, Dix ans de travaux, 1972–1982* (Paris 1982) 61–68. On the Hittite stamp cylinder, see R. L. Alexander, "The Tyskiewicz Group of Stamp-Cylinders," *Anatolica* 5 (1973–1976) 141–214, pls. 1–4.

5 E. Masson, "Les inscriptions louvites hiéroglyphique d'Emir-gazi," *Journal des Savants* 1979, pls. 11, 12c, fig. 1. For the reliefs, see K. Bittel, *Die Hethiter* (Munich 1976) figs. 198, 214, 230. For the seals, see R. M. Boehmer, "Kleinasiatische Glyptik," in W. Orthmann ed., *Der Alte Orient* (PK 14, Berlin 1975) 437–57, nos. 375, 376a.

6 The closest parallel for this motif occurs on a silver plaque from Syria: W. Andrae, *Die Kleinfunde von Sendschirli* (Ausgrabungen in Sendschirli 5, Berlin 1943) 103, pl. 47b. For floral motifs on Syrian, Kassite, and Hurro-Mitannian seals, see H. H. von der Osten, *The Ancient Oriental Seals in the Collection of E. T. Newell* (OIP 22, Chicago 1934) no. 417, and *Altorientalische Siegelsteine der Sammlung Hans Silvius von Aulock* (Uppsala 1957) nos. 290, 307; W. E. Forte, *Ancient Near Eastern Seals. A Selection of Stamp and Cylinder Seals from the Collection of Mrs. William H. Moore* (Metropolitan Museum of Art, New York 1976) no. 12.

7 For the headdress of King Shulumeli, see T. H. Bossert, *Altanatolien* (Berlin 1942) nos. 267–71; R. M. Boehmer, "Hörnerkrone," in *RLA* 4 (1975) 432, no. 36.

8 Similar wings appear on Middle and Neo-Assyrian genii: E. Strommenger, *Fünf Jahrtausende Mesopotamien* (Munich 1962) 186, 191, 192.

9 It is possibly a *lituus*: Bittel (supra n. 5) pls. 167–68; B. Buchanan, *Early Near Eastern Seals in the Yale Babylonian Collection* (London 1981) nos. 1244, 1248; von der Osten 1934 (supra n. 6) nos. 207, 226, 246.

10 This is a Hittite winged disc: Bittel (supra n. 5) nos. 234, 242, 243, 246; Uzunoğlu (supra n. 1) pl. 9.2, fig. 2; Porada (supra n. 4) 47, 48.

11 On meaning and iconography, see J. Börker-Klähn, "Greif," *RLA* 3 (1971) 637, no. 6.

12 For a similar headdress on a sphinx, see W. Orthmann, "Hethitisches Kunsthandwerk," in Orthmann ed. (supra n. 5) pl. 372a.

13 Bittel (supra n. 5) pls. 246, 257, 341; Orthmann (supra n. 5) pl. 372a, b; Boehmer (supra n. 5) pl. 375d.

14 B. Buchanan, *Catalogue of the Ancient Near Eastern Seals in the Ashmolean Museum 1. Cylinder Seals* (Oxford 1966) nos. 849–52; D. Collon, *The Alalakh Cylinder Seals* (BAR 132, Oxford 1982) nos. 106–9.

15 E. Porada, *Corpus of Ancient Near Eastern Seals in North American Collections 1. The Collection of the Pierpont Morgan Library* (Washington, D.C., 1948) nos. 17–21, 89, 103, 104, 105 E, 108 E, 116; A. Moortgat, *Vorderasiatische Rollsiegel* (Berlin 1940) nos. 9–19, 26–28; von der Osten (supra n. 6) no. 51.

16 Buchanan (supra n. 14) nos. 849–52.

17 N. Özgüç, *The Anatolian Group of Cylinder Seal Impressions from Kültepe* (TTKY ser. V, 22, Ankara 1965) nos. 94–97.

18 Collon (supra n. 14) no. 75; Buchanan (supra n. 14) nos. 942–48.

19 Bittel (supra n. 5) pl. 187; cf. R. M. Boehmer, *Die Reliefkeramik von Boğazköy. Grabungskampagnen 1906–1912, 1931–1939, 1952–1978* (Berlin 1983) pls. 20–34.

20 Cf. Buchanan (supra n. 14) nos. 1021–25.

21 A seal from Meskene-Emar bears the depiction of a griffin and a lion: Beyer 1982 (supra n. 4) 67, fig. 13. For other Hittite lions, see Bittel (supra n. 5) pls. 188, 236, 237.

22 Boehmer (supra n. 7) 432, no. 34; Bittel (supra n. 5) pls. 191, 193, 207.

23 Bittel (supra n. 5) pls. 183, 193.

24 This motif appears in many different media in Hittite art: Bittel (supra n. 5) pls. 76, 78, 215. It was also used as a decorative border on the Tabrammi seal: Schaeffer (supra n. 3) 55, figs. 76–77.

25 Cf. Bittel (supra n. 5) pls. 182, 186, 194, 206–7.

26 Strommenger (supra n. 8) pl. 202 above and middle; L. Delaporte, *Catalogue des cylindres orientaux et de cachets de la Bibliothèque Nationale* (Paris 1910) no. 372; Porada (supra n. 15) 659–63.

27 D. G. Hogarth et al., *Carchemish 3* (London 1952) pl. B. 41a, 42a, b; Bossert (supra n. 7) pls. 764, 767.

28 See examples cited supra nn. 26 and 27.

29 Porada (supra n. 15) nos. 653, 661, 662.

30 See examples cited supra n. 27.

31 J. D. Hawkins, "Karkamiš," *RLA* 5 (1976–1980) 439–42.

32 G. A. Eisen, *Ancient Oriental Cylinder and Other Seals with a Description of the Collection of Mrs. William H. Moore* (OIP 47, Chicago 1940) no. 74.

33 The classification of this seal was made by Edith Porada at a lecture on the Moore seals at the Metropolitan Museum of Art, New York.

# Appendix: The Hieroglyphic Inscription on Cylinder Seal No. 6948

ALI M. DINÇOL and BELKIS DINÇOL

Cylinder seal no. 6948, according to the records of the Istanbul Archaeological Museum, came from Carchemish and represents one more example of inscribed Hittite cylinders, which are relatively rare.[1] This shape was not in common use in Hatti proper and is evidence of Mesopotamian influence on the customs of the Hittites.

Hieroglyphic signs are clearly seen both on the cylinder and on its impression. L.327 and L.377 appear in front of the horse harnessed to the chariot, and L.363 above the head of the figure with the bow. In 1942 I. Gelb argued that sign L.327 means SEAL, and he furnished additional supporting evidence in 1949.[2] Despite some disagreement,[3] Gelb's proposal was generally accepted.[4] On two seals[5] sign L.327 is accompanied by L.377, to which the phonetic value "za" was recently ascribed on the basis of the Altıntepe graffiti—a value confirmed by the bigraphic seals of Meskene-Emar.[6] The combination of these two signs was interpreted by Gelb as the ideogram for SEAL and its phonetic complement, and this suggestion has not been questioned.[7] After the "small revolution"[8] in the values of L.376 (and consequently that of L.377), the signs in question are now to be read SEAL-za, which stands for the phonetic writing sasaza.[9] On the seals mentioned above, this word is used in the formula "za-wa SEAL-za PN," which means: "this (is) the seal (of) PN."

Obviously the conventional function of an inscribed seal was to give the name and/or title of its owner. It is therefore surprising that this word occurs on our seal without any other sign representing the name of its user. The absence of a personal name would not be as strange if a full official title were given, as in the case of the anonymous tabarna seals. Here, on the contrary, only the sign L.363 (GREAT) may be part of a title. We are inclined to think that the sign GREAT in combination with the hunting figure may represent a title. An official GAL$^{l\acute{u}}$ŞA'IDU ("great hunter") is not attested among the Hittites of the Imperial and the Late Hittite periods, but since hunting was a royal activity in Assyria, a hunting figure may have symbolized a member of the royal family and/or an officer of a higher rank at Carchemish, which was culturally linked with Syria.

Such a combination of a hieroglyphic sign with a "real" depiction would, however, be unique, and such "playful" writing suggests another possibility related to the word SEAL-za. These signs could be a personal name, $Sa_5$-za, if the sign L.327 is read phonetically ($sa_5$). In this case the two signs may represent both the personal name and the word SEAL at the same time, thus meaning "(This is) the SEAL (of) Saza." Unfortunately, this interpretation can be supported neither by a parallel nor by evidence that a personal name Saza existed.[10]

## NOTES

1 For a list of hitherto-unknown Hittite cylinder seals, see G. Beckman, "A Hittite Cylinder Seal in the Yale Babylonian Collection," *AnatSt* 31 (1981) 131. For the seal impressions from Meskene, see Beyer, "Notes préliminaires sur les empreintes de sceaux de Méskéne," in J. C. Margueron ed., *Le moyen Euphrate. Zone de contacts et d'échanges. Actes du Colloque de Strasbourg 10–12 Mars 1977* (Leiden 1980) 265–83, and "Les empreintes de sceaux," in D. Beyer ed., *Meskéné-Emar, Dix ans de travaux, 1972–1982* (Paris 1982).

2 I. J. Gelb, "The Word for Seal in Hieroglyphic Hittite," *Orientalia* n.s. 18 (1949) 68–72.

3 See, e.g., H. T. Bossert, *Asia* (Istanbul 1946) 150–51.

4 *HH* no. 327; Meriggi, *Glossar* 2, no. 346.

5 Gelb (supra n. 2) figs. 4, 5; cf. also fig. 6.

6 J. D. Hawkins, A. Morpurgo-Davies, and G. Neumann, *Hittite Hieroglyphs and Luwian: New Evidence for the Connection* (Göttingen 1973) 50, table 1, and 153–56; J. D. Hawkins and A. Morpurgo-Davies, "Hieroglyphic Hittite: Some New Readings and Their Consequences," *JRAS* 1975, 121–33; J. D. Hawkins, "The Negatives in Hieroglyphic Luwian," *AnatSt* 25 (1975) 119–56, esp. 154–55, table 2; A. Morpurgo-Davies and J. D. Hawkins, "Il sistema grafico del luvio geroglifico," *AnnPisa* 3.3 (1978) 767–82; E. Laroche, "Les hiéroglyphes de Meskene-Emar et le style Syro-Hittite," *Akkadica* 22 (1981) 13, and "Documents Hittites et Hourrites," in Beyer ed. 1982 (supra n. 1) 57, no. 10; also "Langues et civilisation de l'Asie Mineure," in *Annuaire du College de France* 1981–82, 526–27.

7 See Meriggi, *Glossar* 2, 108 (where the first reference is not the sign M.346 but undoubtedly L.326 = SCRIBE, as correctly drawn by S. Alp, *Zur Lesung von manchen Personennamen auf den hieroglyphenhethitischen Siegeln und Inschriften* [Ankara 1950] fig. 82, and later by D. Kennedy, "Sceaux hittites conservés à Paris," 65 [1959] no. 12); see also Laroche (supra n. 4) 327.

8 The expression is Laroche's, in *Annuaire* (supra n. 6) 526–27.

9 P. Meriggi, *Schizzo grammaticale dell'Anatolico* (Rome 1980) 276; M. Poetto, *La collezione anatolica di E. Borowski* (Pavia 1981) 37 n. 65; Morpurgo-Davies and Hawkins 1978 (supra n. 6) 777.

10 A similar-sounding name, *Sasi*, the king of Unqi, occurs in the Assyrian records; J. D. Hawkins, "Assyrians and Hittites," *Iraq* 36 (1974) 81.

# A Subject for Continuing Conversation

## 8

EDITH PORADA

The main subject of this essay is a cylinder seal of Middle Assyrian style exhibiting what appear to be Hittite elements in its design. A full understanding of the seal and its likely historical background requires the encyclopedic knowledge and insights of Machteld Mellink. Conversations led by her about the problems involved, conversations that belong to the joys of this writer's life, however, will continue. Here only details of style and ramifications of the subject matter are discussed.

Before we proceed to the analysis of the cylinder, let us first briefly review the historical relationship between the Assyrians and Anatolia. The fullest textual evidence comes from the tablets of the Old Assyrian merchant colonies. Texts were found in the last two of four levels excavated at the site of Kültepe in the plain of Kayseri. Assyrian merchants resident at Kültepe called the area of the site in which they lived Karum Kaneš. The older of the two levels—Karum II—lasted from approximately 1920 to 1840 B.C.,[1] when the area was destroyed. A second Karum—phase I b—was established on the same site about fifty years later, in the time of the great Šamši-Adad I of Assyria, who dominated northern Mesopotamia, including Mari on the border of Syria, for thirty-three years after about 1813 B.C.[2] K. R. Veenhof describes the partial integration of the merchants with the local population through occasional marriages with Anatolians.[3] No material evidence remains, however, of these contacts between Assyrians and Anatolians except for the styles of cylinder seals. Of the various styles used on the tablets from Kültepe, only the sharply gouged Early and Late Old Assyrian styles[4] were also used on those of some Babylonian towns.[5] A Late Old Assyrian cylinder

was found at Ga.sur,[6] an Old Assyrian town later called Nuzi. But only Assur has also yielded some seals of other styles used in the Karum Kaneš: the Old Syrian[7] and the Anatolian.[8] Curiously, only a single typically Late Old Assyrian cylinder[9] was excavated at Assur.

The Karum Kaneš was part of the town of Neša, the seat of princes who appear in Hittite historical sources at the inception of the Old Hittite kingdom.[10] The Hittites had probably immigrated to Anatolia in the middle of the third millennium B.C. In 1956 Machteld Mellink explored the possibility of associating the first intrusion of the Hittites with the princely graves of Alaca Höyük.[11] She pointed out some of the features supporting such a contention—for example, the distinctive subterranean chamber tombs, which differ from early burial types common in Anatolia, but could be compared to graves in the Kuban region of the northern Caucasus area, as well as later ones at Mycenae and, in the first millennium, those of the Phrygians and Scythians. But she left open the problem of the association of the Alaca Höyük tombs with the Hittites, although elsewhere[12] she drew attention to the continuation in later Hittite art of the depiction of the red deer stags and bulls earlier seen in the magnificent standard finials from the Alaca Höyük tombs.

The history of the Old Hittite kingdom can be partly reconstructed from cuneiform records found in the later Hittite capital of Hattuša (modern Boğazköy)[13] and other sites. This phase of Hittite rule culminated under Hattušili I, who seems to have unified the country and who incorporated areas of northern Syria such as Alalakh (modern Atchana in the Aleppo region) into his kingdom about 1650 B.C. He brought rich treasures from the temples and palaces of the conquered towns to the temples of the Hittite deities. The expansive phase of the Old Hittite kingdom terminated with Muršili I, adoptive son of Hattušili, who continued his predecessor's military successes in Syria and proceeded to Babylon, which he destroyed in a conflagration in 1595 B.C. Muršili was murdered shortly thereafter, an event that initiated a period of internecine feuds in the Hittite royal family and ultimately weakened the country. This situation was reversed by Telepinu (ca. 1515–1500 B.C.), who created a rule of succession for the throne that was retained until the end of the Hittite empire. The beginning of the empire is generally placed about 1400 B.C., but the actual founder of the Hittite realm as a major power was Šuppiluliuma I (ca. 1380–1340 B.C.), who made the Hittite country the most powerful state of the age: he extended its frontiers to northern Syria and its influence to northern Mesopotamia at the expense of the Mitannian empire. After the fall of Babylon in 1595, Kassites had taken over the rule of Babylonia, and Mitannians dominated northern Mesopotamia and parts of Syria. Assyria was completely surrounded by the Mitannian empire, but, as is known from later Assyrian king lists, it maintained its autochthonous kings. These kings were probably tributaries of the Mitannians, although the extent to which they were dependent on their overlords appears to have varied.[14]

Relations between Assyrians and Hittites in the following centuries were summarized by P. Machinist as follows[15]: in the period from Assur-uballit to Shalmaneser I (1273–1244 B.C.), Assyria sought to gain hegemony over the area occupied by Mitanni-Hanigalbat and then, under Tukulti Ninurta I (1243–1207 B.C.), to extend its power farther into the upper Euphrates and Tigris regions. The Hittite response was both diplomatic and military. There was also an economic reaction, attested in the documents bearing on the period of Tukulti Ninurta I and in the sanctions that the Hittite king Tuthaliya IV established against the Assyrian king in an attempt to cut off the latter's access to Syrian and Mediterranean trade. According to Machinist, whether or not there was a cultural dimension to Assyrian-Hittite contact remains problematic, since little contact of any kind can be demonstrated.

The only object of Hittite art known to have been found in levels of the Middle Assyrian period is a small relief of lapis lazuli from the Ištar Temple at Assur, showing a Hittite god holding a hare and a bird.[16] It is therefore all the more interesting that Hittite elements appear in a cylinder seal of Middle Assyrian style acquired at Nineveh by F. J. Jones of the Indian Navy, who in 1846 and 1848 mapped the course of the Tigris and the contours of the terrain covering the ruins of Nineveh (fig. 8-1; ill. 8-1). The cylinder was acquired by the British Mu-

Fig. 8-1. Modern impression of the carnelian cylinder seal British Museum 89806, bought at Nineveh between 1846 and 1848; enlarged a little less than 1:3. (Published here with the kind permission of Terence Mitchell, acting keeper of Western Asiatic Antiquities, the British Museum)

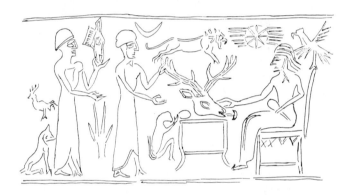

Ill. 8-1. Nineveh, Middle Assyrian cylinder seal, British Museum 89806: drawing of the impression. (Published here with the kind permission of Terence Mitchell, acting keeper of Western Asiatic Antiquities, the British Museum)

seum in 1854.[17] The seal, made of carnelian, is 2.1 cm high and has a diameter of 1.0 cm.

The scene engraved on the cylinder shows an important personage—probably a ruler, since he lacks a divine headdress—enthroned on a high-backed chair. In front of him is a table on which an attendant deposits the head of a stag, out of whose mouth protrudes the crescent-shaped handle of a dagger. This object resembles Hittite daggers more than Assyrian ones.[18] The cake or roll on the table beside the stag head may indicate that the head is part of a meal set out before the ruler. Furthermore, the cylinder shows the head of a second animal, which I take to be a horse, brought by a second attendant. This head is probably a vessel. It looks manmade (note espe-

Fig. 8-2. Silver vessel in the form of a stag protome with a drinking cup attached, New York, Metropolitan Museum of Art, Norbert Schimmel Collection. (Photograph courtesy of Norbert Schimmel)

Fig. 8-3. Stag Vessel, New York Metropolitan Museum of Art, Norbert Schimmel Collection (detail). (Photograph courtesy of Norbert Schimmel)

cially the pattern on the neck) and may represent a decorated cup, joined to the head in the manner of the stag head vessel of the Norbert Schimmel Collection (figs. 8-2 and 8-3). Moreover, the vessel is supported by the attendant's cupped hand. This is how cups are shown being raised on ivories from Megiddo (ills. 8-2 and 8-3). It is different, however, from the manner in which a Hittite offering bearer carries an animal head in the fragment of a Hittite relief vase of bronze from Boğazköy-Hattuša (ill. 8-4). As is more obvious in a photograph of this fragment, the head looks like that of a sheep, which is still considered a great delicacy in the Near East. It is not impossible, then, that the different gestures indicate different types of objects.[19]

One of the Megiddo ivories (ill. 8-2) also shows that drinking vessels in the shape of animal heads were used in Syria-Palestine in what seems to have been a royal banquet. They were carried above the large jar that presumably held the liquid to be consumed at the feast.

In the cylinder from Nineveh, a monkey sits beside the table with its hand raised toward the bread roll or cake on the table. A dog sits behind the second attendant, and a cock appears in the field above. A bird of prey with spread wings extends its foot toward the top of the ruler's chair. The bird forms a visual counterweight to a lion leaping through the upper field above the stag's head on the other side of a winged disc with an inscribed eight-pointed star. A moon crescent also appears in the sky. A highly schematized frontal gazelle head between the two attendants may be a later addition. The size and distribution of the figures find their closest affinities in impressions of cylinder seals on tablets from Assur, dated to the thirteenth century B.C.[20] Several features point to that date. The high-backed chair is characteristic of the Middle Assyrian period; see, for example, a sealing of the thirteenth century from Assur, the drawing of which (ill. 8-5) shows only partly the pendant fringe bound in small tassels below the bottom of the seat. A clearer indication of such a fringe occurs on another thirteenth century sealing (ill. 8-6), which resembles the Nineveh cylinder in that it depicts two attendants, one carrying a vessel.

Another characteristic piece of furniture is the table, the legs of which curve in before splaying out at the bottom in imitation of lions' legs. A more detailed representation of this type of table is seen on a sealing from Assur (ill. 8-7), dated on stylistic grounds to the thirteenth century B.C.[21] Both the chair and the table recur on the

Ill. 8-2. Incised ivory plaque, probably from a footstool, from Megiddo. (Reproduced from G. Loud, *The Megiddo Ivories* [OIP 52, Chicago 1939], pl. 4, fig. 2)

Ill. 8-3. Detail of ivory plaque with relief carving from Megiddo. (Reproduced from G. Loud, *The Megiddo Ivories* [OIP 52, Chicago 1939], pl. 32, fig. 160b)

Ill. 8-4. Fragment of a Hittite bronze vessel with representations in repoussé from Hattuša-Boğazköy. (Reproduced from R. M. Boehmer, *Die Reliefkeramik von Boğazköy* [Boğazköy-Hattuša 13, 1983], p. 43, fig. 35)

Ill. 8-5. Middle Assyrian sealing from Assur. (Reproduced from A. Moortgat, "Assyrische Glyptik des 13 Jahrhunderts," *ZAssyr* n.s. 13 [47] [1941] 83, fig. 70)

Ill. 8-6. Middle Assyrian sealing from Assur. (Reproduced from A. Moortgat, "Assyrische Glyptik des 13. Jahrhunderts," *ZAssyr* n.s. 13 [47] [1941] 83, fig. 73)

Ill. 8-7. Middle Assyrian sealing from Assur. (Reproduced from U. Moortgat Coorens, "Beiträge zur mittelassyrischen Glyptik," in K. Bittel et al., eds., *Vorderasiatische Archäologie. Studie und Aufsätze Anton Moortgat zum fünfundsechzigsten Geburtstag gewidmet* [Berlin 1964] 167, fig. 2)

White Obelisk, the reliefs of which belong to the Middle Assyrian period.[22]

The representation of animals in the Nineveh cylinder is equally characteristic of Middle Assyrian style. Most distinctive is the alert posture of the dog, which differs from the Old Babylonian columnar representation of what may have been the same breed of mastiff.[23] An Old Babylonian clay plaque showing a seated dog (fig. 8-4) can be compared with a Middle Assyrian sealing from Tell al-Rimah, also with a seated dog (ill. 8-8), to illustrate the difference between the styles. The upright ear of the Middle Assyrian dog gives him a tense expression, which is enhanced by the outline of his back, creating the impression of a natural pose. Moreover, both hindlegs are shown, imparting a slight sense of three-dimensionality. This effect is not unique in Middle Assyrian glyptic[24] and is typical of the limited naturalism of this art, which sets it off from that of the preceding and following periods.

Another Middle Assyrian element is the cock. It is seen on one of the rare objects preserved from this period, an engraved ivory pyxis (ill. 8-9), which shows little cocks perched on branches in the crowns of trees. Such cocks must have been Indian fowl, much smaller than modern chickens, which could fly high into trees. Chickens were imported also into Egypt in the middle of the second millennium,[25] and it is assumed that they came from Mesopotamia, although they seem to have become common there only in the Neo-Babylonian period, during the sixth century B.C., probably having been brought earlier from Iran and ultimately from India, their original homeland. The occurrence of the cock in Middle Assyrian designs therefore had some special significance, probably religious or magical.

Ill. 8-9. Engraved ivory pyxis from a Middle Assyrian tomb at Assur. (Reproduced from A. Haller, *Die Gräber und Grüfte von Assur* [WVDOG 65, Berlin 1954] 135, fig. 161)

Fig. 8-4. Old Babylonian clay plaque, British Museum 129095, reproduced from R. Opificius, *Das altbabylonische Terrakottarelief* (Untersuchungen zur Assyriologie und vorderasiatische Archäologie 2 [1961]), pl. 270, no. 659. (Photograph: British Museum)

The bird of prey with spread wings behind the king is shown as if alighting on the back of the chair, still fluttering before coming to rest. Birds of this type frequently appear on Middle Assyrian seals in the sky of scenes in which animals are the principal figures.[26] The scene under analysis here, however, seems to indicate a specific relation between the bird of prey and the enthroned figure. The same may be true of the leaping lion, a figure paralleled nowhere else in the upper field of a cylinder except for a hunting scene on a cylinder seal from Thebes. Both animals seem to flank the winged disc, which was connected with kingship in Hittite Anatolia but not, as far as is known, in contemporary Assyria.[27]

So far I have stressed the features that link the design of the cylinder from Nineveh to other Middle Assyrian seals or sealings. I shall now point out the features that set off the Nineveh cylinder from those so far known, beginning with the human figures. The first attendant—reading from left to right—seems to wear a plain cap,

Ill. 8-8. Middle Assyrian seal impression from Tell al-Rimah. (Reproduced from B. Parker Mallowan, "A Middle Assyrian Seal Impression," *Iraq* 36 [1974] 185, fig. 1)

set off from the head by a thin line that curves down toward the back, thus differing from the stiff line that indicates the brim of a cap in other Middle Assyrian representations: for example, a cylinder in the Pierpont Morgan Library (fig. 8-5). The cap of the second attendant may have a different shape, since a slight indentation in the back suggests perhaps the edge of a broad, upturned brim, not seen elsewhere in this period. Neither attendant has single strands of hair, as does the enthroned figure, whose hairstyle resembles that of the worshiper on a carved pedestal usually associated with King Tukulti Ninurta I.[28] But there is a striking difference: the enthroned figure on the Nineveh cylinder is beardless, unless a line on the cheek slightly projecting from the chin was meant to indicate a short beard of the type worn by the human figures on the ivory from Megiddo (ill. 8-2). The ruler seems to wear a necklace of crossed strings ending in tassels that hang down from the neck opening of the garment, comparable to the device worn by the heroic figure on the Morgan cylinder

Fig. 8-5. Cylinder seal of Middle Assyrian style in the Pierpont Morgan Library (impression): *Corpus of Ancient Near Eastern Seals in North American Collections* (Washington, D.C., 1948), vol. 1: *The Collection of the Pierpont Morgan Library*, no. 599.

(see fig. 8-5). All garments are otherwise unadorned except for the broad belt worn by the second attendant and indicated by lightly engraved lines. The garments of both attendants leave one leg uncovered below the knee, the other covered to the ankle. H. G. Güterbock has suggested that the closest parallels are Hittite garments (see, e.g., ill. 8-4).

Very striking are the number and variety of animals represented on the Nineveh cylinder. The dog so closely resembles in posture the one shown on a pedestal within a temple as symbol of the goddess Gula (ill. 8-10) that its meaning in our scene may be similar; perhaps it stands

for an inscribed dedication to that goddess. The cock above the dog, unconnected with any figure of the scene, may also be considered a divine symbol, although the identity of the deity it represents has not been established.

Ill. 8-10. Middle Assyrian sealing from Assur. (Reproduced from A. Moortgat, "Assyrische Glyptik des 12. Jahrhunderts," *ZAssyr* n.s. 14 [48] [1942], fig. 46)

The next pair of animals consists of the roaring, leaping lion, surely a symbol of military aggression, and a bird of prey in flight, which recalls the eagles or other raptors flying above the army of the later King Assurnasirpal II (883–859 B.C.).[29] Thus, the bird of prey complements the lion compositionally and iconographically, both animals symbolizing the ruler's military might.

The pairing of the animals so far discussed is unique, but, except for the cock, the single animals could find parallels in appearance and posture on other Middle Assyrian cylinders. Not so the monkey as a figure active in what appears to be a ritual scene. Machteld Mellink has drawn attention to the role of the "monkey-with-pitcher" as a magic attendant of rituals in Anatolian representations.[30] She associates the appearance of the monkey in sealings from Kaneš and in ivories from the palaces of Acemhöyük with the international trade that flowed through Carchemish, Alalakh, Aleppo, and Byblos and ultimately to Egypt. In fact, the Egyptians, especially on scarabs, show the monkey with its hand raised to its mouth as if eating (although it does not hold any food).[31] Such representations approximate the action of the monkey on the Nineveh cylinder but not its participation in the ritual scene, for which only Anatolian examples can be cited. Moreover, association with the stag head, which is preeminently Hittite in origin, confirms the Anatolian connection of the monkey on our seal.

From the time of the royal cemetery at Alaca Höyük to the end of the Hittite empire, the majestic red deer stag appeared in the art of Anatolia, nowhere with greater dignity and beauty than in the silver "stag rhyton" of the Schimmel collection (see figs. 8-2 and 8-3), which is considered one of the greatest works of ancient Near Eastern art known today. It was a vessel from which the king drank to the great sun goddess of Arinna and the other gods.[32]

A close association existed between the drinking vessel in the form of a stag head and the stag as a game animal, as shown by the relief representation on the Schimmel vessel. There a stag lies with its limbs folded, a posture that probably means that the animal is dead, surrounded by two spears, a quiver, and what S. Alp convincingly interprets as the sacred fleece.[33] Presumably the stag was killed in the course of a divine or royal hunt. The same combination of hunting symbols appears with the head of a stag in the outer band of a Hit-

Fig. 8-6. Hittite stamp seal, British Museum 115655 (formerly 17804). (Photograph: British Museum)

Fig. 8-7. Design on the base of Hittite stamp seal, British Museum 115655 (formerly 17804): enlarged impression. (Photograph: British Museum)

tite stamp seal in the British Museum (figs. 8-6 and 8-7), to which H. Güterbock drew my attention and which S. Alp also associates with the Schimmel silver stag head.[34]

For our representation the most important fact is that the stag head, a standard Hittite design, appears to have been known in Assyria, probably because of its association with major Hittite gods and also with the king. That it appears on the only Middle Assyrian cylinder for which an origin at Nineveh may be assumed—a cylinder showing several differences from the style prevalent at Assur—demonstrates the variety that may have existed in Middle Assyrian glyptic, a variety that is perhaps attributable to various foreign influences.

The challenge now is to find why a Hittite stag head—for no such representation is known in Middle Assyrian art[35]—appears on a table before an Assyrian ruler, and why a monkey participates in the ritual, another figure for which one must look to Anatolia for comparisons. The explanation can only be undertaken with the great knowledge, the disciplined imagination, and the wisdom of Machteld Mellink.

### NOTES

This article was written during my tenure as a fellow of the John Simon Guggenheim Foundation.

1 For the dates of the Karum Kaneš, see M. Trolle Larsen, *The Old Assyrian City-State and Its Colonies* (Mesopotamia 4, Copenhagen 1976) 366.
2 For the dates of Šamši-Adad I, see D. O. Edzard, *Die zweite Zwischenzeit Babyloniens* (Wiesbaden 1957) 164.
3 K. R. Veenhof, "The Old Assyrian Merchants and Their Relations with the Native Population of Anatolia," in H.-J. Nissen and J. Renger eds., *Mesopotamien und seine Nachbarn* (Berliner Beiträge zum Vorderen Orient 1, 1982) 147–60.
4 For a characterization of the Old Assyrian style, see N. Özgüç, *Seals and Seal Impressions of Level Ib from Karum Kanish* (TTKY ser. V, 25, Ankara 1968) 47–49. For the terms "Early" and "Late" Old Assyrian style, see my article "Kaniš, kārum. C. Die Glyptik," *RLA* 5 (1980) 384–85. Most of the seals that I called "provincial Babylonian" in *Corpus of Ancient Near Eastern Seals in North American Collections* (Bollingen Series 14, Washington 1948; hereafter cited as *Corpus* 1) 109–12, belong to the Late Old Assyrian style.
5 An Early Old Assyrian cylinder was used on a tablet from Larsa, dated to the 25th year of Rīm-Sin, reproduced in L. Delaporte, *Musée National du Louvre, Catalogue des cylindres, cachets et pierres gravées de style oriental 2. Acquisitions* (Paris 1923; hereafter cited as *Louvre* 2) pl. 113.3 (A. 509). The animals recognizable in the lower part of that seal resemble those on typical Early Old Assyrian cylinders: *Corpus* 1, 852, 854. Examples of Late Old Assyrian cylinders were used on tablets from Sippar (some of them found in excavations by V. Scheil) published by F. Thureau-Dangin, *Lettres et contrats de l'époque de la première dynastie babylonienne* (Textes cunéiformes, Musée du Louvre 2, Paris 1910) no. 74; *Louvre* 2, pl. 113.5a (A. 517, F, G) and no. 76, *Louvre* 2, pl. 114.2a (A. 520, B). None of the other seal impressions is as clearly recognizable as Late Old Assyrian. Lamia Al-Gailani Werr has published drawings of dated cylin-

ders and seal impressions of the Old Babylonian period which include those of officials of King Šamši-Adad of Assyria, in "Chronological Table of Old Babylonian Seal Impressions," *Bulletin of the Institute of Archaeology, London* 17 (1980) 50–51, no. 32a–d. Of these only one, no. 32a, is carved in characteristic Old Assyrian style. The others are engraved in fine Old Babylonian style, as was the cylinder used by Šamši-Adad I himself on the bullae found at Acemhöyük in Anatolia: see N. Özgüç, "Seal Impressions from the Palaces at Acem-höyük," in E. Porada ed., *Ancient Art in Seals* (Princeton 1980) fig. III:1.
Old Assyrian impressions on tablets from Tell Harmal and Tell Diba'i have been assembled by Al-Gailani Werr, *Studies in the Chronology and Regional Style of Old Babylonian Cylinder Seals* (forthcoming).

6 R. F. S. Starr, *Nuzi* (Cambridge, Mass., 1937) pl. 62.B. The seal was found between the levels in which Nuzi was known as Ga.sur and the later ones but was correctly assigned to the earlier period (p. 381).

7 A. Moortgat, *Vorderasiatische Rollsiegel. Ein Beitrag zur Geschichte des Steinschneidekunst* (Staatliche Museen, Berlin 1940) pl. 61.513.

8 Moortgat (supra n. 7) pl. 61.505.

9 Moortgat (supra n. 7) pl. 61.516.

10 For the identification of Neša with Kaneš, see the initial study by H. G. Güterbock, "Kaneš und Neša," *Eretz-Israel* 5 (1958) 46–50; also S. Alp, *Belleten* 27 (1963) 107, 377–86, and H. Lewy, *JCS* 17 (1963) 103–104.

11 M. J. Mellink, "The Royal Tombs at Alaca Höyük and the Aegean World," in S. S. Weinberg ed., *The Aegean and the Near East. Studies Presented to Hetty Goldman* (Locust Valley 1956) esp. her remarks on the Indo-European question, pp. 54–57.

12 M. J. Mellink, "The Art of Anatolia Until c. 1200 B.C.," in *Art Treasures of Turkey* (Smithsonian Institution, Washington, D.C., 1966) 10.

13 This brief survey is based on H. Otten, "Hethiter, Hurriter und Mitanni," in E. Cassin, J. Bottéro, and J. Vercoutter eds., *Die altorientalischen Reiche* (Fischer Weltgeschichte 2–4, Frankfurt-a-M. and Hamburg 1965) 102–76, and K. Bittel, *Die Hethiter* (Munich 1976) passim.

14 E. Cassin, "Assyrien," in *Die altorientalischen Reiche* (supra n. 13) 71.

15 P. Machinist, "Assyrians and Hittites in the Late Bronze Age," in *Mesopotamien* (supra n. 3) 265–67. More recently, however, G. Beckman has stressed contacts between Assyrians and Hittites, especially scribes and ambassadors: "Mesopotamians and Mesopotamian Learning at Hattuša," *JCS* 35:1–2 (1983), esp. p. 108, fig. 4.11.

16 W. Andrae, *Die jüngeren Ischtar-Tempel in Assur* (WVDOG 58, Berlin 1935) 50, and W. Orthmann, *Der alte Orient* (PK 14, Berlin 1975) 435, fig. 371c. The figure called "Schutzgott" by Orthmann, however, lacks the characteristic mount—a stag—and a bow, as noted by H. G. Güterbock, "Hethitische Götterdarstellungen und Götternamen," *Belleten* 7 (1943) 314–15, who suggested that several deities had the function of protector. He recently reiterated this suggestion in connection with the stag rhyton in the Schimmel collection: "Hethitische Götterbilder und Kultobjecte," *Beiträge zur Altertumskunde Kleinasiens. Festschrift für Kurt Bittel* (Mainz am Rhein 1983) 207.

17 It is registered as no. 89806. I owe the references concerning this cylinder to Dominique Collon, who also drew my attention to Seton Lloyd's remarks about Captain Felix Jones in *Foundations in the Dust* (London 1947) 157–60. A drawing of the cylinder was published by W. H. Ward, *Seal Cylinders of*

*Western Asia* (Washington, D.C., 1910) no. 733. F. Hancar assumed that the seated figure was the goddess Ištar and therefore advanced an unlikely interpretation of the seal design: *AfO* 13 (1939–1941) 295, fig. 11.

18 The sword of the Assyrian king Adad Nirari I (1305–1274 B.C.) in the Metropolitan Museum of Art (Acc. no. 11.166.1) corresponds to the Egyptian sickle sword of the Late Bronze Age (Y. Yadin, *The Art of Warfare in Biblical Lands* [New York, Toronto, London 1963] 207) in the one-sided curve of the handle, whereas the dagger of the god on the so-called Royal Gate at Boğazköy-Hattuša shows a clearly defined crescentic handle: Bittel (supra n. 13) fig. 268, opp. p. 233. The later development of Assyrian daggers shows a tendency toward an only slightly everted top. It has to be admitted, however, that several of the daggers inscribed with the names of Babylonian rulers of the Second Dynasty of Isin in the twelfth and eleventh centuries B.C. have handles ending in a crescentic shape: W. Nagel, "Die Königsdolche der Zweiten Dynastie von Isin," *AfO* 19 (1959–1960) 97 and 99, figs. 3, 4, 6, 7–9. One cannot be sure, therefore, whether some earlier Assyrian daggers had a similar shape.

19 H. G. Güterbock read the first draft of this article and, among other important suggestions, made reference to this fragment, which is well known by now. I reproduce the drawing, although a photograph (cf., e.g., Bittel [supra n. 13] 164, fig. 177) would provide better support for my view that the head is meant as real, not as a vessel. A comparable head is seen on the table placed in front of Ahiram on his sarcophagus: P. Montet, *Byblos et l'Egypte* (Paris 1929) pl. 131.

20 A. Moortgat, "Assyrische Glyptik des 13. Jahrhunderts," *ZAssyr* n.s. 13 (47) (1942) 50–88.

21 U. Moortgat-Correns, "Beiträge zur mittelassyrischen Glyptik," in K. Bittel et al. eds., *Vorderasiatische Archäologie. Studie und Aufsätze Anton Moortgat zum fünfundsechzigsten Geburtstag gewidmet* (Berlin 1964) 167, fig. 2.

22 Some of the reasons for dating the reliefs on the White Obelisk to the Middle Assyrian period were discussed by J. E. Reade, "Ashurnaṣirpal I and the White Obelisk," *Iraq* 37 (1975) 129–50.

23 See the remarks by U. Seidl on the two principal breeds of dogs depicted in the ancient Near East: *RLA* 4 (1975) 497, s.v. *Hund*. The dog with a cane of the Old Babylonian period and the dog shown on our cylinder belong to the heavy "Molosser" type.

24 The same slightly three-dimensional effect was obtained by showing the tip of the farther horn of a bull or goat in such a way as to suggest a three-quarter view of the animal's horns; see, e.g., *Corpus* 1, 595, and two cylinders from Thebes as well as one in the Bibliothèque Nationale: *AfO* 28 (1981) 57–59 and figs. on those pages. Perhaps this quasi-three-quarter view and the concomitant three-dimensional effect were due to Aegean influence on Kassite and Middle Assyrian art, to which Machteld Mellink first drew attention in her review of *Archaeologica Orientalia in Memoriam Ernst Herzfeld* in *BibO* 12 (1955) 122.

25 They seem to have been imported from Mesopotamia, according to D. Opitz in *RLA* 1 (1928) 49, who cites a text in which Tuthmosis III refers to the chicken as the bird that gives birth daily. See also W. Heimpel and P. Calmeyer, s.v. *Huhn*, in *RLA* 4 (1975) 487–88.

26 Moortgat (supra n. 20) 71, figs. 38, 41, 43.

27 "The Cylinder Seals Found at Thebes in Boeotia," *AfO* 28 (1981/1982) 65–66, no. 37, a cylinder of uncertain origin. On the question of the association of the winged disc with the Hittite king, see D. Beyer, "Le sceau-cylindre de Shahurunuwa, roi de Karkemish," in *La Syrie au Bronze Récent*

(XXVIIᵉ Rencontre Assyriologique Internationale, Paris 1980) 71–72 and relevant references in n. 14.

28 Andrae (supra n. 16) pls. 30, 31a; also H. Frankfort, *The Art and Architecture of the Ancient Orient* (Baltimore 1955) pl. 73B.

29 R. D. Barnett, *Assyrian Palace Reliefs* (London n.d.) pl. 15.

30 M. J. Mellink, "Anatolian Libation Pourers and the Minoan Genius," in E. Porada ed., *Monsters and Demons. Death and Life in the Ancient and Medieval World* (forthcoming).

31 E. Hornung and E. Staehelin, *Skarabäen und andere Siegelamulette aus Baseler Sammlungen* (Ägyptische Denkmäler in der Schweiz 1, 1976) 107.

32 S. Alp, *Beitränge zur Erforschung des hethitischen Tempels* (Türk Tarih Kurumu Basımevi, Ankara 1983) 125 (no. 21) lines 8–9.

33 Alp (supra n. 32) 99.

34 Alp (supra n. 32) 99 and fig. 12a. R. L. Alexander, "The Tyskiewicz Group of Stamp-Cylinders," *Anatolica* 5 (1973–1976) 208 n. 102, remarks on the seals in Dresden and in the Louvre (Alp [supra n. 32] figs. 11, 13), which are so closely related to the one in the British Museum that their authenticity should be carefully considered.

35 By Middle Assyrian art I mean the subtly modeled style to which the Nineveh cylinder belongs. Cylinders in Mitannian style do show stag heads; see, e.g., T. Beran, "Assyrische Glyptik des 14. Jahrhunderts," *ZAssyr* n.s. 18 (52) (1957) 195, fig. 96.

## 9

# Royal Statements of Ideal Prices: Assyrian, Babylonian, and Hittite

## J. D. HAWKINS

This study is dedicated to Machteld Mellink, who has always taken such a keen interest in the hieroglyphic inscriptions of Karkamiš and Anatolia.

The newly discovered Hieroglyphic Luwian stele of TAKSARAY[1] contains a remarkable passage which provides the key to three comparable passages in longer-known inscriptions, KARKAMIŠ A 2 and A 11 *a* and SULTANHAN. It will be shown that these passages can be interpreted by reference to tariffs of "ideal prices" found in the royal inscriptions of Babylonia and Assyria. These latter have been often discussed.[2] They fall into two distinct groups, the Old Babylonian (ca. 1900–1800 B.C.), including the inscriptions of Sin-iddinam and Sin-iqišam(?) of Larsa, Sin-kašid of Uruk, and Šamši-Adad I, and a late group from the inscriptions of Aššurbanipal (666–626 B.C.) and Nabonidus (556–539 B.C.). The recurrence of the theme after so long a gap might be supposed to be due to the learned and antiquarian interests of the two later kings, but the proposed identification of this literary topos in some earlier Hieroglyphic Luwian texts implies a greater continuity of usage.

We should begin with an examination of the Assyrian and Neo-Babylonian examples, both for the sake of comparison with the Hieroglyphic passages and because there are some new points of interest about them which deserve to be noted.

1. Aššurbanipal (A)
*ina* BAL ^meš-*ia* HÉ.NUN *ṭuh-du*
*ina* MU.AN.NA ^meš-*ia ku-um-mu-ru hé-gál-lum* (var. *lu*)
10 (var. 12) ANŠE ŠE.PAD 1 (var. 2, 3) ANŠE GEŠTIN ^meš
2 BÁN Ì^meš 1 (var. -) GÚ.UN SIG ^meš
*ina nap-har* KUR-*ia* KI.LAM *nap-šú*
*i-šam-mu ina* 1 GÍN *kas-pi*

In my reign (there was) plenty (and) wealth,
in my years abundance was heaped up:
10 (var. 12) homers of barley, 1 (var. 2, 3) homers of wine,
2 seah of oil, (1) talent of wool,

throughout my land, a cheap price,
they buy for a shekel of silver.

This passage is found in Aššurbanipal's "Annals," editions B, D, and C (650–646 B.C.). Most of it has been known since A. C. Piepkorn[3] and R. Campbell Thompson,[4] but it is only since 1967–1968 that new Nimrud and Nineveh fragments have been published which give the crucial "*ina* 1 *šiqil kaspi*" ("for one shekel of silver"), without which the passages does not make sense.[5]

2. Aššurbanipal (B)
*ina* 1 GÍN KÙ.BABBAR 30 GUR *š[e]-am* [ . . . *ina*] ^uru*aš-šur liš-šá-a*
*ina* 1 GÍN KÙ.BABBAR 3 BÁN Ì.GIŠ [ . . . *in*]*a* ^uru*aš-šur liš-šá-a*
*ina* 1 GÍN KÙ.BABBAR 30 MA.NA SÍG [ . . . ]*ina* ^uru*aš-šur liš-šá-a*

For one shekel of silver 30 kor of barley [ . . . ] may one get in Aššur,
for one shekel of silver 3 seah of oil [ . . . ] may one get in Aššur,
for one shekel of silver 30 minas of wool [ . . . ] may one get in Aššur!

In his edition of this prayer,[6] E. Weidner noted the preposterous character of the equation of 30 kor of barley to one shekel of silver and reasonably suggested the correction to "3! kor," which would bring this price more or less into line with the other two, and with other implausibly optimistic statements.

The breaks in the middle of each line, each of which has space for 3–4 signs, may have accommodated further measures of other commodities—perhaps, by comparisons with the other tariffs, dates, fine oil, and wine. It is curious that the text, cast in the form of a prayer by a priest in the Šamaš Temple at Aššur, should employ the Babylonian *kor* rather than the Assyrian homer as the top unit of measure.

3. Nabonidus
*ina a-mat* [d]30 LUGAL DINGIR [meš] [d]IM ŠÈG *ú-ma[š-š] i-ra-am-ma*
[d]*é-a ú-paṭ-ṭi-ra naq-bu-šú*
*meš-ru-ú nu-uh-šú u hé-gál-la ina* KUR-*ia iš-ku-un*
1 GUR 2 (PI) 3 BÁN ŠE.BAR *a-na* 1 GÍN KÙ.BABBAR
1 GUR 2 (PI) 3 BÁN ZÚ.LUM [*a*]-*na* 1 GÍN KÙ.BABBAR
1 (PI)(?) 5 BÁN ŠE.GIŠ.Ì *a-na* 1 GÍN KÙ.BABBAR
3 BÁN *ú-li-e a-na* 1 GÍN KÙ.BABBAR
5 MA.NA SÍG[hi-a] *a-na* 1 GÍN KÙ.BABBAR
1-*en* MA.NA [ . . . ] *a-na* 1 GÍN KÙ.BABBAR
[GEŠ]TIN KAŠ.SAG KUR-*i ša ina qí-rib* KUR-*ia ia-a-nu*
3 BÁN(?) GEŠTIN *a-na* 1 GÍN KÙ.BABBAR
[ . . . ] *meš-ru-ú ina* KUR-*ia iš-ku-un*

At the word of Sin, king of the gods, Adad let go the rain,
Ea released his ground water,
riches, plenty, and abundance he brought about in my land:
1 kor 15 seah of barley for one shekel of silver,
1 kor 15 seah of dates for one shekel of silver,
11(?) seah of sesame for one shekel of silver,
3 seah of fine oil for one shekel of silver,
5 minas of wool for one shekel of silver,
1 mina of [ . . . ] for one shekel of silver,
wine—the beer of the mountain, which is not in my land—
3(?) seah of wine for one shekel of silver,
[so wealth and] riches he brought about in my land.

In his recent edition of the passage,[7] Röllig comments on the prices recorded and compares them with actual known figures. Collation of the piece in the British museum suggests the following for the doubtful figures given for barley, sesame oil, and wine:[8]

Barley: 1 GUR 2' (PI) (a broken vertical, as in the following quantity of dates) 3 BÁN—thus, a total of 270 *qa*.

Sesame oil: 1 (PI) (vertical definitely present) 5 BÁN—thus, a total of 66 *qa*, an abnormally high figure (i.e., low price), as Röllig was aware (see his comment supporting the reading of 5 BÁN only).[9]

Wine: of the BÁN sign, only two horizontals are definitely visible—thus, a minimum of 2 BÁN, as suggested by L. W. King in his original publication,[10] but not excluding a possible restoration of 3 BÁN.

A. K. Grayson has pointed out that both groups of tariffs tend to list the same basic commodities in the same general order.[11] In fact, if we list them for comparison, we observe the following pattern:

Old Babylonian
Sin-iddinam: barley, dates, wool, (sesame) oil, lard
Sin-iqišam(?): barley, oil, wool, dates
Sin-kašid: barley, wool, copper, (sesame) oil
Šamši-Adad I: barley, wool, oil

First Millennium B.C.
Aššurbanipal (A): barley, wine, oil, wool
Aššurbanipal (B): barley, [ . . . ], (sesame) oil, [ . . . ], wool, [ . . . ]
Nabonidus: barley, dates, sesame (oil), "best oil," wool, [ . . . ], wine

Prices are always expressed in terms of one shekel of silver, and barley is always listed first. Otherwise the commodities vary in their order, but wool and oil are always included, though different types of the latter appear. Wine only joins this list of staples in the first millennium, and Nabonidus specifically notes its foreign provenance. All commodities are measured by volume, except wool, which is measured in weight (as is copper when it occurs).

The unreality of these "ideal prices" has attracted comment.[12] They have been measured not only against actual prices found in contemporary commercial documents but also against the tariff in the Laws of Ešnunna (ca. 1850 B.C.), which can be seen to be comparatively sober and realistic.[13] The Nabonidus prices, though on the optimistic side, are not ridiculously out of step with current prices.[14] It is of relevance here to attempt to assess the Aššurbanipal claim, for which purpose prices are reduced to the lowest common denominator, based on the usually accepted metrological assumptions for the various periods (table 9-1).[15]

From the comparative table it would appear that the boasted prices in Aššurbanipal's Annals are fairly comparable to the Old Babylonian "ideal" prices, except that of wool, which is markedly cheaper.[16] One might make the point that the variation in the prices of barley and wine between the different recensions indicates the unrealistic nature of the claims. The Aššurbanipal prayer produces more moderate figures, once the price of barley has been emended from 30 to 3 kor (a figure of 5,400 instead of the emended 540 would be evidently ludicrous).

Before proceeding to the Hieroglyphic Luwian passages, we should consider the evidence from the tariff of prices in the Hittite Laws.[17] Comparison with the Mesopotamian information is not easy, on account of uncertainties in our knowledge of Hittite metrology, in particular the relative quantities in the Hittite *PARISU-SUTU* system, borrowed from Mesopotamia,[18] and also the value of the Hittite 40-shekel mina.[19] We may, however, offer the following relevant prices for comparison:

1 sheep, price 1 shekel of silver
. . .
3 *PA(RISU)* of wheat for 1 shekel of silver
4 *PA* [of barley for 1/2 shekel of silver][20]
1 *PA* of wine for 1/2 shekel of silver

Oil cannot usefully be brought into the comparison, since only "sweet oil" (Ì DÙG.GA) is priced (besides lard and butter), and in any case it is measured by the *zipattani*, a measure of unknown size.

The Hittite *PARISU* has been shown to consist of 6 *SUTU*, which equates it with the Mesopotamian *NIGIDA* (Akk. *panu*/*parsiktu*.)[21] The Hittite *SUTU*,

Table 9.1. Quantities of commodities valued at one shekel of silver

| | Old Babylonian Price | | | | | First Millennium Price | | |
| | "Ideal" | | | | Laws | "Ideal" | | |
| | 1 | 2 | 3 | 4 | 5 | 6 | 7 | 8 |
|---|---|---|---|---|---|---|---|---|
| Barley | 1,200 | 600 | 900 | 600 | 300 | 270 | 1,000/1,200 | 540[?!] |
| Dates | 3,600 | 3,000 | — | — | — | 270 | — | [?] |
| Wool | 15 minas | 10 minas | 12 minas | 15 minas | 6 minas | 5 minas | 60 minas (?) | 30 minas |
| Oil (sesame) | 30 | 20 | 30 | 20 | 12 | 66[?!] | 20 | 18 |
| Best oil | — | — | — | — | 3 | 18 | — | [?] |
| Wine | — | — | — | — | — | 18[?] | 100/200/300 | [?] |

Key: 1 = Sin-iddinam; 2 = Sin-iqišam; 3 = Sin-kašid; 4 = Šamši-Adad I; 5 = Laws of Ešnunna; 6 = Nabonidus; 7 = Aššurbanipal (A) (Annals); 8 = Aššurbanipal (B) (prayer).
Note: All quantities have been reduced to SILÀ (*qa*, approx. one liter) for the sake of comparison, except those given for wool.

however, seems to have consisted of varying quantities of the smallest subdivision, the *UPNU: SUTU* of 12, 20, and 24 *UPNU* have been identified. In this it resembles the Mesopotamian *SUTU*, whose value could range between 5 and 10 SILÀ.[22]

In an attempt to gain an approximate idea of Hittite prices, we can do no better than assume that the Hittite *SUTU* had the same range as the Mesopotamian and estimate maximum and minimum prices based on *SUTU* of 10 and 5 SILÀ. This somewhat arbitrary procedure gives us the following possible amounts—in SILÀ—of commodities available for 1 shekel of silver:

wheat: maximum, 180; minimum, 90
[barley: maximum, 480; minimum, 240]
wine: maximum, 120; minimum, 60

It is also important to note the equation 1 sheep = 1 shekel of silver, regardless of the exact weight of the Hittite shekel, for it indicates Hittite agreement with Mesopotamia in this very general equivalence, which is shown to be approximately realistic in actual transactions.[23] Also of interest is the way in which the Hittite Laws reckon meat prices in terms of sheep, not silver, although as Gurney observes, given the basic equivalence, there would be little practical difference.[24]

We should now turn to the Hieroglyphic Luwian passages mentioned above, which may be tabulated as shown in table 9-2 for the sake of comparison (another passage, BOR, which shows similarities, has been included). It should be noted that three of the passages—AKSARAY, SULTANHAN, and BOR—come from inscriptions from the Anatolian plateau dating to the late eighth century B.C.[25] The two KARKAMIŠ inscriptions were both written by the ruler Katuwas and thus date to the beginning of the ninth century,[26] and since the two cited passages come from almost identical contexts, they can be used to restore and supplement each other.

In fact, the other two main citations are also found in very comparable contexts, preceded by descriptions of god-given abundance and followed by statements that the authors returned favors to the gods. Thus, it has been generally recognized that these passages too are a further description of some feature of great prosperity.[27]

It is the new AKSARAY context which provides the key to the other passages. Its "in those years" confirms the generally recognized "in my *days*" of the KARKAMIŠ passages,[28] although the phonetic rendering and exact interpretation of the word for "days" have not been established.[29] Furthermore, comparison of the remainder of each of the passages with that of AKSARAY permits the grammatical structure of the clause to be clearly discerned. We may identify the following elements:

(*a*) the word "sheep" in the dat. sing. (AKSARAY, also KARKAMIŠ A 2). SULTANHAN has "2 sheep," which may have no phonetic complement to indicate the case, but perhaps should be read with a -*sa* indicating nom. or gen. case.[30] In KARKAMIŠ A 11 *a*, although damage obscures the content, it is possible to restore some combination of (OV[IS.ANIMAL]*ha*]-*wa/i*[-*i*].[31] There are, however, two further signs [x]-*pi*/DARE: for a consideration of these see further below, p. 98 and n. 66.

(*b*) a numeral (missing from KARKAMIŠ A 11 *a* but presumably to be restored from the closely comparable KARKAMIŠ A 2)

(*c–e*) AKSARAY thrice repeats this phrase, each time with a different element (*d*). The other inscriptions only show phrases corresponding to the first of the three repetitions.

(*e*) the verb CRUS + *RA/I* with a probable original sense of "stand," as argued below

Table 9.2. Hieroglyphic Luwian passages on prices

| Source | Introduction | Elements (a) | (b) | (c) | (d) | (e) |
|---|---|---|---|---|---|---|
| AKSARAY, 3 | \| à-wali a-[pa]-tá-za$_x$ ("ANNUS")u-sá-za | (OVIS.ANIMAL)ha-wali-i | 30 20 [ . . . ] | ti-wáli-ta-li-sa ti-wali-tá-li-sa ti]-wali-tá-li-sa | "冊" -za "χ" -ti-sa (VINUM)ma-tú-sà | \| CRUS + RA/I [ . . .]-ta \|CRUS + RA/I |
| KARKAMIŠ A 11 a, 3–4 | [à]-wali mi-ia-za-' DEUS.AVIS-tá-ní-ia-za | OV[IS . . . ]-wali(-) . . . | [ . . . ] | ASINUS.(ANIMAL) | "冊" | \| CRUS + RA/I |
| KARKAMIŠ A 2, 4 | à-wali mi-ia-za-' LITUUS.AVIS-ta-ni-ia-za | \|OVIS.ANIMAL-i | 10 | ASINUS | — | CRUS + RA/I |
| SULTANHAN stele 3 | \| REL-i-pa-wali \| ("TERRA")ta-sà-REL + RA/I(-sa?) | \| 2 "OVIS"(sa?) | 80 | — | "冊" | CRUS + RA/I |
| BOR, 7–8 | \| wali-mu-u | — | 100 [ . . . ] | ti-wali-[ta]-li-[sa ti-wali]-ta-li-sa | . . . ma-tu-sà | |

(d) the logogram 冊 (HH no. 179), now known from the KULULU lead strips, especially strip 1, as a common commodity issued to named recipients and parallel to "sheep" in strip 2.[32] In KARKAMIŠ A 11 a, the sign is damaged but restorable by comparison with AKSARAY and SULTANHAN. In KARKAMIŠ A 2 there is nothing corresponding to this sign, but comparison with the other contexts suggests that it should be understood here. In AKSARAY its phonetic complement -za, found also on KULULU lead strip 1, presumably marks it as nom./acc. sing. N. In the two repetitions of the (c–e) passage, this logogram is replaced by other words, "χ" -ti-sa and ("VINUM")ma-tù-sá.

(c) In AKSARAY the word *tiwatalis*, occurring three times in the repetition of the parallel phrases, corresponds to the ASINUS of KARKAMIŠ A 2, to which KARKAMIŠ A 11 a adds (ANIMAL).[33] SULTANHAN has no corresponding element. The word *tiwatalis* is clearly nom. sing. MF (an acc. sing. *tiwatalin* is attested: see Appendix below), and is thus identifiable as the subject. ASINUS (ANIMAL) may be assumed to occupy the same grammatical position.

Enough should now be clear of the structure of the statements to offer as a tentative rendering:

(a) For (/of?) one (/two) sheep (b) so-many (c) *tiwatalis*/ASINUS (d) commodity (e) *stood*.

In the context of descriptions of prosperity, this formula suggests the comparison with the Mesopotamian literary topos of the ideal price. We should therefore examine the component elements in greater detail to see whether such an interpretation can be plausibly sustained.

(a) "for a sheep": Mesopotamian statements of price are all expressed in terms of one shekel of silver (*ina 1 šiqil kaspi*). Given, however, the very standard equivalent 1 sheep = 1 shekel of silver, together with the practice in the Hittite Laws of expressing meat prices in terms of sheep, (as noted above) we may well understand that the sheep here stands as the unit of value.

30 *tiwatalis* "*179-za*": lack of grammatical congruence between the latter two elements has already been noted,[34] but this feature resembles the phrase 4 (SCALPRUM)*ma-na-zi* *257-za, argued to mean "4 *minas* (of) silver."[35] The present phrase could be explicable in the same terms—that is, numeral + measure + commodity.

[x] ASINUS(ANIMAL) "*179" / 10 ASINUS: if, in element c, *tiwatalis* expresses a measure, we should examine the corresponding ASINUS to see whether it lends itself to such an interpretation, which does in fact turn out to be the case. In the actual "donkey" marked by the addition ANIMAL, we may recognize the well-known Assyrian measure, the *donkey-load* or *homer*.[36] It is hardly surprising to find this measure in use in Karkamiš, an important commercial center and the immediate neighbor of Assyrian-controlled Upper Mesopotamia.[37] The ease with which ASINUS may be interpreted as a measure surely strengthens the case for regarding *tiwatalis* as another such.[38]

(d) The commodities:

(i) *179-za* is, as noted, a common commodity found on KULULU lead strip 1.[39] Although the phonetic rendering of the logogram *179 remains for the present undemonstrable, the fact that it stands first in all these postulated statements of price allows a strong presumption that it denotes *grain*, probably barley. This would revive an old and apparently abandoned suggestion of Meriggi, who identified *179 as "barley" simply on the basis of the appearance of the sign, as found in the writing of three words on AŠŠUR letter e.[40]

The form *179-za appears as noted to be sing. N. None of the Luwian words for grain have been definitely identified;[41] in Hittite several of these words are neuter, but not *halkiš* (ŠE), "barley."[42]

The other main occurrence of *179 is in the writing of the name of a deity in the lists of gods on the TELL

AHMAR stelae 1 and 2: DEUS.*179(-)*matili-*.[43] This deity comes immediately after the grain god *Kuparma*, and could thus be another grain god, or perhaps Kuparma's consort.[44]

(ii) ("VINUM")*ma-tú-sà*: the word is found without the logogram on SULTANHAN stele and BOR (see Appendix, below). In the latter context it is again preceded by the word *tiwatalis*, and in the former by the numeral 9(x)100 and linked with an ox as an offering to a god. These contexts, the measuring by *tiwatalis* (apparently a measure of volume, not weight) and the offering to a god, serve to define it as a certain type of commodity.

The logogram "VINUM,"[45] with which it is now found, surely provides direct evidence for the interpretation of *ma-tú-sà*.[46] VINUM is used elsewhere to determine *wiyani-*, "vine" (see below); *tuwarsa-*, "vineyard"; (-)*tipariya-*, the wine god; (-)*hara/i-* (= Phoenician [*t*]*rš*), "vintage"; and *sarlata-*, "libation." Thus *matus(a)* is clearly a substance associated with the vine, and, since measured by volume and offered to the god of vineyards, most probably a type of wine.

The form of the word could be nom. sing. MF *matus* or, equally well, nom./acc. sing. N. *matu*(+*sa*). The latter form could well be compared with Cuneiform Luwian *maddu-*, itself already compared by Meriggi with Greek μέθυ[47] and thus implicitly with Indo-European *medhu*, "mead." The identification of Cuneiform Luwian *maddu-* with Indo-European *medhu* encounters a phonetic obstacle,[48] but the location of Hieroglyphic *matu-* in such a comparatively well-defined context must increase the plausibility of the triple equation.

If the identification is correct, *matu-* could denote sweet or honeyed wine, corresponding to Hittite GEŠTIN KU₇.[49] Consideration of the Hieroglyphic attestations of *wiyani-* shows, however, that in each case it may be translated "vine" in preference to "wine," so it is possible that it was restricted to this sense. If so, it is further possible that *matu-*, attested only three times (AKSARAY; SULTANHAN and BOR, see Appendix below), was generalized as the term for "wine" in the Hieroglyphic inscriptions of the Iron Age.

(iii) ⸢*χ*⸣*-ti-sa*: the partially destroyed logogram is identified as FONS by Kalaç, followed by Poetto.[50] The sign FONS is attested elsewhere only in the writing of the name *Suppiluliuma*, whence its interpretation was drawn.[51] This name is found in the Late Hittite period only on BOYBEYPINARI,[52] where the sign form, a solid relief circle with surface incisions, does not resemble the present sign, apparently a hollow circle with a vertical central division showing signs of surface incision. There is thus no compelling reason to identify the AKSARAY logogram as FONS.

If the three commodities in AKSARAY element (*d*) begin with some kind of grain (*179) and end with *wine* (*matusa*), the most obvious missing commodity of a type measured by volume, not weight, is *oil*, so it could be that the damaged logogram stands for this. The Cuneiform Luwian word for oil is *tain-*,[53] and here a form of this word with the common -*ti*- suffix could lie behind the present writing. But this proposal might make oil implausibly cheap. In Mesopotamian tariffs the oil is valued at so many seah to the shekel against barley, which is measured by the kor or homer. So it might be more plausible to suppose that we have here simply another, somewhat more expensive, kind of cereal.[54]

(e) CRUS + *RA/I*:[55] apart from the present contexts, the sign is found expressing a verb, both simple and causative, only three times.[56] In all writings of the simple verb, it is written without any verbal endings, which is sufficiently unusual to have led scholars to seek the verbal ending in the + *RA/I*,[57] but this possibility is to be ruled out because CRUS + *RA/I* on one occasion represents the 3 plur. (pret.) and because of the causative CRUS + *RA/I-nu-*.[58]

Parts of the body used logographically to write verbs are usually of a fairly transparent sense and range of meaning.[59] CRUS normally represents *ta-*, "stand," presumably cognate with Hittite *tiya-*, which has the same meaning.[60] CRUS + *RA/I* must be taken to represent a different root within the same semantic range, and one would suppose that *RA/I* is probably a phonetic indicator. In the context, one thinks of Hittite *ar-* (med.) "stand," though the root is not otherwise attested in Cuneiform or Hieroglyphic Luwian. But it remains curious that CRUS + *RA/I* is never found written with a verbal ending. If comparison with Hittite *ar-* is correct, it is conceivable that we have here a fossilized form: *media tantum* are either nonexistent or extremely rare in Hieroglyphic Luwian, which could explain the peculiar usage of this verb.

In any case it seems legitimate to posit a basic sense of "stand" for the logogram in these contexts of "standing" for a value.[61] The verb was perhaps used in a diluted sense comparable to that of Hittite *ar-* used in place of *eš-*, "be";[62] we may note also the KARATEPE use of (CRUS)*taza-* = Phoenician *kn*, "be," and CRUS = Phoenician -.[63]

It is hoped that these arguments will have served to show that the four cited passages should be interpreted as statements of ideal prices, a literary topos expressing great prosperity. The following renderings of the passages may now be offered.

AKSARAY
|*à-wa/i a-[pa]-tá-za*ₓ ("ANNUS") *u-sá-za* |(OVIS.ANIMAL)
*ha-wa/i-i* 30 *ti-wá/-í-ta-li-sa* *179-za* |CRUS + *RA/I*

20 *ti-wa/i-tá-li-sa* "[X"]-*ti-sa* [ . . . ]-*ta*
[ . . . *ti*]-*wa/i-ta-li-sa* ("VINUM")*ma-tú-sà* |CRUS + RA/I

In those years for (one) sheep 30 *measures* (of) *barley* stood,
20 *measures* (of) ⌜oil(??)⌝ [ . . . ]-ed,[64]
[x] *measures* (of) wine *stood*.

KARKAMIŠ A 11 *a*
[*à*]-*wa/i mi-ia-za-´* DEUS.AVIS-*tá-ní-ia-za* OV[IS . . . ]-*wa/i*
[-*i*?]⌜x⌝-*pi*/DARE [ . . . ] ASINUS.ANIMAL "⌜*179*⌝" | CRUS +
RA/I

In my *days* [for] (one) sheep[65] (as) [pr]ice(??)[66] 10 homers (of)
[*ba*]*rley* stood.

KARKAMIŠ A 2
*à-wa/i mi-ia-za-´* LITUUS.AVIS-*ta-ni-ia-za* |OVIS.ANIMAL-*i* 10
ASINUS CRUS + RA/I

In my *days* for (one) sheep 10 homers (of *barley*) stood.

SULTANHAN[67]
|REL-*i-pa-wa/i* |("TERRA")*ta-sà*-REL + RA/I |2 "OVIS"-*sa* 80
"*179" CRUS + RA/I

When(?) in(?) the land[68] two sheep stood (i.e., cost) 80 (*measures* of) *barley*.

We may conclude this inquiry by comparing the postulated topos of ideal prices in the Hieroglyphic Luwian
inscriptions with those in Mesopotamian to see whether
they tally. It is striking how the boast of Katuwas on
KARKAMIŠ A 2 and A 11 *a* that 10 homers of *barley* cost
one sheep corresponds with Aššurbanipal's boast that
the same quantity cost 1 shekel of silver, and this very
correspondence may be urged in favor of accepting the
interpretation as correct. In the case of AKSARAY, the
measure corresponding to the homer, the *tiwatalis*, is
not known, so no direct comparison can be made. This
inquiry, however, would not be complete without some
further consideration of what kind of measure the *tiwatalis* might be. Since this question involves an examination of its other attestations, it is most conveniently relegated to an appendix.

APPENDIX: *Tiwatalis*
We have seen that the word *tiwatalis* occurs in AKSARAY
as element *d*, where KARKAMIŠ has ASINUS (ANIMAL), argued to mean "homer." The inference is that *tiwatalis*
too stands for a measure of volume. The SULTANHAN
passage lacks an element (*d*), but *tiwatalis* does appear
elsewhere in this inscription, and it would seem that it
has simply been omitted, as measures often were in
Cuneiform inscriptions, and should be understood. The
other attestation of *tiwatalis* is on BOR (twice), and since
both this and the SULTANHAN occurrence are contexts
connected with the statements of price which we have
been investigating, we should consider them here. We
may also note that BOR belongs to the group of inscriptions represented by SULTANHAN, AKSARAY, and KULULU,

both geographically (the Anatolian plateau) and chrono-
logically (the period of Tiglath-pileser III–Sargon).

SULTANHAN stele, lines 5–6
(i) |*à-wa/i* |TONITRUS-*hu-za-sa* |*za-´* |*tu-wa/i* + *ra/i-sà-zá* |*ma-
sa-ha-ni-i-ti*
(ii) |*à-wa/i* |*wa/i-ia-ni-i-sa* |PUGNUS-*ri* + *i-ti-i*
(iii) |*tara/i-sa-zi-pa-wa/i* |*ia* + *ra/i-ti-i*
(iv) |*à-wa/i* |MILLE *ti-wa/i-ta-li-na* |*á-ia-ti-i*
(v) |*wa/i-tu-u* |BOS(ANIMAL)-*sa* 9 (x) CENTUM-*ha ma-tu-sà*
(vi) |POST + RA/I-*ta-pa-wa/i à-ta* |*sa₅* + *ra/i-wa/i-ia*
(vii) *wa/i-tu-u-ta* |*ti-na-ta-za* |POST + RA/I-*ta*
(viii) |*u-sa-li-pa-wa/i-tu-u* |2 OVIS(ANIMAL)-*zi*

(i) Tarhunzas shall make this vineyard grow,
(ii) and the vine shall come up,
(iii) and it will *put forth shoots*,
(iv) and it will make one thousand *measure(s)* (of wine),
(v) and (there shall be) to him an ox and 900 (*measures* of)
wine (or "nine oxen and 100 (*measures*) of wine"; see
below).
(vi) But in future *it will increase*(?)
(vii) and to him (there shall be) a *tithe* in future,
(viii) and to him annually two sheep.

Textual Notes
(i) *mashani-*, "cause to grow": see F. Starke, *KZ* 93
(1979) 259.
(ii) PUGNUS-*ri* + *i*-, "rise, raise": see J. D. Hawkins,
*AnatSt* 30 (1980) 149 and 156, addendum 4.
(iii) *tara/i-sa-zi*: order of reading (as against *tara/i-zi-
sa*) and interpretation by comparison with A. Goetze,
*The Hittite Ritual of Tunnawi* (American Oriental Series 14, New Haven, 1938) col. IV, line 18 (pp. 22 and
97), though ᴳᴵˢ*tarša*, "shoots(?)," is there plur. N., and
*tarsa-* here would be MF.
*ia* + *ra/i*-: presumably the same verb as MANUS +
RA/I(-)ia + *ra/i*(-*ia*)-, which is of uncertain sense and
not clearly transitive or intransitive (cf. paper by J. D.
Hawkins and A. Morpurgo Davies in the forthcoming
Festschrift for Hans Güterbock). It would be possible to
translate here "the shoots shall come forth"; but for the
sense offered, cf. *KUB* 29, 1 iv 13–15: ᴳᴵˢGEŠTIN-*wa
ma-ah-ha-an* . . . *ša-ra-a* . . . ᴳᴵˢ*ma-ah-lu-us si-i-ia-iz-zi*,
"as the vine . . . pushes up the tendrils."
(iv) MILLE?: the KULULU lead strips have confirmed
the reading of the sign for "hundred" (CENTUM), and
there now seems little reason to doubt that "thousand"
is written with the present sign, hence MILLE.
*a-ia-*, "make": see Hawkins and Morpurgo Davies,
"Hieroglyphic Hittite: Some New Readings and Their
Consequences," *JRAS* 1975/2, 128.
(v) read in this way, as against Meriggi's *u-s-nu-ha*, in
order to take account of the ANIMAL marker following
BOS, which thus cannot be read *u*. It would also be possible to read BOS(ANIMAL)-*sa* 9, "nine ox(en)," but nu-
merals are generally written before their noun, and this
would give rather a large offering.

9 (x) CENTUM: the KULULU lead strips show the CEN-
TUM sign written up to four times for 400, and CEKKE
writes it six times for 600. It is assumed here that 900
could be meant by this method of writing and that the
writing of CENTUM nine times was avoided for reasons of
space. For comparison, 1 (x) CENTUM is twice found
(BOR, line 7, see below; BOHÇA line 4, see J. D. Hawkins
and A. Morpurgo Davies, *Studia Mediterranea P. Meriggi dicata* [Pavia 1979] 388–89. This system is of
course parallel to the Cuneiform writings of 1–9 ME for
100–900.

(vi) *a(n)ta sarwa-*: sense guessed from context.

(vii) *ti-na-ta-za*, "tithe": cf. (*257.DARE)*ti-na-tá* J. D.
Hawkins and A. Morpurgo Davies, *Serta Indogermanica*
(*Festschrift G. Neumann*) (Innsbruck 1982) 95,n. 3.

It would appear that (iv) omits the commodity, so that
one must understand MILLE *tiwatalin* (*matusa*); and (v)
omits the measure, so that one must understand 9 (x)
CENTUM (*tiwatalis*) *matusa*. Thus (iv–v) seem to state
that the god will receive 90 percent of the produce as
well as an ox, apparently in the first year. Subsequently
he is to receive a *tinata(n)za*, probably "tithe," and (annually) two sheep. Such omissions of measure or commodity have been seen in the statements of ideal price:
KARKAMIŠ A 2 omitted element (*d*), the commodity; and
SULTANHAN element (*c*), the measure.

BOR, lines 7–8
*wa/i-mu* 1 (x) CENTUM *ti-wa/i-[ta]-l[i]-s[a* . . .
. . . *ti-wa/i]-ta-li-sa ma-tu-sà*
to me (there shall be) 100 *measures* [of . . .
. . . and X *meas]ure(s)* (of) wine.

The context is very similar to that of the other passages considered here: the author, Warpalawas of
Tuwana, has planted a vineyard over which he has set
Tarhunzas of the Vineyard. This broken passage is doubtless a statement of the produce expected. One can only
speculate about the identity of the missing first commodity (or possibly commodities: the space might permit the restoration of another measure + commodity).
Would ancient Anatolian vineyards have produced ex-
clusively grapes and their products?

Finally, it is appropriate to give some consideration to
the type of measure which might be represented by the
word *tiwatalis*. Here some relevant points should be
noted, although no definite conclusions can be reached
on the basis of the present evidence. Approaches to
*tiwatalis* as a measure can be both etymological and
practical. The former will start with the obvious observation that the word appears to be a derived form of
*tiwat-*, "sun" (and possibly also "day," although this

connotation is not attested for Cuneiform or Hieroglyphic Luwian). But while there might be many obscure
reasons why a measure should be named with a deriva-
tive of the word for "sun," no obvious or well-attested
connection is discernible.

In practical terms, we have seen reason to think that
Karkamiš employed the Assyrian homer as its top measure of volume, and future discoveries may lead to the
identification of the homer's subdivisions, the seah and
even the *qa* in Hieroglyphic texts. The Hittite Empire
used a different system of volume measures, the *PA-
RISU-seah-hazzil-UPNU* (discussed above and in n. 18
below). It would seem likely that the *tiwatalis* corresponds to a unit in one system or the other, although we
may have to reckon with the possibility that it was a part
of a completely different system. To attempt to judge the
approximate size expected for the *tiwatalis*, we have the
possibility of comparing the AKSARAY boast with that of
Katuwas of Karkamiš. If the two statements were exact
equivalents, 10 homers would equal 30 *tiwatalis*—that
is, the *tiwatalis* would be 1/3 homer (3.3 seah or 33 *qa*).
SULTANHAN, of course, has a slightly more extravagant
boast, which would give the equivalent 10 homers = 40
(*tiwatalis*), so that the *tiwatalis* would be 1/4 homer (2.5
seah, 25 *qa*). There is no obvious division of the homer
into 1/3 or 1/4 with which such a *tiwatalis* could readily
be compared. If we give up the idea that the KARKAMIŠ
and AKSARAY or SULTANHAN boasts were approximately
equivalent, we might try comparing the *tiwatalis* with
the seah; but this would give a very meager boast, since
the seah is only 1/10 homer, so that instead of 1,000 liters (approx.), only 300 (AKSARAY) or 400 (SULTANHAN)
liters would stand for one sheep, a price down to the realistic level of the Laws of Ešnunna (see table 9-1). It
would seem that the *tiwatalis* does not fit easily into the
Assyrian homer system of volume.

The Hittite Empire *PARISU* system, as we have seen,
does not readily lend itself to comparisons because of
the uncertainty of the size of the *PARISU* and seah, but
allowing the maximum attested Mesopotamian range of
the seah between 10 *qa* and 5 *qa*, we have estimated that
the *PARISU* of 6 seah was probably within the range of
60 to 30 *qa* (or, approximately, 60 to 30 liters). The
latter figure lies between 1/3 and 1/4 homer, and thus, if
the KARKAMIŠ and AKSARAY-SULTANHAN boasts are approximately on a level, the *tiwatalis* would lie within the
range of a light *PARISU*; that is, AKSARAY would boast
about 900 liters to the sheep and SULTANHAN about
1,200 liters. This is probably as far as speculation can
profitably go. The closest that we can approach the possible size of the *tiwatalis* is to recognize that in known
systems it is the *PARISU* which provides the most plausible correspondence with the *tiwatalis*.

## NOTES

The abbreviations used in this article follow, for Akkadian references, those employed by the *Chicago Assyrian Dictionary*, W. von Soden's *Akkadisches Handwörterbuch*, R. Borger's *Handbuch der Keilschriftliteratur*, and the *Keilschriftbibliographie* in *Orientalia*; and, on the Hittite side, those used by Friedrich-Kammenhuber, *Hethitisches Wörterbuch*, the *Chicago Hittite Dictionary*, and E. Laroche's *Les Hieroglyphes hittites*. See also J. D. Hawkins, A. Morpurgo Davies, and G. Neumann, "Hittite Hieroglyphs and Luwian: New Evidence for the Connection," *Nachrichten der Akademie der Wissenschaft in Göttingen*, Phil.-Hist. Klasse 6 (1973), preliminary note on p. 3. The system of transliteration employed is the one tabulated in *AnatSt* 25 (1975) 153–55 and *AnatSt* 31 (1981) 148.

As usual I am immensely indebted to Professor Anna Morpurgo Davies, not only as specifically acknowledged, but especially for her patient discussion of the problems, reading of the drafts, and invaluable suggestions and criticism.

1 Published by Mustafa Kalaç, "Ein Steinbruchstück mit Luwischen Hieroglyphen in Aksaray bei Niğde," *KZ* 92 (1978) 117–25; a further edition and discussion are offered by Massimo Poetto, "Osservazioni sull'iscrizione luvio-geroglifica di Aksaray," in *Serta Indogermanica* (*Festschrift G. Neumann*, Innsbruck 1982) 275–84.

2 For convenient reference, see A. K. Grayson, *Assyrian Royal Inscriptions* 1 (Wiesbaden 1972) 20–21 and n. 64.

3 A. C. Piepkorn, *Historical Prism Inscriptions of Ashurbanipal* (Assyriological Studies 5, Chicago 1933) 29–31, lines 34–38 and n. 11.

4 R. Campbell Thompson, "A Selection from the Cuneiform Historical Texts from Nineveh (1927–32)," *Iraq* 7 (1940) 98, lines 26–29 (with incorrect restoration *ina qabalti mātīya*) and fig. 6, no. 14.

5 See E. E. Knudsen, "Fragments of the Historical Texts from Nimrud—II," *Iraq* 29 (1967) pl. 23, col. 1 (5524), lines 7–12; A. R. Millard, "Fragments of Historical Texts from Nineveh: Ashurbanipal," *Iraq* 30 (1968) 110–11 and pl. 25, col. i (BM 127896), lines 17–21; cf. M. Gogan and H. Tadmor, "Ashurbanipal's Conquest of Babylon: The First Official Report—Prism K," *Orientalia* 50 (1981) 237–38 and n. 21.

6 E. Weidner, "Assurbânipal in Assur," *AfO* 13 (1939–1941) 210–12, pl. 13 and n. 38.

7 N. Röllig, "Erwägungen zu neuen Stelen König Nabonids," *ZAssyr* 56 (1964) 247–49.

8 Collation supports the reading of the figures for barley and sesame oil given in C. Bellino's copy (published in C. J. Rich, *Narrative of a Journey to the Site of Babylon* [London 1839] pl. 8.2), although none of the figures for wine were registered there.

9 Röllig (supra n. 7) n. 87.

10 L. W. King, *Babylonian Boundary Stones and Memorial Tablets in the British Museum* (London 1912) no. 26; see p. 129 n. 2.

11 A. K. Grayson, *Assyrian and Babylonian Chronicles* (New York 1975) 286–88.

12 *In extenso* by B. Meissner, *Warenpreise in Babylonien* (Berlin 1936) passim; only the inscriptions of Sin-kašid, Šamši-Adad, and Nabonidus (= "Saosduchin") were available to him; see also D. O. Edzard, *Die "zweite Zwischenzeit" Babyloniens* (Wiesbaden 1957) 154; A. Goetze, *The Laws of Eshnunna* (AASOR 31, New Haven 1956) 28–30; E. Sollenberger, *Ur Excavations Texts* [8] (London 1965) 15; Weidner (supra n. 6) 211–12 n. 38; W. Röllig (supra n. 7) 248–49 and n. 89; Grayson (supra n. 11).

13 See references cited supra n. 12.

14 Röllig (supra n. 7), basing his argument on Meissner (supra n. 12).

15 Namely, Old Babylonian: 1 GUR (kor) = 30 BÁN (seah) = 300 SILÀ (*qa*); Neo-Babylonian: 1 GUR + 5 PI = 30 BÁN = 180 SILÀ; Neo-Assyrian: 1 ANŠE (homer) = 10 BÁN = 100 SILÀ. These equations are based on the information presented by F. Thureau-Dangin, *RAssyr* 18 (1921) 136–37. For possible variables in ratio and absolute size, see, for the Old Babylonian, J. N. Postgate, "An Inscribed Jar from Tell al Rimah," *Iraq* 40 (1978) 71–75; for Neo-Assyrian, J. N. Postgate, *Fifty Neo-Assyrian Legal Documents* (Warminster 1976; hereafter cited as *FNAD*).

16 In Aššurbanipal's Annals the figure may be either 60 or 30 minas, depending on whether the heavy or light talent is intended: see Postgate, *FNAD* (supra n. 15) 64–65.

17 Especially §§ 178–186; see A. Goetze, *Kleinasien*[2] (Munich 1957) 121–22; O. R. Gurney, *The Hittites* (rev. ed., Harmondsworth 1980) 86–88.

18 G. F. Del Monte, "Metrologia Hittita I, Le Misure di capacità per Aridi," *OrAnt* 19 (1980) 219–26.

19 N. F. Parise, *DialAr* 4 (1970) 3–36.

20 For the restoration, see H. Hoffner, *Alimenta Hethaeorum* (American Oriental Series 55, New Haven 1974) 67 and n. 123, where Goetze's earlier view is emended.

21 Del Monte (supra n. 18) 219 n. 1.

22 *Akkadisches Handwörterbuch* s.v. *sūtu(m)*.

23 Meissner, *Warenpreise* (supra n. 12) 18–19.

24 *Hittite Laws* § 185b–186; Gurney (supra n. 17) 85.

25 Cf. J. D. Hawkins, "Some Historical Problems of the Hieroglyphic Luwian Inscriptions," *AnatSt* 29 (1979) 162–67.

26 Cf. J. D. Hawkins, "Assyrians and Hittites," *Iraq* 36 (1974) 70–72; *RLA* 5 (1980) 439–43 s.v. Karkamiš.

27 E.g., by P. Meriggi, *Manuale* II.1, 54, citing L. R. Palmer's interpretation, *TPSoc* (1958) 52–53; so also Kalaç and Poetto (supra n. 1).

28 In the Mesopotamian statements of ideal price, we find the corresponding Sumerian ud bala sa₆-ga-gá/mu, "at the time of my good reign" (Sin-iddinam, Sin-iqišam); bala nam-lugal-la-ka-ni, "in the period of his kingship" (Sin-kašid); Akkadian *ina* BAL^mes-*ia . . . ina* MU.AN.NA^mes-*ia*, "in my reign . . . in my years" (Aššurbanipal).

29 The phonetic rendering *i + si* for LITUUS + AVIS postulated by Palmer (supra n. 27), 52–53, appeared to yield the word *istana-*, as was accepted by Meriggi, *Glossar* 2 s.v.; but these values can no longer be maintained—see Hawkins (supra n. 25) 157 n. 31; J. D. Hawkins, "The Logogram 'LITUUS' and the Verb 'To See' in Hieroglyphic Luwian," *Kadmos* 19 (1980) 141.

30 See infra p. 98 and n. 67 for discussion.

31 This inscription was reassembled from fragments at this point, and it is unfortunately not certain that all the pieces are still extant to permit collation. It is, however, clear from photographs, and from the squeeze (preserved in the British Museum) from which the text was published, that only half the first sign, the front half of a sheep's head, was preserved; this was restored in the published text as the syllabogram *m[a]* with no good reason, since the restoration OV[IS] is epigraphically just as acceptable and is now supported by the parallel passages.

32 Now edited by M. Poetto, "Note alle strisce di piombo di Kululu," in E. Neu ed., *Investigationes Philologicae et Comparativae, Gedenkschrift H. Kronasser* (Wiesbaden 1982) 97–115; for Poetto's remarks on the logogram, see p. 100. Kalaç (supra n. 1), 121, has shown that in TOPADA, 4, *HH* no. 179 alternates with REL₂ with a presumed value *hu(i)*, but I cannot accept his derivation of this from ≪ *humma-*, "pig-sty."

33 This addition clearly indicates that the sign is to be read logographically as ASINUS, not phonetically as *ta*, both in KAR-

KAMIŠ A 11 *a* and in the parallel KARKAMIŠ A 2, where in the past it has been read as *ta*—e.g., by Meriggi, *Manuale* II.1, 54 fr. 8; and Poetto (supra n. 1) 278.

34 Kalaç (supra n. 1) 123; and Poetto (supra n. 1) 278.

35 J. D. Hawkins and A. Morpurgo Davies, in *Serta Indogermanica* (supra n. 1) 96–97.

36 For the area of usage of the homer, see now M. Powell, "A Note on the 'imērum' Measure at Mari," *RAssyr* 67 (1973) 77–78.

37 We may compare the use of the mina, doubtless the well-known mina of Karkamiš, which is also now identified in the Hieroglyphic inscriptions: see supra n. 35.

38 For a consideration of what type of measure could be denoted by the *tiwatalis*, see Appendix.

39 An edition by myself of the KULULU lead strips has been waiting for some years to appear in *Belleten* and is now (1984) in page proof. Since KULULU belongs to the same area and date as AKSARAY and SULTANHAN, it seems likely that in lead strip 1's "numeral" + *179-za* the measure *tiwatalis* is to be understood.

40 Meriggi, *Glossar* 1, 113 s.v. GETR(EIDE); the words *179.*347.5(-) *wa/i-sà-pa-*, *179(-)REL-la-ia-na-*, and *179(-)sa-lá/í/u-ma-sa-* (in our current readings). The first word has now been identified also in CEKKE (rev., § 12: see Hawkins and Morpurgo Davies [supra n. 35] 96 and 98). If the sign *179 does indeed denote "gram," it will be difficult to maintain the suggestion that *179.*347.5(-)*wa/i-sà-pa-* might be identified with Cuneiform Luwian *waš(ša)pa-*, "garment."

41 I have proposed that the IVRIZ image of the god with vines and corn-stems springing from his feet is described on SULTANHAN, §§ 5–7; this in addition to *wiyanis*, "vine," gives *parwalis* (initial consonant uncertain), "corn-stem." See *CAH³*, revised plates volume, 86 with fig. 123.

42 Hoffner (supra n. 20) 59–83.

43 J. D. Hawkins, "The 'Autobiography of Ariyahinas's Son': An Edition of the Hieroglyphic Luwian Stelae TELL AHMAR 1 and ALEPPO 2," *AnatSt* 30 (1980) 146; further collation of TELL AHMAR 1 (squeeze in the British Museum) and TELL AHMAR 2 (in the Louvre) confirms the identity of *HH* no. 454 with no. 179. It is uncertain whether (-)*matili-* is the full phonetic writing.

44 For the identification of Kuparma as a late Hieroglyphic form of the god Kumarbi, see J. D. Hawkins, "Kubaba at Karkamiš and Elsewhere," *AnatSt* 31 (1981) 166. We could compare the deity (-)*matili-* with the Hittite goddess *Maliya*, "mother of wine and grain" (*KUB* 43, 23 rev. 50–51); cf. also R. Lebrun, in J. Quaegebeur, ed., *Studia Naster* 2 (Orientalia Lovanensia Analecta 13, Louvain 1982) 123–30. I owe the reference to Dr. Hatice Gonnet. The inexact correspondence between *Maliya* and *Matili* is, however, disturbing.

45 So identified by Kalaç (supra n. 1) 118 and 123. Photographs enable one to see more clearly the form of the sign, which resembles most the monumental form seen on TELL TAYINAT VII 1B, line 1, and the linear forms of KARATEPE 271 and 319. There is no need to identify a new sign form, as does Poetto (supra n. 1) 279.

46 I cannot agree with the suggestions of J. A. C. Greppin, "Hieroglyphic-Luwian *ma-tú-sà* 'Artibus,'" *KZ* 94 (1980) 119–21.

47 P. Meriggi, *Wiener Zeitschrift für die Kunde des Morgenlandes* 54 (1957) 198 n. 17; see also now F. Starke, "Das luwische Wort für 'Frau,'" *KZ* 94 (1980) 79 n. 23.

48 From Indo-European **dh*, we would expect a Cuneiform Luwian spelling with a simple *-d/t-* instead of the *-dd-* as found: see A. Morpurgo Davies' examination of this problem in "Dentals, Rhotacism, and Verbal Endings in the Luwian Languages." *KZ* 96 (1982–1983) 250. She points out that, if

the present identification is correct, Indo-European **d/dh* might conceivably have yielded Common Luwian -**t-* after a short, accented vowel, but more evidence is needed.

49 H. Hoffner, "A Hittite Text in Epic Style about Merchants," *JCS* 22 (1968) 40–41, nn. 74, 76.

50 Kalaç (supra n. 1) 118; Poetto (supra n. 1) 279.

51 Cuneiform TÚL = Hieroglyphic *HH* no. 215.1 (i.e., FONS), shown by H. Bossert, *Ein hethitisches Königssiegel* (IstForsch 17, Berlin 1944) 198; sign form distinguished from *HH* no. 212.2 (*ha*) by T. Beran, in K. Bittel et al., *Boğazköy* 3 (Berlin 1957) 44 n. 14.

52 J. D. Hawkins, "A Hieroglyphic Hittite Inscription from Porsuk," *AnatSt* 20 (1970) 77–78; (supra n. 26), 80; and J. D. Hawkins, review, Orthmann, *Späthethitischen Kunst*," *ZAssyr* 63 (1974) 311, which together confirm the reading of *Suppiluliuma* by the appearance of an Assyrian reference to *Ušpilulume* of Kummuh. The possibility of reading the name PURUS.FONS.MI as *tu-ha-me* can now be categorically denied; PURUS is not the same sign as *tu*, nor is FONS *ha*. For the form of the sign FONS on BOYBEYPINARI, see the form drawn in *AnatSt* (supra n. 44) 148.

53 E. Laroche, *Dictionnaire de la langue louvite* (Paris 1959) s.v. dain(i) "huile," p. 89.

54 Compare the relative values of Hittite *halki-* ("barley") and *zíz* ("wheat"): supra p. 94 and n. 20, and Hoffner's remarks (supra n. 20) 61, 66–67.

55 It should be noted that in the three repeated phrases of AKSARAY, only the first and the last have the verb CRUS + *RA/I*; the middle has [x]-*ta*, restored as *[sa]-ta* by Kalaç and *[ta]-ta* by Poetto. The photograph shows traces of the first sign, and possibly collation might indicate what it was. Conceivably this could be a phonetic writing of CRUS + *RA/I*; alternatively, it could represent a synonym. Either way it would be of considerable interest to establish the reading.

56 KARKAMIŠ A 11 *a*, 2, and ADIYAMAN 1, 1 (simple CRUS + *RA/I*), and ALEPPO 2, 3 (causative CRUS + *RA/I-nu-*): see Hawkins (supra n. 43) 148 and 151; "The Negatives in Hieroglyphic Luwian," *AnatSt* 25 (1975) 140 n. 41; and (supra n. 52) 102–104. The sign is also used on other occasions, apparently with a syllabic value.

57 P. Meriggi, *ta⁵* + *r* (3 plur. pret.; *Glossar* 2 s.v. *ta₅-*); E. Laroche, *ta₆* + *ta* (*HH* no. 82.1); Hawkins (supra n. 52) 104.

58 Morpurgo Davies (supra n. 48) 247 n. 8.

59 Thus, OCULUS (/LITUUS), "see" etc. (J. D. Hawkins [supra n. 29] 123–25); CAPERE, "take" (A. Morpurgo Davies and J. D. Hawkins, "The Hieroglyphic Inscription of Bohça," in O. Carruba ed., *Studia Mediterranea P. Meriggi dicata* [Pavia 1979] vol. 2, 397–98); MANUS, "fill; extend" (*HH* no. 59); PONERE, "put" (*HH* no. 65); DARE, "give" (*HH* no. 66); AURIS(+), "hear" (Hawkins [supra n. 56] 151–52); CRUS + CRUS, "follow" Hawkins [supra n. 29] 128); PES, "come" (J. D. Hawkins, "'To Come' and 'To Build' in Hieroglyphic Hittite," *RHA* 29 [1971] 113–16); PES₂, various verbs of going (Hawkins [supra n. 29] 131); PES₂ + PES, "trample" (*HH* no. 96); PES₂ + PES, "go" (*HH* no. 95).

60 N. Oettinger, *Die Stammbildung des hethitischen Verbums* (Nuremberg 1979) 350, citing C. Watkins and B. Eichner.

61 For a meaning shift from "stand" to, e.g., "cost, be worth," Morpurgo Davies compares the value of Latin *stare*, "stand" in such sentences as *scribit centum talentis eam rem Achaeis stetisse*, "he writes that that thing cost (lit. 'stood') 100 talents to the Achaeans" (Liv. 34.50.6).

62 E. Neu, *Studien zu den Boğazköy-Texten* 5 (Wiesbaden 1966) 6 with nn. 7, 8.

63 KARATEPE LXXIV–LXXV; J. D. Hawkins and A. Morpurgo-Davies, "Hieroglyphic Hittite: Some New Readings and Their Consequences," *JRAS* 1975/2, 125–26, 129–30.

64 For the two damaged words, see supra p. 97.

65 For the restoration, see supra n. 31.

66 The two signs ⌐x⌐ -*pi*/DARE have no corresponding word in the other passages. A possibility, not excluded by examination of photographs and the squeeze preserved in the British Museum, would be to restore [ARGEN]TUM.DARE, a combination which is examined by Hawkins and Morpurgo Davies (supra n. 35), 95–97 and n. 3, and which is also found in this same inscription (line 5) in the form ARGENTUM(-)*pi*/DARE-*si-ia*, of uncertain interpretation. Here, whatever word lay behind the compound logogram, it might indicate "price," in which case it would correspond to the KI.LAM element found in the Mesopotamian statements of price (all the Sumerian ones, and Šamši-Adad I and Aššurbanipal's boasts).

67 The most natural order of reading is that given—that is: |("TERRA") *ta-sà*-REL+*RA/I* | 2 "OVIS"-*sa*, where *tas*REL*ra/i* must be taken as dat. sing. and "OVIS"-*sa* as nom. or gen. (sing.), in contrast to the dat. sing. of the parallel passages. It would, however, be conceivable to read the -*sa* at the end of *tas*REL*ra/i*- instead of "OVIS." This would permit the interpretation of OVIS as dat. sing. as in the parallel passages, but results in the perhaps less easy translation "of the land for two sheep." It seems that the SULTANHAN passage is slightly different in construction from the others: the translation offered assumes that OVIS-*sa* is nom. sing.

68 The sense with this reading is perhaps parallel to Aššurbanipal's *ina naphar mātīya*, "throughout my land" (see supra p. 93).

# Hartapus and Kızıldağ

## 10

KURT BITTEL

On a day in the middle of May of the year 1905, Gertrude Bell went to Binbirkilise on Karadağ, north of Karaman in ancient Lycaonia.[1] Her achievements in the Near East still elicit admiration, but she was, nevertheless, not the first visitor to the ancient site with its remains of many churches—Laborde, Davis, Smirnov, Crowfoot, and other travelers and scholars had preceded her.[2] Yet her visit, which had been prompted by Josef Strzygowski's book on the artistic wealth of Asia Minor,[3] had most significant repercussions, not only on the exploration of the Byzantine monuments, but especially on the study of the remains of earlier civilizations on Karadağ. When Gertrude Bell returned there two years later with W. M. Ramsay, to whom she had already reported her observations in 1905 in Konya, she discovered "a very queer inscription" on a rock, which the more experienced Ramsay immediately recognized as a Hittite hieroglyphic inscription.[4] In the course of that same expedition, several inscriptions of the same type were found on nearby Kızıldağ, as was a large rock relief which was then considered to depict a god or a priest-king.[5] Today the reading of the inscription accompanying the rock relief no longer presents any difficulty. The relief shows a king named Hartapus seated on a throne (fig. 10-1).

Karadağ belongs to the chain of volcanic mountain ranges which extend across Lycaonia and Cappadocia from the Taurus to the Erciyazdağı (Argaios).[6] In my opinion, no recent picture of the whole of Karadağ rivals the colored print which E. J. Davis included in his book more than a century ago, even if one grants that the distance between Karaman and the mountain massif is too short as he rendered it.[7]

The actual relationship of Kızıldağ to Karadağ cannot be easily determined from more recent literature, not even with the help of the available maps, because the name Kızıldağ (Red Mountain), which is frequent in Anatolia, appears in several instances precisely here, in

Fig. 10-1. Kızıldağ, relief of Hartapus

the immediate vicinity.[8] Ramsay has, however, adequately described the position of these mountains and, in addition, has marked them on a map.[9] According to this information, Kızıldağ lies 12 km north-northwest of Mahalıç, where the 1:200,000 map has a "Kızılkale." E. Forrer has correctly marked it on his map, published in 1937 ("Der Südosten des Hatti-Reiches").[10] Kızıldağ is a rocky mountain on the edge of an ephemeral lake, which largely dries out in the summer and which extends to the west and southwest of the small settlement of Hotamış. Together with the more sharply profiled neighboring mountains, Kızıldağ can be counted among the northern extensions of Karadağ only in a fairly general sense. In actuality, between the two mountain ranges lies a relatively flat area including the small Acıgöl (Bitter Lake) in the immediate vicinity of the village of Suleimanhacı. On its slopes, which are not uniformly steep, a trachyte rock appears in many places. The so-called throne—a natural formation which owes its striking shape to the cleaving properties of trachyte—is situated on the northern slope of Kızıldağ about three-quarters of the way up (fig. 10-2).

Fig. 10-3. Kızıldağ, rock on which relief of Hartapus is carved

The upright, needlelike rock bears on its western side the image of Hartapus (figs. 10-3 and 10-4).[11] H. G. Güterbock visited Kızıldağ in 1939 and made important observations on the general layout and the inscriptions. In 1965 S. Alp worked intensively on the inscriptions and made good copies and photographs of the remains in the course of a trip to the site.[12] Both authors have also brought back photographs of the Hartapus monument, of which the one by Alp reproduces best. Much earlier, a plaster cast of the rock relief was made, several replicas of which have reached various museums.[13]

In comparison with the attention received by the Kızıldağ inscriptions, the rock relief has remained somewhat in the background. Moreover, its style and date have been disputed. Usually it is described as an engraved linear design, which is only partly true. In comparison with Hittite high reliefs, the linear quality of the rock carving is, of course, very obvious, but the outlines of the costume, the body (including the arms and the face), and the throne were all made by closely set, continuous chisel strokes, which transcend the effect of a merely engraved linear design and provide instead a certain depth to the image, although it remains in one plane. That true relief sculpture was also known and used at the time is shown by the hieroglyphic inscription before the king's head, which is, surprisingly, executed in relief.[14] The accomplishment of the artist who carved the image becomes obvious from a close study of the face with its large eye and full nose, and especially the area around the mouth, conveying force and energy. As far as the extant monuments permit judgment, the sculptor of the Hartapus image seems to have had few contemporary equals (fig. 10-5).

Opinions on the date of the sculpture range from the later period of the Hittite Empire and the eighth century B.C., but in the main they cluster toward the lower end of this time span. They have been recently summarized elsewhere,[15] so that it is unnecessary to repeat them here. E. Akurgal believes that the monument shows dependence on the later phase of Late Hittite sculpture in North Syria, and, in general, he is probably right, although I cannot believe that Hartapus wears an "Aramaic tiara," since the visible headdress is not specific enough for such an unequivocal classification.[16] The hairstyle and the form of the beard, however, which is shaved off around the lips, are so similar to North Syrian examples that a fashion common to both regions must be assumed. In the area beyond the Taurus, which has so far yielded a greater number of monuments, the fashion is documented from the reliefs of Kilamuwa of Sam'al, of the ninth century B.C., down to at least those of Barràkib at the same site, dating to the eighth century B.C. The god and king of the rock relief at İvriz, not far from

Fig. 10-4. Kızıldağ, rock on which relief of Hartapus is carved

Fig. 10-5. Kızıldağ, relief of Hartapus (detail)

*Hartapus and Kızıldağ* 105

Fig. 10-7. Urartian bronze bowl

Fig. 10-6. Kızıldağ, relief of Hartapus (detail)

Kızıldağ, have beards of the same general fashion, although theirs are more artistically rendered. Probably this latter feature was derived from Assyrian prototypes. The shape of the throne points to the same chronological placement, as stressed by H. Kyrieleis.[17] To it should be added the evidence of the bowl, which has so far gone unnoticed.[18] The king holds that bowl on the stiffly spread fingers of his right hand, a customary ancient formula for carrying an offering (fig. 10-6). From the photograph itself it is clear that it undoubtedly is a shallow-ribbed bowl with low rim such as is known in Urartu (fig. 10-7) and also in the East Phrygian area of Anatolia.[19] These bowls characteristically have a pattern of relief tongues and an upright rim which sometimes—as on the Urartian examples—exhibits a row of punch-engraved arches above the upper ends of the tongues. Some of these bowls are engraved with the names of Iš-puini, Menua, and Sarduri II; that is, they date from the end of the ninth to the middle of the eighth century B.C. The inscriptions, to be sure, merely provide an indication of the time when these objects were made and used, not an absolute date applicable to all such bowls. The bowl held by Hartapus shows that these vessels were

known not only in Urartu and Phrygia but also in eastern Anatolia. In fact, they may even have been made there, for the domain of Hartapus, which extended to the east beyond Aksaray, bordered directly on Tabal, if it did not actually include it from time to time. Tabal was explicitly mentioned as an artistic center for metalwork in texts from the time of the Assyrian king Sargon II (721–705 B.C.).[20]

Since the time of Ramsay's visit to Kızıldağ, it has been known not only that the rock relief of Hartapus and several Hittite hieroglyphic inscriptions existed there, but also that there were architectural remains. Güterbock has confirmed their existence from first-hand observation and has related reports of fortification walls and a rock-cut stairway. These reports are, however, brief and therefore do not convey a thorough picture of the entire complex.[21] I myself can make no definite contribution because I could not visit Kızıldağ. I do, however, owe to Hans Thoma valuable information and, above all, the use of his topographical sketch of the site (ill. 10-1). Missing on the sketch is the lower ring wall mentioned by Güterbock as connected with the entrance staircase and with the podium carrying the inscription Kızıldağ 4. The staircase and "gate" with podium actually presuppose that wall, so that Thoma himself does not question its existence. It would have been important to know its course, if it can still be traced without gaps, because it would show whether the rock with Hartapus' image was within or immediately outside this lower fortification ring. If one considers the contour of the mountain, the first possibility is the more likely. The upper ring of walls is almost circular and consists of cyclopean masonry. Today there are numerous gaps, which (allowing for natural shifts in the rock) were at one time surely filled with smaller stones (figs. 10-8 and 10-9). No remains of towers have so far been noted.

The technique of the masonry largely corresponds to that of other known fortifications dating from the early centuries of the first millennium B.C. in the southeastern part of central Anatolia, among which we may consider comparable not only Göllüdag, Hisarcık, and Karaburna

Village of
Adakale

N

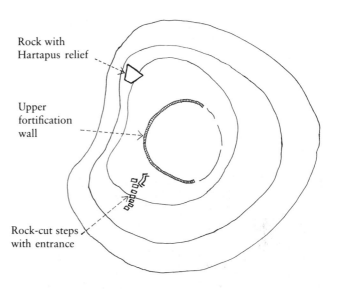

Rock with
Hartapus relief

Upper
fortification
wall

Rock-cut steps
with entrance

Village of
Suleimanhacı

Ill. 10-1. Plan of Kızıldağ, 1975—not drawn to scale. (Sketch by Hans Thoma)

Fig. 10-8. Kızıldağ, upper ring wall

Fig. 10-9. Kızıldağ, upper ring wall

in Tabal and Kerkenezdağ north of the middle Halys course, but also Pursuk near the Cicilian Gates and even Karatepe in eastern Cilicia.[22] As for those of the plateau—that is, Lycaonia and Cappadocia—it is the natural cleavage pattern of andesite and trachyte which determines to a considerable extent the general similarity in the shape of the stones and the way in which they are laid. All the sites mentioned clearly correspond to one another in this respect, while differing from a more recent fortification on Kılbasankızıldağ, which uses regular blocks with cut edges and is most likely Hellenistic.

Nothing is known of building remains within the upper fortification ring at Kızıldağ.[23] The carefully worked steps (fig. 10-10), which at the top end in a pierlike finial, strongly recall not only similar constructions in Phrygia but also, as Machteld Mellink has pointed out, a related monument near İvriz.[24] They obviously do not

Fig. 10-10. Kızıldağ, steps and finial

belong to the same period because the stepped arrangement near Beşkardeş, southeast of Fraktin in Cappadocia, leads up to the facade of a small temple whose surface is decorated by a bucranium of Roman Imperial times.[25] Considering the entire context, however, the rock-cut steps of Kızıldağ with their finial must belong to the same period as the fortress—as implied by Hartapus' rock-inscription nearby (Kızıldağ 4), which is not decisive but is, nevertheless, suggestive. It is the same text in the second line of which, to the right, P. Meriggi almost twenty years ago wanted to read the name of Muški—that is, according to a widely held opinion, the Phrygians.[26] This reading has not remained unchallenged; but that in Tabal there existed considerable Phrygian elements has been shown on the one hand by Machteld Mellink and on the other by Akurgal and

R. M. Boehmer on the evidence of the pottery and of several ornaments on textiles, such as those on the relief of the king of İvriz and the so-called Stele of Bor.[27] All these observations and considerations are, of course, insufficient to pinpoint the dating of Hartapus and his dynasty. Yet, although he closely patterned his royal cartouche, in form and content, after common Hittite Imperial conventions, and although his father was called Muršili—a name which occurs several times in the course of the second millennium—there can be no doubt that the rock relief was created in the ninth or eighth century B.C. A more precise assignment within this span, however, does not seem to me possible at present.

Few finds are known from Kızıldağ aside from the rock relief and the inscriptions. A small fragment of a vessel, now in the Ashmolean Museum, Oxford, shows a pattern of branches in black on a red ground.[28] Thoma collected more sherds on the slope between the upper fortification wall and the rock with Hartapus' relief. Among them are two pieces which may belong to the Late Bronze Age—that is, to the time of the Hittite Empire. Most of the others have shapes and decoration common in the Early Iron Age. Not one sherd, however, exhibits painted decoration in Early Phrygian style. Monochrome pottery predominates, but the polished Phrygian gray ware is totally unrepresented. Brown to gray striped patterns on light gray ground are prevalent, as is the well-known black-on-red ware which was also widespread in this part of Anatolia and whose precise date is hard to determine, especially if the pieces are as small as those from Kızıldağ. J. Mellaart once dated this fabric to the time span between the eighth and the sixth century B.C.[29] We still, however, lack the stratigraphically well-placed material from the plateau necessary for its precise assessment. In Porsuk, to which one immediately turns, this pottery is represented by only a few examples from Level III.[30] Among the sherds found by Thoma there is only one piece which probably comes from the Roman Imperial period. There is no later pottery, which may be accidental.

Güterbock was the first visitor who noted two groups of "footprints" on the horizontal surface of the rock on which the royal cartouche (Kızıldağ 2) is also carved. One group has the outlines of two, the other of four, pairs of feet. The surface of the "throne," toward which Hartapus' image on the steep rock pillars is turned, therefore bore the separate royal name as well as the footprints.[31] Did all these symbols together form a chronological and iconographic unit? As far as the royal name and the image on the rock are concerned, it can scarcely be doubted: they probably lent a special ideological significance to the entire rock. But did the footprints go with them from the beginning?

Although it is known that such foot marks appeared in antiquity from early times—for instance, on megalithic structures—and that they did not have the same significance in every place,[32] it is certain in our case that they are much more recent than the rock image because there is a Greek inscription associated with the first group of imprints, which names a priest who apparently carried out some cultic rite at this place.[33] The foot marks and the inscription seem so closely connected that the text can hardly be a later addition (fig. 10-11). I owe Michael Wörrle the information that the letter forms are Hellenistic or early Imperial. Thus, the possibility is excluded that there was here a contemporary outpost of the neighboring great church and monastery complexes of Binbirkilise. Moreover, no building remains of that late a period were observed on Kızıldağ. It is therefore not completely impossible that Hartapus' image received renewed attention centuries after its own time, albeit under completely different circumstances, even if the footprints and the priestly inscription are not oriented toward the rock portrait and likewise apparently point toward the west.

Fig. 10-11. Kızıldağ, footprints and Greek inscription

Once again one should recall that Ramsay said of Kızıldağ and its fortifications: "Excavations of this fort, if complete, might prove valuable."[34] Since that time, some seventy-five years have passed, but the statement has lost none of its validity. It has instead gained in importance, if one considers the lack of methodically excavated sites in this part of Anatolia—sites which belong to the "Dark Ages" of the early centuries within the first millennium B.C., sites located between Phrygia on the one hand and Tabal and Cilicia on the other, sites which promise important evidence because of their geographic position.

With its rock-cut image and inscriptions, Kızıldağ is surely not the least important among these sites. A precise recording of the remains still visible on the surface would constitute a contribution. To stimulate such an undertaking has therefore been the purpose of this paper, dedicated to a highly respected colleague who has for so long been recognized for her knowledge of this particular area of Asia Minor.

NOTES

This contribution has been translated from the original German [Eds.].

1  Letter to her father written on 13 May 1905 in "Binbirkilise." See *The Letters of Gertrude Bell* (London 1947) 184–87.

2  Cf. S. Eyice, *Karadağ (Binbirkilise) ve Karaman çevresinde arkeolojik incelemer* (Istanbul 1971) 2–12.

3  J. Strzygowski, *Kleinasien, ein Neuland der Kunstgeschichte* (Leipzig 1903) 1–27 (photographs by J. W. Crowfoot).

4  Bell (supra n. 1) 200 (25 May 1907). She visited Binbirkilise briefly again in 1909: *Amurath to Amurath* (London 1911) 358.

5  On the discovery, see W. M. Ramsay, *Luke the Physician and Other Studies in the History of Religion* (London 1908) 159–60. On early attempts at interpretation, cf. J. Garstang, *The Hittite Empire* (New York 1930) 155–58.

6  For the geological structure in general, see N. Güldalı, *Geomorphologie der Türkei* (TAVO A.4, Wiesbaden 1979) 51–55.

7  E. J. Davis, *Life in Asiatic Turkey. A Journal of Travel in Cilicia (Pedias and Trochoea), Isauria, and Parts of Lycaonia and Cappadocia* (London 1879) 300.

8  According to Garstang (supra n. 5) 155, Kızıldağ lies "about eight miles to the north-west" of Karadağ. According to W. Orthmann, "Karadağ," *RLA* 5 (1976–1980) 402, the top of Kızıldağ is about 5 km northeast of Mahalıç, the main peak of Karadağ. S. Alp says Mahalıç, the highest peak of Karadağ, is about 12 km east of Kızıldağ: See *Anatolian Studies Presented to Hans Gustav Güterbock on the Occasion of His Sixty-Fifth Birthday* (Istanbul 1974) 25. The only generally accessible map on a large scale has a Kızıldağ southeast and another one northeast of Mahalıç (also called Mihalıç). In order to differentiate the two mountains, the map combines the name with that of the closest large settlement, labeling them Kilbasaninkızıldağ and Madenşehirkızıldağ. The map further gives a Kızılkale north-northwest of Karadağ on the edge of the Hotamışbataklık. (The map I used, the latest available to me, is the 1:200,000 Konya-Ereğlisi version.)

9  W. M. Ramsay and G. L. Bell, *The Thousand and One Churches* (London 1909) 18–19, 294 map, 505 n. 1, 507.

10  E. Forrer, *Klio* 30.2 (1937), Beil.

11  Unfortunately, treasure hunters have dynamited the so-called throne in recent times. See H. Gonnet, "L'inscription no. 2 de Kızıldağ," *Hethitica* 25 (1983) 25–26. The extent of the damage can be seen by comparing the old photograph published by Güterbock ("Alte und neue hethitische Denkmäler," in *In Memoriam Halil Edhem* 1 [Ankara 1947] fig. 9) with the more recent one in Alp (supra n. 8) pl. 3, fig. 5.

12  Güterbock (supra n. 11) 52–54, 63–66, figs. 9–12; Alp (supra n. 8) 21–25.

13  The poor reproduction in H. T. Bossert, *Altanatolien* (Berlin 1942) 180, no. 761, was made from the cast in the Near Eastern section of the Staatlichen Museen in Berlin. Of another cast, in the Museum of the Ancient Orient in Istanbul (illustrated in B. Hrozny, *Les inscriptions hittites hiéroglyphiques* 3 [Prague 1937] pl. 93), unfortunately only approximately the upper third could be found in 1983.

14 To cite a parallel within this same area of Anatolia, the situation is reversed in the stele of Çiftlik/Eğriköy; a good photograph is published in I. J. Gelb, *Hittite Hieroglyphic Monuments* (OIP 45, Chicago 1939) pl. 30.

15 K. Bittel, "Die archäologische Situation in Kleinasien um 1200 v. Chr. und während der nachfolgenden vier Jahrhunderte," *SBÖstAkadWiss* 418 (1983) 42. Long after this paper was written, H. Gonnet published "Nouvelles données archéologiques relatives aux inscriptions hiéroglyphiques de Hartapusa à Kızıldağ," *Archéologie et religions de l'Anatolie Ancienne* 10 [Louvain-La-Neuve 1984] 119–25. She advocates "une datation haute de l'ensemble de Kızıldağ," that is to say, a date sometime during the reign of the last kings of the Hittite Empire (p. 123). Her arguments do not convince me. I hope to comment further on Mme. Gonnet's hypothesis in the near future.

16 E. Akurgal, *Späthethitische Bildkunst* (Ankara 1949) 3 n. 18, 13, and n. 102 (in both cases under "Karadağ"); W. Orthmann, *Untersuchungen zur späthethitischen Kunst* (Bonn 1971) 115 and n. 5 (also under "Karadağ"). Alp (supra n. 8), 21, therefore is correct in stating that a number of authors list the monuments of Kızıldağ under Karadağ, which leads to confusion. Akurgal and Orthmann mentioned only briefly the rock relief of Kızıldağ. Heinz Genge, *Nordsyrisch-südanatolische Reliefs. Eine archäologisch-historische Untersuchung, Datierung und Bestimmung* (Copenhagen 1979), omits it entirely, perhaps because he does not consider it a relief in the proper sense of the term.

17 H. Kyrieleis, *Throne und Klinen* (*JdI–EH* 24, Berlin 1969) 63. A fragment of a vessel from Porsuk (Level III) with the depiction of a seated figure shows that such seats were common, even if they varied in details: S. Dupré, *Porsuk I. La céramique de l'Age du Bronze et de l'Age du Fer* (Paris 1983) 119, no. 180, pls. 93, 95. Also essential is Ruth Mayer-Opificius, "Rekonstruktion des Thrones des Fürsten Idrimi von Alalaḫ," *Ugarit-Forschungen* 15 (1983) 119–26. Thronelike chairs of a somewhat different construction are already attested in the old Hittite period: see, for instance, T. Beran, *Die hethitische Glyptik von Boğazköy* 1 (Berlin 1967) pl. 3, no. 134.

18 Ramsay and Bell (supra n. 9) 508: "[the "priest-king's"] left hand supports a round flat object, which I understood while drawing it to be a patera." Garstang (supra n. 5) 165: it "seems to be a cup." Alp (supra n. 8) 22: "hält in der rechten Hand einen Becher." But Ramsay later considered this interpretation as doubtful: see A. H. Sayce, "The Hittite Inscriptions Discovered by Sir W. Ramsay and Miss Bell on the Kara Dagh," *PSBA* 31 (1909) 83–84 n. 1.

19 Bowl of Hartapus: Alp (supra n. 8) pl. 4, fig. 7. In N. Cappadocia: Boğazköy—K. Bittel and H. G. Güterbock, *Boğazköy* 1. *Neue Untersuchungen in der hethitischen Hauptstadt* (Berlin 1935) 53 and pl. 21.2; Kerkenes Dağ—*American Journal of Semitic Languages* 45 (1929) 272–73, figs. 73–74. In Urartu: H. J. Kellner, "Ein datierter Silberfund aus Urartu," *Anadolu* 19 (1975–1976) 61–64, fig. 1, pl. 5.1–2; B. Piotrovski, *Karmir Blur* (Leningrad 1970) figs. 73–74. In contrast, a silver ribbed bowl with high omphalos found in Büyükkale Level I (Boğazköy) is somewhat later: K. Bittel et al., "Vorläufiger Bericht über die Ausgrabungen in Boğazköy, 1936," *MDOG* 75 (1940) 49 and fig. 9.1

20 D. D. Luckenbill, *Ancient Records of Assyria and Babylonia* 2 (Chicago 1927) 109–10, no. 213; M. Wäfler, "Zu Status und Lage von Tabäl," *Orientalia* 52.1 (1983) 193.

21 Ramsay and Bell (supra n. 9) 507 ("slight remains of a fortress"), 511 ("the fort on the top of Kizil Dagh is entered by a gate on W"); A. H. Sayce (supra n. 18) 83 ("the remains of a fortress"); Güterbock (supra n. 11) 64 (staircase "zwischen einer unteren und einer oberen Ringmauer" and steps with "einer Art Postament"). See also Güterbock fig. 11.

22 Göllüdağ: *TürkTarDerg* 3 (1936) 26, fig. 12; Hisarcık: Gelb (supra n. 14) pl. 41 upper; Karaburna: *Le Muséon* 70 (1957) fig. 9; Kerkenes Dağ: H. H. von der Osten, "Explorations in Hittite Asia Minor, 1927–28" *OIC* 6 (1929) 21 fig. 12; Porsuk: O. Pelon, "Rapport préliminaire sur la première campagne de fouilles à Porsut-Ulukışla (Turquie)," *Syria* 47 (1970) pl. 17.2; Karatepe: H. T. Bossert and U. B. Alkım, *Kadirli ve Dolayları* (Istanbul 1947) pl. 24. 118, 119, pl. 25.120, and cf. p. 25. The wall of Domuztepe is of a similar type: H. T. Bossert et al. *Karatepe Kazıları birinci ön-rapor. Die Ausgrabungen auf dem Karatepe (Erster Vorbericht)* (TTKY, ser. V, 9, Ankara 1950) pl. 28.131–32.

23 To judge by a number of rummaged places within the upper wall, treasure hunters have also been at work there. The same is true for the area between the southwestern foot of Kızıldağ going in the direction of the village of Hacısüleyman, where a settlement belonging to the fortress on the mountain could have been located.

24 M. J. Mellink, "Midas in Tyana," in *Florilegium Anatolicum. Mélanges offerts à Emmanuel Laroche* (Paris 1979) 252.

25 It was occasionally considered Phrygian, if not Hittite, admittedly with proper reservations: F. Steinherr, "Zu den Felsinschriften Taşçı I and II," *IstMitt* 25 (1975) 316–17; M. J. Mellink, "Archaeology in Asia Minor," *AJA* 80 (1976) 271–72. F. Prayon has explained the situation.

26 P. Meriggi, "Una prima attestazione epicorica dei Moschi in Frigia," *Athenaeum* 42 (1964) 52–59. The inscription: Alp (supra n. 8) 23–24, pl. 7, figs. 13–14.

27 In general: Mellink (supra n. 24) 252–56 and nn. 11 and 13.

28 H. Frankfort, *Studies in Early Pottery of the Near East* 1 (London 1924) 71, fig. 8.B; his "Kizil Dagh" is most probably identical with ours. J. Mellaart, "Second Millennium Pottery from the Konya Plain and Neighbourhood," *Belleten* 22, no. 87 (1958) 326 (map), places Kızıldağ in the right place to be the find-spot of such pottery, but no evidence is given in the text.

29 J. Mellaart, "Iron Age Pottery from Southern Anatolia," *Belleten* 19, no. 74 (1955) 122–23.

30 Dupré (supra n. 17) 82–83.

31 Güterbock (supra n. 11) 64 and fig. 10 (sketch plan): (*a*) Hartapus; (*b*) royal cartouche; (*d*) contours of feet. On the vertical rockface immediately under the cartouche is the inscription Kızıldağ 3 (Alp [supra n. 8] n. 12, pl. 6), in which Hartapus refers to himself as son of a Great King Muršili. The interferences mentioned supra (n. 11) have in the meantime considerably changed the situation. Only one group of footprints remains today; the other was dynamited.

32 To give only a few examples: A. Jeremias, *Das Alte Testament im Lichte des Alten Orients*[4] (Leipzig 1930) 785; F. W. Hasluck, *Cyzicus* (Cambridge 1910) 292 n. 1; L. Robert, *Études Anatoliennes* (Paris 1937) 201; L. Castiglione, "Inverted Footprints, a Contribution to the Ancient Popular Religion," *Acta Ethnographica Academiae Scientiarum Hungaricae* 17 (1968) 121–37, and "Vestigia," *Acta Archaeologica Academiae Scientiarum Hungaricae* 22 (1970) 95–132. I thank E. Porada for the reference to an important example, the large artificial footprints on the steplike threshold of a temple in Ain Dara in North Syria (tenth–ninth century B.C.). They point toward the interior of the temple. Cf. Ali Abou Assaf, "Ain Dara—eine neuentdeckte Residenzstadt," in *Land des Baal, Syrien—Forum der Völker und Kulturen* (Mainz 1982) 351. See now also *Da Ebla a Damasco. Diecimila anni di archeologia in Siria* (Exhibition at the Campidoglio, Rome, 15 Feb.–26 Mar. 1985) 55 right;

L. Castiglione, "Footprints of the Gods in India and the Hellenistic World: Influence or Parallelism?" *Annales Archéologiques Arabes Syriénnes* 21 (1971) 33.

33 ΚΡΑΤΕΡΟΣ ΕΡΜΟΚΡΑΤΟΥ ‖ ΙΕΡΕΥΣ ΕΠΗΔΗΣΕ. The photograph of this inscription (here fig. 10-11) was taken by Hans Thoma. To him, as to Sedat Alp, Hans Gustav Güterbock, and Wulf Schirmer, I am indebted for much assistance and for kindly supplying photographs.

34 Ramsay and Bell (supra n. 9) 512.

# Sirens and Rephaim

## 11

R. D. BARNETT

During the period from 1964 to 1966, Vassos Karageorghis excavated at Salamis in Cyprus one of the most spectacular archaeological finds of the century—Tomb 79, containing the rich and virtually untouched burial of (we may suppose) a late eighth-century Phoenician king of Salamis or possibly of a wider area. The possibility cannot entirely be dismissed that this might be the tomb of the exiled king of Sidon, Luli, whose flight by sea from Tyre to Cyprus in 700 B.C. before Sennacherib's army was depicted in the sculptured reliefs in the latter's palace at Nineveh.[1] The richly furnished tomb was excavated with remarkable skill and published with exemplary thoroughness.[2] Among the rich and well-preserved furniture was a large bronze cauldron, which still stood on its tripod base in the corner of the propylaeum of the tomb. It is of a type long known to science, its rim ornamented with four large griffin protomes and having four ring handles shaped into the form of (in this case) large, janiform human-headed birds. Beside it was a smaller cauldron of different type, its rim decorated only with a pair of large ring handles, each of which was ornamented with three bulls' heads, cast in high relief, above a large Hathor head.[3] The publication of this important material in 1973–1974 drew fresh attention to the subject of such ornate cauldrons, which form one of the most striking and stately, but bizarre, products of the Early Iron Age in the ancient Near East. These objects clearly played an important role in both ancient commerce and art history, having been exported to both Greece and Etruria in considerable numbers. Their ornamentation with bronze griffin protomes and handles in the form of human- or animal-headed birds, sometimes called *Sirenen-* or *Fi-*

*gurattaschen* in German, has formed the subject of a series of studies over the last hundred years, from Furt-wängler onward.[4] In 1966 H. V. Herrmann published as vol. 6 of the Olympia excavation reports the most thorough and detached study of the subject so far made and drew up a catalogue of seventy-eight known *Sirenenattaschen* of Oriental type. In an appendix was added another (B6099) found at Olympia in 1965,[5] and five Greek imitations were also recorded. P. Amandry, in a brilliant review, added to the Oriental series three more (two from Samos and one from Delphi) that Herrmann had overlooked, but took away three others which he considered nonexistent.[6] Total: eighty, of which thirty came from Greek shrines and six from Etruscan tombs at Praeneste and Vetulonia. One more, of unknown provenance, has since turned up and is now in the Glencairn Museum,[7] bringing the grand total to eighty-one. The source of these works of art, however, is hotly disputed. The strongest evidence pointed—or was deemed to point—to Urartu; the earliest example to appear was found in a rock-cut tomb in Iranian territory opposite the Russian frontier post of Alistair on the Aras River, in or before 1859.[8] Five more turned up on the market in Istanbul, apparently from Toprak Kale, in the 1880s, and this was considered strong enough proof by C. F. Lehmann-Haupt to launch a theory that these cauldrons were typical Urartian artifacts.[9] Their ascription to the art of Urartu was generally accepted among the principal archaeologists of the Near East. But was it correct? Greek archaeologists began raising awkward questions, and it was soon seen that the subject bristled with problems, although some could be and were eliminated. Urartu was certainly a very important center of metal-

Fig. 11-1. Olympia A1. (Athens, Nat. Mus. 6122)

working in the eighth century B.C., as Lehmann-Haupt had proclaimed and the full publication of the material from Toprak Kale demonstrated.[10] But did the ornaments of the cauldrons—the griffin and lion protomes and human-headed bird figures alike—all emanate together from the same source as the cauldrons? Or were the protomes in griffin and animal form added in Greek lands, to the possibly Urartian cauldrons, of which the human-headed birds alone were the original components? This was Herrmann's view in 1966, restated in 1979 at length.[11] Certainly the Gordion examples have *Attaschen* but no protomes. Amandry had little difficulty, on the other hand, in pointing out that the Salamis example was already fully equipped, yet was clearly Oriental;[12] so clearly there was variation in practice, even in the Orient.

The origin of the shape of the metal cauldron in the Near East has been traced back to Elam.[13] It was probably common also to other areas, such as Babylonia. Elaboration of the swinging ring-handle bases into winged figures seems to have taken place in an area comprising Southwest Iran, Assyria, and North Syria—which gives us a pretty wide choice, one might say. Where, then, was the center where these products were made, if not Urartu? (We discount from this argument the Phoenician and Greek variations.) Kunze[14] half a century ago and after him Herrmann[15] opted for North Syria, at some city or cities well placed to distribute their goods alike to Greece, Italy, and Urartu, such as Carchemish or Zincirli-Samal or Malatya. Their view was accepted by Muscarella,[16] Kyrieleis,[17] and van Loon,[18] but strongly rebutted by Akurgal.[19] Amandry pointed

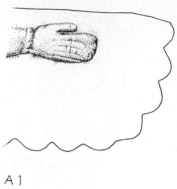

A 1

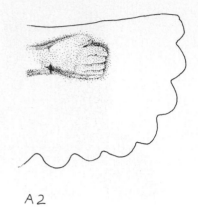

A 2

A 12

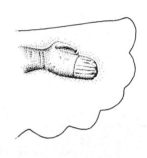

A 19

DELPHI 1666

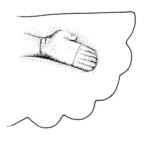

A 20

Ill. 11-1. Six-fingered hands. (Drawings by Gillie Newman)

Fig. 11-2. Olympia A2

out that it was curious logic to take these works of art away from Urartu, where some had been found, and give them to Syria,[20] where they had not. But the difficulties remain. For one thing, excavation and discovery in North Syria have been anything but thorough and consistent. The excavation of Carchemish was interrupted by World War I after a very promising start and never resumed. That of Zincirli, like that of Malatya, produced neither cauldrons nor *Attaschen*. Yet what, for example, do we know of the art of an area such as Kummukh, reported by the Assyrian kings to have been rich in metallurgy? Its capital, Samosata, is receiving some attention before it disappears forever beneath the waters of a new

Euphrates dam; but again no such objects as these are reported as having been found there.

The possibility remains that they were made at several centers. Herrmann has marshaled all the internal evidence as to place or places of origin of the cauldron figures on grounds of style, costume, hairstyle, wings and tails, and so on and divided them in the best classical manner into three main groups or workshops. There is no need here to go over these groups. On some of the figures, however, a curious point of detail has remained hitherto unnoticed. It is the recurrence of six fingers on one of the outstretched hands which occur on: Olympia A1 (Herrmann pl. 7, the right hand; here fig. 11-1, and

Fig. 11-3. Olympia A12

see also ill. 11-1 for details of all the following); A2 (Herrmann pl. 8, the right hand; here fig. 11-2); A12 (Herrmann pl. 18, the right hand; here fig. 11-3); and the Greek imitations A19 (Herrmann pl. 29, the right hand; here fig. 11-4) and A20 (Herrmann pl. 30, the right hand; here fig. 11-5). To these we may add two more from Delphi.[21] There may be more examples, but the details are not always clear enough in photographs or the objects are too corroded to be certain.

I have recently made a study of this most extraordinary feature which I hope to publish in full elsewhere.

Suffice it to say that polydactyly is a fairly common genetic abnormality, especially in isolated or inbred groups, occurring in cats and mice as well as humans. As a birth anomaly, it was classified by the Assyrian priests as an omen of good (left hand) or evil (right hand) portent.[22] It is frequently illustrated in art from the Neolithic period in the Jordan Valley,[23] in prehistoric Malta,[24] the Cyclades,[25] Iran,[26] and Palestine,[27] and under Oriental influence in Greece in the ninth and eighth centuries B.C.[28] and in Hellenistic Egypt.[29] Extinguished in classical art by notions of the "perfect man," it was revived in

Fig. 11-4. Olympia A19. (Courtesy of German Archaeological Institute, Athens)

the late Middle Ages and Renaissance[30] to linger on in Malta until the eighteenth century.[31] Polydactyly was evidently felt to mark the owner as possessing supernatural or special powers.

What, then, is or was the significance of this feature on some of the bronze cauldrons and in other contemporary and later Levantine works of art—the Deir el-Balah sarcophagi (fig. 11-6) or some carved tridachna shells (ill. 11-2)?[32] A passage in the Bible (II Samuel 21.18–22) gives us a possible clue. It tells of a giant at Gath in the Philistine country who is slain by Jonathan, David's nephew. This giant, we are told, "had on every hand six fingers and on every foot six toes, four and twenty in number, and he was also born to the Rephaim." Hence, we learn explicitly that polydactyly—and by inference its explanation—was associated with the Rephaim, at least in Philistia; and indeed we have illustrations of such polydactyly from the cemetery of

Fig. 11-5. Olympia A20. (Courtesy of German Archaeological Institute, Athens)

Deir el-Balah, near Gaza (fig. 11-6). What then do we know about the Rephaim? Recently the ritual ceremony or festival called the *marzeah* in Syria and Palestine has come under scrutiny.[33] It has been shown that this was an important ritual celebrated usually in honor of a particular but variable deity, from at least the fourteenth century B.C. at Ras Shamra to the second or third century A.D. in Greece and Syria. At Dura and Palmyra the celebrants lay on ivory couches, banqueted on calves' flesh, and drank wine from bowls—all as described in the Book of Amos.[34] It is claimed that at these celebrations the Rephaim, the divinized ancestors of the celebrants, were invited to be present and to participate. Such invitations to ancestral spirits were known in Baby-

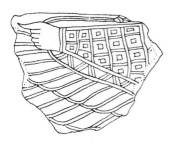

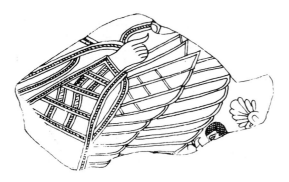

Ill. 11-2. Tridachna shell fragments: Stucky 6 and 46. (Courtesy of *Dédalo*, Saõ Paulo)

Fig. 11-6. Anthropoid sarcophagus from Deir el-Balah, near Gaza. (Dayan Collection, Israel Museum; photograph courtesy of Dr. Izhack Beit-Arie, Tel Aviv University)

Ionia; for example, King Ammizadduga invites his ancestors and their slain warriors to a funeral feast, or *Kispu.*[35]

Figures of birds with women's heads were associated with the dead and the dead person's soul in Egypt and elsewhere—the Ba in Egypt, the so-called Harpies on the monument from Xanthos now in the British Museum, the *Seelenvogel*[36] and the siren in archaic and classical Greece.

I conclude therefore that these winged figures fluttering toward the interior of the cauldron, as if to drink from it, are meant to represent the Rephaim or divinized ancestors or their equivalents who are invited to a funeral feast. Whether the cauldrons or their figured attachments were made in Syria or elsewhere, I leave to others to decide.

I offer these notes as a token of appreciation of Machteld Mellink's great contributions to Near Eastern and classical archaeology.

## NOTES

1  R. D. Barnett, "Phoenicia and the Ivory Trade," *Archaeology* 9 (1956) 93, fig. 9; D. B. Harden, *The Phoenicians* (Harmondsworth 1952) pl. 51.
2  V. Karageorghis, *Salamis* 5. *Excavations in the Necropolis of Salamis* 3 vols. (Nicosia 1973–1974).
3  Karageorghis (supra n. 2) pls. 2, 12–14, 243–46.
4  A. Furtwängler, "Bronze aus Olympia," *AZ* 37 (1879) = J. Sieveking and L. Curtius eds., *Kleine Schriften* 1 (Munich 1912) 336–38, pl. 10.
5  H.-V. Herrmann, *Die Kessel der orientalisierenden Zeit* 1. *Kesselattaschen und Relief-Untersätze* (OlForsch 6, Berlin 1966).
6  P. Amandry, review, *Gnomon* 41 (1969) 796–802.
7  D. G. Romano and V. C. Pigott, "A Bronze Siren Cauldron Attachment from Bryn Athyn," *MASCA Journal* 1983, 124–29.
8  B. B. Piotrovsky, *Urartu* (trans. P. Gelling, London 1967) 36, 82, figs. 59–61; M. van Loon, *Urartian Art* (Istanbul 1966) 107.
9  C. F. Lehmann-Haupt, *Armenien einst und jetzt* 2.2 (Berlin 1931) 183–85, nn. 21–22.
10 R. D. Barnett, "The Excavations of the British Museum at Toprak Kale near Van," *Iraq* 12 (1950) 1–39; and "The Excavations of the British Museum at Toprak Kale near Van—Addenda," *Iraq* 14 (1954) 5–22.
11 Herrmann, *Die Kessel der orientalisierenden Zeit* 2. *Kesselprotomen und Stabdreifüsse* (OlForsch 11, Berlin 1979) 137 60.
12 Amandry (supra n. 6) 796–97.
13 P. Calmeyer, "Kessel," in *RLA* 5 (Berlin 1980) 573–74.
14 E. Kunze, *Kretische Bronzereliefs* (Stuttgart 1931) 271–80.
15 Herrmann (supra n. 5) 54–55, 176–77.
16 O. W. Muscarella, "The Oriental Origin of Siren Cauldron Attachments," *Hesperia* 31 (1962) 317–29.

17 H. Kyrieleis, *Marburger Winckelmannsprogramm* 1966, 1–25.

18 Van Loon (supra n. 8) 107–10.

19 E. Akurgal, *Urartäische und altiranische Kunstzentren* (Ankara 1968) 44–48. So also Piotrovsky (supra n. 8).

20 Amandry (supra n. 6) 798–99.

21 Herrmann (supra n. 5) pl. 35, the left hand; P. Perdrizet, *Fouilles de Delphes* 5 (Paris 1908) no. 364, the left hand. The sirens are grouped differently by Herrmann (supra n. 5) 74–84, into "ältere Stufe (Werkstatt 'A' und 'B')" and "jüngere Stufe," and by Akurgal (supra n. 19) 37–44, into "Typus A" and "Typus B."

22 E. Leichty, *The Omen Series šumma izbu* (New York 1970).

23 Clay figures from 'Ain Ghazal: A. H. Simpson and G. O. Rollefson, "Neolithic 'Ain Ghazal (Jordan): Interim Report on the First Two Seasons, 1982–1983," *JFA* 11 (1984) 394. Garstang found a fragment of a left foot with six toes at Jericho. This piece is unpublished, but Simpson and Rollefson (p. 394 n. 13) cite a photograph of it in the "Palestine" (Rockefeller) Museum, Jerusalem.

24 National Museum, Valletta; from Hagiar Kim, ca. 1300 B.C., H. about 1 cm (six fingers on each hand).

25 Ashmolean Museum, Oxford, 1946.118, from Naxos, H. 2 cm (six fingers on each hand).

26 Clay figures from Marlik: E. Negahban, *A Preliminary Report on Marlik: Gohar Rud Expedition* (Teheran 1964) pl. 11 (six

27 toes on each foot). Other examples of polydactyly exist in Iranian art.

27 Fourteenth-century B.C. sarcophagi from Deir-el-Balah: T. Dothan, *Excavations at the Cemetery of Deir-el-Balah* (Qedem 10, Jerusalem 1979) pl. 32 (six fingers on each hand).

28 Terracotta centaur: V. Desborough, "A Euboean Centaur," *BSA* 65 (1976) 21–30 (six fingers on right hand).

29 Painted mummy cloth in Columbia, Missouri, Museum, 61.66.3 (six toes on each foot). I owe this information to the kindness of Professor Saul Weinberg.

30 E.g., painting of Adam and Eve attributed to Jan van Scorel (ca. 1525), now at Hatfield House (six fingers on right hand). Other examples in art from this period exist.

31 Eighteenth-century fresco in the refectory of the Seminary, St. Caledonius Square, Floriana, Malta, illustrating Daniel 1.12.

32 R. A. Stucky, "The Engraved Tridachna Shells," *Dédalo* 10.19 (June 1976) nos. 6 and 46.

33 J. C. Greenfield, "The *marzeah* as a Social Institution," *Acta Antiqua* (Hungary) 22 (1974) 451–54; M. H. Pope, "The Cult of the Dead at Ugarit," in G. D. Young ed., *Ugarit in Retrospect* (Winona Lake 1981) 169–79.

34 Amos 6.4–7.

35 J. J. Finkelstein, "The Genealogy of the Hammurapi Dynasty," *JCS* 20 (1966) 95–118. I owe this reference to the kindness of J. D. Hawkins.

36 G. Weickert, *Der Seelenvogel* (Leipzig 1902).

COMPOSED BY G & S TYPESETTERS, INC., AUSTIN, TEXAS
MANUFACTURED BY MALLOY LITHOGRAPHING, INC., ANN ARBOR, MICHIGAN
TEXT AND DISPLAY LINES ARE SET IN TIMES ROMAN

Library of Congress Cataloging-in-Publication Data
Ancient Anatolia: aspects of change and
cultural development.
(Wisconsin studies in classics)
Includes bibliographies.
1. Turkey—Antiquities.   2. Turkey—Civilization.
3. Hittites.   4. Mellink, Machteld J. (Machteld Johanna)
I. Mellink, Machteld J. (Machteld Johanna)
II. Canby, Jeanny Vorys.   III. Series.
DR431.A66   1986      939'.2       86-40059
ISBN 0-299-10620-9